The Grover E. Murray Studies in the American Southwest

Also in the series

MY WILD LIFE

DISCARD

A Memoir of Adventures within America's National Parks

MY WILD LIFE

Roland H. Wauer   Foreword by Jonathan B. Jarvis

Texas Tech University Press

This book is typeset in Monotype Amasis. The paper
used in this book meets the minimum requirements of
ANSI/NISO Z39.48-1992 (R1997). ∞

Designed by Kasey McBeath
Cover photographs by Roland H. Wauer and Betty
Wauer

Library of Congress Cataloging-in-Publication Data
Wauer, Roland H.
    My wild life : a memoir of adventures within Amer-
ica's national parks / Roland H. Wauer; foreword by
Jonathan B. Jarvis.
        pages cm—(The Grover E. Murray studies in the
American Southwest)

Summary: "A retired National Park Service employee
details his life working within the national parks; including photographs of landscapes and wildlife within
multiple parks"—Provided by publisher.
    Includes bibliographical references and index.
    ISBN 978-0-89672-885-1 (paperback : alkaline
paper)—ISBN 978-0-89672-886-8 (e-book) 1. Wauer,
Roland H. 2. Park rangers—United States—Biography.
3. United States. National Park Service—Officials
and employees—Biography. 4. National parks and
reserves—United States—History—20th century. 5.
National parks and reserves—West (U.S.)—History—
20th century. 6. Natural history—United States. 7.
Natural history—West (U.S.) I. Title.
    SB481.6.W38A3 2014
    363.6'8092—dc23
    [B]   2014015674

14 15 16 17 18 19 20 21 22 / 9 8 7 6 5 4 3 2 1

Texas Tech University Press
Box 41037 | Lubbock, Texas 79409-1037 USA
800.832.4042 | ttup@ttu.edu | www.ttupress.org

I dedicate this book to the memory of my father
for teaching me a love of nature; and to my wife,
Betty, for her many years of love and support.

Table of Contents

Illustrations

Color plates, following page 106

Foreword

Ro Wauer is my hero. There are only a few people who have significantly influenced my nearly four decades with the National Park Service (NPS), and Roland Wauer is in the top tier of the list yet probably does not even know that. His vision and values plus his ability to turn those into actual policy and programs intersected my early years and shaped my entire career path and philosophy of national park protection. From joining the NPS in March 1976 to the spring of 1982, I worked as a seasonal interpreter on the National Mall and as a law enforcement ranger at Prince William Forest Park, but with a degree in biology and a love of nature and the outdoors, I longed to work in natural resources. But such jobs did not even exist at the time. The management of the resources was delegated to the park rangers, among other duties such as fire prevention, law enforcement, interpretation, maintenance of campgrounds, and fee collection. As a park ranger, I performed all those duties at Prince William Forest Park, though I was drawn to exotic plant control, restoration of impacted park sites, surveys of deer populations, and documentation of the flora and fauna of this unique park on the southern skirts of Washington, D.C. I did not know that simultaneously, in the Washington Office (WASO), Chief Scientist Ro Wauer was creating my job description.

Ro envisioned a new type of position in the NPS: the resource manager, a professional who is scientifically literate but not a practicing researcher, a person who is at home in wild places but just as comfortable around the meeting table discussing policy, a person who sees the bigger picture of ecosystem integrity but has the skills to act locally to protect a vital component, a person who can absorb the technical details of a scientific journal article and evaluate the implications for the understanding of superintendents, interpreters, and the public. With this vision, Ro created a training program to launch a new cadre of resource managers into the NPS. So in 1982, after a brief stint at Guadalupe Mountains National Park as a district ranger, I was selected along with thirty-seven others to participate in the Natural Resource Management Trainee program, the brainchild of Ro Wauer. I was reassigned to Crater Lake National Park, Oregon, where Ro Wauer had begun his career. My wife, now pregnant with our first of two, had been planning to give birth in the mild Texas winter in El Paso. Now we were headed to Crater Lake, one of the snowiest places on the planet. But she is tough, our son was born there during a howling snowstorm, and it was just another step in our family adventure in the national parks, but that is another story.

In the fall of 1982, I joined the rest of the trainees in Fort Collins, Colorado, to get our charge from Chief Scientist Ro Wauer. I will never forget it. He stood in front of us like a winning coach before a great game. We were his team; he wanted us to succeed and said that through us the natural resources of the NPS would be in skilled hands; that we would be given the formal training and form a peer network; that we would cut our teeth on the natural re-

source challenges of the day like exotic plant and animal control, air and water pollution, external threats from development; and we would learn to fight the good fight. He suggested that some of us would advance to become chief scientists and superintendents, and maybe even a future NPS director was in the room. Ro set the tone that the protection of park resources was a mission, not just a job, and we needed to be prepared with the best science and the best training available. The next two years were designed to prepare us for that mission.

The rest, as they say, is history. Like inserting genetically engineered cells into a body, the number and influence of resource managers in the NPS grew and spread. There were five more trainee classes, launching the careers of over one hundred professional resource managers into parks and programs across the country. Complete new Resource Management Divisions appeared, and new funding streams were created. Today, over thirty years later, the NPS is a different organization as a result. I would suggest that many of the programs we consider essential to park management and protection today are the direct result of this early idea and investment by Ro Wauer and his trainees: the Natural Resource Challenge, the CESU Network, the I&M network, the State of the Parks reports, the Air Quality program . . . the list goes on and on. Today, the National Park Service is a visible leader in communication, adaptation, and mitigation and monitoring of the effects of climate change because of the professional resource managers spawned from Ro Wauer's early initiative.

In the winter of 1983, a small group of our trainee class traveled to Washington as a part of our program. I vividly remember the visit to Ro's office. It was empty, the desk clear of papers, a single wire coat hanger hung forlornly on the wall near an outdated government-issue calendar. Ro had been purged, reassigned to a field position because of his relentless advocacy for the protection of park resources and because of the petty jealousies and party politics that are so common in Washington. Our small group was solemn, like we were visiting a shrine to a lost leader. Word of his purge spread through the trainees, and our resolve and commitment only deepened. Ro had started something that could not be stopped, and with his own sacrifice, there too was a lesson. That day, for me and for the other trainees, as well as the successive trainees, solidified the belief that the protection of the national parks is worth the risk, even to our careers. For me, Ro Wauer stands among John Muir, George Melendez Wright, and A. Starker Leopold, each setting a new course for the National Park Service toward greater stewardship of the exemplars of our nation's natural heritage.

Jonathan B. Jarvis *was in the first class of the Natural Resource Management trainees in 1982. He has served in the NPS for thirty-seven years as interpreter, ranger, resource manager, superintendent, and regional director in five regions and nine park areas. In 2009, he was confirmed by the US Senate as the eighteenth director of the National Park Service.*

March 6, 2013

Preface

Many folks, on finding out that I worked for the National Park Service (NPS) for thirty-two years, express envy for the kind of life I lived. Few people have such an extraordinary opportunity. Working and living within America's crown jewels was a wonderful way of life. Looking back at those years as a park ranger, naturalist, and biologist, I can't help wanting to share some of those marvelous memories.

Quite often those same folks ask questions about the individual parks, about the park's wildlife, and which one of all the parks is my favorite. Everyone seems to love the national parks, and many show an interest in learning more about them. More than once I have been told, "You should write about your adventures so we could enjoy them too." I have thought that such a project would be a worthy one, but one that would be of interest primarily to my wife, my kids, and a few friends. I also thought that it would be a long-term project and one that might never see the light of day.

Being a park interpreter was important to me; I have always enjoyed sharing my outdoor experiences. And writing my autobiography has provided me with that special opportunity. It is a way to share my personal experiences with and about wildlife. Additional comments about the people and places along the way can't help being part of the narrative.

I would not have been able to include so many of those experiences if it weren't for the daily journal entries that I kept for all of those years. Although the majority of my entries were little more than lists of the birds I found at the various sites, additional notes about habitats, plants, and wildlife in general helped provide the necessary memories.

From day one as a seasonal park ranger at

Crater Lake, through the years at Death Valley, Pinnacles, Zion, Big Bend, and Great Smoky Mountains National Parks, I lived a life that I enjoyed and cherished on a daily basis. My first park, Crater Lake, was a wonderful experience, and I quickly fell in love with the area and the National Park Service. But as a seasonal, I knew that my tenure at Crater Lake was limited. So the opportunity to move on to Death Valley, where I eventually received permanent status, was an even greater opportunity. There I was introduced to a whole new environment, the hottest and driest place in North America, an area where the majority of the plants and animals were also new for me. The move to Zion, the most intimate of the national parks, will forever be remembered as another of those special opportunities. And Big Bend was, for me, the single most exciting opportunity of all. For a biologist and an avid birder, Big Bend was the ultimate.

When I left the field to work in a regional office and then Washington, D.C., I still felt that I was connected to the field. From that perspective I believed that I was able to provide the parks with special expertise because of those many years in the field. But after the years in the regional and then Washington offices, when I returned to the field, it was not the same. My perspective had changed, and I never regained the closeness of being one of the uniformed park employees.

Now, many years after retirement, I finally have written about those wonderful years in the parks and the abundant experiences that I had with park wildlife. Whether that wildlife consisted of birds banded in my backyard or grizzly bears and humpback whales in far different environments, they all held special memories. To be able to share my wildlife experiences with others, I have once again become a park interpreter through my writing. I hope those who read this will not only enjoy the stories but will appreciate even more the values of our national parks.

Acknowledgments

I am most grateful for the hundreds of NPS personnel that I encountered throughout my thirty-two-year career. A few of those individuals are mentioned within the ten chapters of this book. Those that I most want to mention include Roby "Slim" Mabery and Tom Williams at Crater Lake; Fred Binnewies, Bill Bullard, Bill Lukens, and Leroy Rutledge at Death Valley; Russ Mahan at Pinnacles; Dennis Carter, Alan Hagood, Bruce Moorhead, and Frank Oberhansley at Zion; Sue Claybaugh, Bill Jensen, Ruth Jessen, and Roger Siglin at Big Bend; Frank Kowski, Joe Rumberg, and Keith Yarborough at the Southwest Regional Office; George Gardner, Al Greene, and Ted Sudia at the Washington, D.C., Office; Stu Coleman, John Cook, and Pat Miller at the Great Smokies; and Tom Bradley at the Virgin Islands. Also over the years I developed close friendships with a few non-NPS individuals, including Destry Jarvis, Clyde Jones, David Riskind, and Fred Sladen.

I am indebted to a few individuals who provided assistance during the preparation of this book. First and foremost is my wife, Betty. She not only provided her love and full support but also responded to my many computer issues and, when preparing the numerous illustrations, worked long hours rehabbing several of the images, many the results of scanned old slides. I also thank Blair Davenport for providing fairy shrimp data from Death Valley; Keith Arnold for references regarding house sparrow research; and Brent Ortego for information regarding deer nematodes.

A few other friends and colleagues kindly helped with gathering photographs. David Marshall, Southwestern Collections at Texas Tech, responded to my request by digging out several slides from those I had earlier donated, copying them, and sending them on to me.

MY WILD LIFE

Introduction

A chance telephone call literally changed my life! As in the Robert Frost poem, two roads lay before me; "I took the one less traveled by, and that has made all the difference." I have wondered numerous times what my life would have been like if I had chosen a route other than the National Park Service. But I doubt if it would have brought me the same amount of adventure and fulfillment. That phone call led to a thoroughly enjoyable career and an "afterlife" that would not have been possible otherwise.

Dr. William Graff, my teacher and adviser at San Jose State, answered the telephone. He talked for a few minutes and then turned to me and said, "There's a summer job at Crater Lake National Park available. Interested?" It was an immediate answer to the very concern that Dr. Graff and I had been discussing. I was on the verge of graduation, about to leave a life in which I had been reasonably secure for three years, without a job or plan for the future. In less than five minutes I had talked to Chief Ranger Jack Broadbent about the Crater Lake job and had agreed to start there two weeks later.

I had gone to San Jose State because of that school's judo program, ranked number one in the NCAA at the time. Coach Yosh Uchida had offered me a job, kind of a scholarship, as editor of the *National Judo Bulletin* that was run out of the school's Athletic Department. It was my job to write and edit monthly bulletins that went to schools, judo clubs, and players throughout the United States and Canada. I also was provided quarters at the Men's Faculty Club, where I was required to keep the place clean, make coffee every morning, and supply the club with doughnuts, sugar and cream, and the like. The Men's Faculty Club was located on campus; the gym and classrooms were all within walking distance.

Coach Uchida had offered me the position

Author at Men's Faculty Club, San Jose State, 1955

after he learned that I was leaving Santa Rosa Junior College (JC), where I had played judo two of my three years there. My initial major at JC was journalism, although I had changed to prelaw and then to preforestry during the last two years. And I was about to change my major to wildlife management at San Jose State.

I played judo all during my three years at San Jose, and that included working out three to four hours daily five or six days every week during the school year. Our team did extremely well, and I won state and national awards in my 170–179-pound weight class. It all came together during the 1956 National Tournament held in Los Angeles in November. There were only seventeen contestants left on the third day; I was one of those individuals, although I lost my first match on the last day, ending up with only a third-place finish.

However, on that final morning, while wait-

San Jose State judo team, 1957

The Korean War was in full swing at the time, and I expected to be drafted right after graduation. So LeMay's offer was an exceptional opportunity for me, a way to continue doing what I was most interested in at the time and also a way to fulfill my military obligation. All three of the San Jose team finalists—Ben Campbell, Johnny Sepulveda, and I—decided to take him up on his offer. We were told to contact him after graduation, and he would see to it that we received the attention he promised.

As it was, of the three of us, only Ben Campbell followed up on LeMay's offer. Ben did get special service, including training in Japan, and worked with the air force judo program throughout his military career. This same Ben Campbell participated in the 1964 Olympics, although he lost his second match because of an injury. Ben was later elected to the Colorado House of Representatives and to the US Congress in 1992. Part Cherokee Indian, Ben is best known as Senator "Nighthorse" Campbell.

My life changed course in February 1957 when a freak accident kept me out of the military. During judo practice, discs in my lower back were damaged when one of our trainees accidentally threw another of the trainees against me. After consulting two physicians, I decided not to undergo an operation, but I was told that it would require me to remain in "good shape" throughout my life or I would have

ing for the competition to begin, we had a visit from General Curtis LeMay, who at that time was head of the Strategic Air Command of the US Air Force. General LeMay explained that he planned to build a judo program in the air force and was looking for instructors. He said that if any of us who were about to graduate would be interested in joining the air force, he would guarantee us "special services" after basic training that would include a detail in Japan for additional training. All of us who had earned black belt status—I was third-degree black belt at the time—already had considerable teaching experience; it was an important part of our training.

Lake Solitude, Grand Teton National Park

serious back problems. In today's world, with the expertise now available on these kinds of back problems, I probably would have selected surgery. But in 1957 there were too many horror stories about similar operations.

That accident now limited my options. Because I had decided to go into the military upon graduation, I had not acquired an appropriate job as all my other classmates had. A few went into the California Division of Parks and Wildlife, and a few others acquired jobs in the US Fish and Wildlife Service. Those kinds of jobs were much easier to obtain in the late 1950s than they are today.

So, I was sitting in Dr. Graff's office bemoaning the fact that I was the only one of his 1957 graduates without a job, when Chief Ranger Jack Broadbent called. Someone else had initially taken the Crater Lake job but had backed out. That coincidence led me to a thirty-two-year career in the National Park Service.

I already had some familiarity with the national parks, acquired during many summers in the Grand Tetons of Wyoming. My father loved the parks, and every summer we visited places like the Tetons, Yellowstone, Glacier, Grand Canyon, Zion, and Bryce. But his true love was the Tetons. Until I was fourteen years old, we lived in Idaho Falls, Idaho, less than three hours away from Jackson Hole. In fact, on a clear day, the Teton Peaks could be seen to the northeast from just outside town. We visited that park area as often as possible. Some of my earliest memories were visits to the Tetons: hiking to Lake Solitude or around String Lake, horseback riding at the old Square-G Ranch, and once being treed by a cow moose at Leigh Lake.

In retrospect, I may have taken the same direction later after the military if given a chance, but in 1957 fate played a crucial role that led me to the National Park Service for my career. The chapters that follow highlight that adventure.

Crater Lake scene from lodge. Concession photo, 1957.

1
Crater Lake National Park, Oregon

I had been to Crater Lake only once before when I began my National Park Service career there. I was hitchhiking back to Santa Rosa, California, with my junior college friend Irwin Kunachima, after spending part of the 1954 summer with friends near Lethbridge in Canada. An elderly couple from Brooklyn, New York, picked us up somewhere in Montana. Although they were heading south, they wanted to see Crater Lake. We were certainly willing, but I was eager to get back to Santa Rosa, where my parents; brother, Brent; and sisters, Helene and Aleta, were living at the time. After a brief visit with them, I planned to continue on to San Jose where I had a job waiting for me. I was scheduled to attend San Jose State in the fall.

That first memory of Crater Lake is of incredibly blue water set in an extremely deep basin. We spent only a few hours in the park that day, taking the Rim Drive and stopping at vari-

ous overlooks, before continuing on to Klamath Falls for the night. At the time, of course, I had no idea that less than four years later I would be living in the park, spending my days along the Rim as a seasonal park ranger.

It wasn't until I lived and worked in the park that I formed a more lasting impression of the area. The park grabbed me right away. There is nothing like it anywhere else. The heart of the park is the lake, the seventh deepest in the world. The lake's deep blue color seems to absorb the blue of the sky, and the high surrounding cliffs tend to punctuate the scene. Below the Rim is a green mantle of forests and meadows that in summer are filled with a profusion of wildflowers.

Park headquarters, where I reported for duty June 18, 1957, as a seasonal park ranger at a salary of $1.64 per hour, was located just below the Rim. It was situated in a green meadow sur-

Ranger Dorm, Crater Lake National Park, 1957

rounded by dark green conifers. The most impressive structure there, besides the headquarters building itself, was the all-log Ranger Dorm where I and the dozen or so other "seasonals" bunked for the summer. Today, more than fifty years later, I remember only a few names of those individuals with whom I shared the summer: Jack Houston, Dave and Hugo Huntzinger, Dan Konapaski, Bob Scott, Bob Topp, and Jim Zink.

Although Chief Ranger Jack Broadbent had hired me two weeks earlier, I reported directly to District Ranger Roby "Slim" Mabery. He issued assignments and was in charge of seasonal training. Slim was a unique individual, very professional and full of enthusiasm, and after work hours he played a guitar and sang old-time sing-along songs. The park superintendent—Tom Williams—was also well liked and highly respected. Three additional full-time park employees—Ranger John Bowdler, Naturalist Dick Brown, and Chief Engineer Bill Loftis—crossed my path on later occasions during my Park Service career. All of the permanent employees lived in adjacent housing.

One evening during that first week of training, the Williamses invited the entire staff to their home for a meal. Although I can no longer recall what we ate, I vividly remember an incident in the upstairs part of the house. Tom had established a wildlife feeding station at a window that opened out to a large tray he had built on an adjacent tree. He and I, and a few others, visited his feeding station right after dinner, taking some meat scraps for bait. Immediately after we opened the window, a pine marten appeared only four or five feet away, and it seemed to ignore our presence as it checked out the handouts. Although I had seen and examined pine marten skins in my mammalogy class at San Jose State, it was my first observation of a wild one. It was truly a beautiful creature with an extremely lush and soft, yellowish-brown coat, a buff throat, and a large bushy tail. It didn't stay long, took a few bites only, and then carried the remainder of the handouts into the adjacent foliage and disappeared.

My only other face-to-face experience with a

My Wild Life

pine marten occurred many years later along a trail near Jackson Lake in Grand Teton National Park. Betty and I had taken a walk away from our campsite, looking for birds, when we noticed a chipmunk sitting on a pile of brush only a few feet off the trail, about thirty feet from where we stood. We were watching it through binoculars when a pine marten suddenly exploded onto the scene and grabbed the chipmunk. It happened so fast that we were unsure if the capture had resulted from a stealthy approach or a rush. But the marten suddenly had the chipmunk in its jaws. The marten sat still a few seconds, with us watching, while it began to consume its prey. Partway through its meal it seemed to realize it was under surveillance and left the scene as unobtrusively as it had arrived.

The Job

My first week at Crater Lake, before we received our summer assignments, was spent in training. Classes were held at the Ranger Dorm, but we also spent considerable time outdoors, involved with various law enforcement activities, fire and rescue, wildland fire control, and people management. At the end of the week I was given the assignment of "Rim Ranger," working at the Crater Lake Rim near the concessions operations and the Sennott Memorial Observation Station, the park's principal interpretive center. I felt fortunate that I was not assigned to an entrance station, which would have limited my freedom of movement and opportunities to observe wildlife. Although my principal responsibility was public contact along the Rim between the store/restaurant complex and the lodge, I also drove Rim Drive once daily to check on visitors who might have questions or need help along the thirty-three-mile route. The majority of my time involved little more than helping visitors properly park their vehicles and answering questions, such as the location of the restrooms, eating places, and the nearest accommodations.

One day a vehicle with an Idaho license plate (with "8B," designating Bonneville County) drove into the parking lot. I walked over to the vehicle and said, "Hi folks, welcome to Crater Lake. How's everything in Idaho Falls?" The driver immediately asked me how I knew where they were from. I told them that I too was from Idaho Falls and that I recognized the license plate. An elderly lady, sitting in the back seat, looked at me very carefully and asked me my name. When I told her, she looked surprised and said, "Well, hello, Roland. I used to take care of you when you were a baby." A small world!

Another time in the parking lot, I watched a passenger roll down her window and throw out an empty soda can. She then rolled the window

rather belligerent and told me that I was being paid to pick up after park visitors. Ignoring her comment, I informed her that I could either write her a ticket for littering and we would go down to park headquarters to see the judge, or she could spend an hour picking up trash in and around the parking area. She glared at me, muttered something or other, but then realized I was serious. The driver, presumably her husband, said, "See, I told you not to throw out your garbage." She got out of the vehicle and spent the next hour picking up trash. Her husband told me afterward that this was the best thing that could have happened to her.

On another day in August, while patrolling Rim Drive, my radio suddenly sprang to life with dialogue that I find hard to forget so many years later. Hugo Huntzinger, who was working the North Entrance Station, had stopped a visitor leaving the park with a sack of golden-mantled ground squirrels that he had trapped within the park. We had been watching for the perpetrator, who was driving a Cadillac with Texas plates. He had been reported by another visitor who had watched the Texan baiting ground squirrels into a sack and then dumping them into a heavier cloth bag. Hugo, after stopping the poacher, had radioed Assistant Superintendent Ray Rundell at his office in Medford for guidance. The conversation went something like the following:

Hugo: "Mr. Rundell, I am holding a Mr. [name] at the North Entrance. He is the one re-

Golden-mantled ground squirrel

back up. I immediately walked over, picked up the discarded can, and knocked on the vehicle window. When she rolled her window down, I asked, "Ma'am, did you accidentally drop your soda can?" I was ready to hand it back when she said, "No, I threw it out." I then explained that the outdoors, especially a national park, was not her personal trash basket. She then got

My Wild Life

ported to be stealing park squirrels. What do you want me to do?"

Ray: "Very good. Is he cooperating?"

Hugo: "Yes, sir." [silence for maybe two to three minutes] "Mr. Rundell, what do you want me to do?"

Ray [after another two to three minutes]: "Hugo, how many squirrels are there?"

Hugo: "I'm not sure, sir. I'll check." [silence for another two to three minutes] "Well, sir, there were four squirrels, but two got out of the bag."

Ray: "Two got out? How did that happen?"

Hugo: "Well, they just jumped out when I opened the sack to count."

Ray: "Hugo, where are they? Can you catch them again?"

Hugo: "I'll try, but they are both running around inside the station. Oops, one just jumped out the window. There goes the second one."

Ray: "Hugo, hold on to the other two. We will need the evidence."

Hugo: "Yes, sir. I think I have them under control." [silence for another two to three minutes] "Mr. Rundell, what do you want me to do?"

Ray [lengthy pause]: "Hugo, did Mr. [name] know that squirrels are protected in a national park?"

Hugo: "Just a minute, sir, I'll ask him. [a lengthy silence] No, he didn't know he wasn't supposed to trap squirrels in a national park."

[an even longer silence] Sir, what do you want me to do?"

Ray: "Hugo, since it's late in the afternoon, go ahead and close the station, and then escort Mr. [name] back to headquarters. I'll ask Slim to meet you there. [pause] And Hugo, don't forget the squirrels."

In spite of loving my job at one of our nation's finest national parks, I realized early on that I was not cut out to be in law enforcement. I was far more interested in the park's animals and plants and in telling people about the national parks and their significant natural and cultural resources. Instead of working in a parking lot, addressing problems and complaints and moderating arguments, I preferred to discuss the park's flora and fauna and document wildlife observations. It appeared to me that none of the other rangers, including the interpreters, knew very much about the park's wildlife. It seemed only natural to me to keep daily notes, both on the job and on my days off, on whatever wildlife I observed.

Crater Lake Birdlife

The birdlife was of particular interest to me. Over the summer I recorded a total of 112 species, including several not previously reported for the park: rough-legged hawk, great gray owl, red-eyed vireo, black-capped chickadee, vesper and tree sparrows, and white-winged crossbill.

The great gray owl was one of my most memorable bird observations that summer. Bob Scott and I had driven to Red Cone Spring in the early morning. We had walked around the area for an hour or more before I discovered the owl perched in the open on a heavy limb near the top of a mountain hemlock. It remained still, allowing us both a great view through binoculars. Its huge size, brownish-gray plumage, heavy ringed facial disks, and yellow eyes were obvious. As long as we stayed put, it remained still, even though it was staring directly at us. But as soon as we began to move closer, it flew into another hemlock and perched so that its head was out of sight, I suppose thinking that it was hidden from view. After studying it a little longer, we moved closer, but it then flew away into the forest. What a marvelous bird! I remember thinking that this bird, more than any other, represented the true wilderness character of Crater Lake National Park.

Another of the wild birds seen almost daily along the Rim was the peregrine falcon. I was sometimes able to point out one or a pair of these large raptors to visitors along the Rim. More often one would simply pass over en route to some peregrine destination. One July day, a pair of peregrines played overhead for several minutes. A few visitors and I watched as the two birds played catch with a prey spe-cies of some sort, probably a ground squirrel. The birds took turns dropping and catching the prey, diving, rolling, and somersaulting all the while. Every few seconds one or both would let out a loud, piercing scream.

Of all Crater Lake's birds, however, none was so obvious and solicited so many questions as the Clark's nutcracker. This high-country relative of crows and ravens was abundant along the Rim, often perching on stumps and rock walls in full view of park visitors. It is slightly smaller than a crow, and its gray, white, and black plumage, with white trailing edges to the black wings, is distinct. And if not readily seen at almost anytime during the daylight hours, its call—a guttural and drawn-out "kr-a-a" or "chaar"—can hardly be missed. It also is a favored "camp robber" in that it readily accepts handouts or steals food off picnic tables. Nutcrackers spend considerable time in the park campground and at picnic sites, where they learn to take handouts. The rangers constantly attempt to discourage people from feeding the wildlife, for their own good, but Clark's nutcrackers especially got plenty of human food.

Its name is derived from its habit of prying seeds from conifer cones in crowbar fashion with its sharp, heavy bill. The birds then hide the seeds on south-facing slopes for winter use. They actually possess a special pouch under their tongues in which they are able to carry up to ninety-five seeds per trip. The nutcracker's scientific name is *Nucifraga columbiana*—the genus name is Latin for "nut breaker," and the species name is derived from the Columbia River, the place where William Clark, of the Lewis and Clark expedition, was the first to collect one in about 1804. Its common name comes from its discoverer.

The Clark's nutcracker unquestionably is Crater Lake's best-known bird. In fact, I once wrote an article for *Birder's World* magazine that I titled "Avian Ambassadors to Our National Parks." "Ambassadors" were the various parks' most common or most renowned birds. Clark's nutcracker was the designated avian ambassador for Crater Lake. A few other park ambassadors included Colima warbler for Big Bend, common raven for Death Valley, trumpeter swan for Grand Teton, phainopepla for Organ Pipe Cactus, western tanager for Yosemite, and canyon wren for Zion.

At the end of my Crater Lake summer, I prepared an article—"Bird Notes from the Crater Lake Area"—on my findings, which was published in *Audubon Warbler* in 1958, a small publication of the Oregon Audubon Society. That article, only two pages in length, was my very first publication. In addition, my *Checklist of the Birds of Crater Lake National Park* (1957), containing 159 species, represented the first complete listing for the park.

Mammals

Mule deer populations within and adjacent to the park were of considerable interest to the park staff. Because so little was known about the park's deer population, I was permitted to spend a day each week attempting to address this issue. On July 10 and 17, I established pellet-count plots along five transects: three near Crater Peak, one near Red Cone Spring, and one along Copeland Creek. Wildlife managers had developed a formula for estimating deer numbers by the number of pellet groups found within predetermined plots within certain time frames. On walking my transect lines on August 9 and 23, I reached the conclusion, however, that Crater Lake had a greater population of elk than deer. My short-term survey, except for providing me with numerous additional wildlife experiences, was not the success anticipated.

The summer of 1957 was drier than normal, and lightning produced a rash of wildfires throughout the park. After one particularly stormy night, several small burns were active at one time. I was given the responsibility to control one of those small fires near Red Cone Spring; additional help was expected within a few hours. The fire was less than an acre in size and the ground was reasonably moist, but the tree hit by lightning was still on fire. As I circled the burn, keeping the fire from spreading by throwing fuel back into the burn, I noticed a fly-

Oregon Caves National Monument entrance sign.
Courtesy of Betty Wauer.

per branches. A very few seconds later it reappeared without its baby, which I assumed had been deposited in a second cavity, ran down the trunk, and headed back to the original tree. It again ran through the low flames, jumping from spot to spot, and right back up the burning tree to where it had first appeared. In another three or four minutes it was en route back down the tree, carrying a second baby, repeating the original performance. I last saw it high in the second tree, second baby and all.

Oregon Caves

In early September, I learned that Bob Smith, chief ranger at Oregon Caves, was going on leave for two weeks, and I was asked to go over there on an interim basis to act for him until his return. Oregon Caves National Monument, located on the western slopes of the Siskiyou Mountains in southwestern Oregon, was a satellite unit of Crater Lake. It contains a three-mile-long solution (worn by water) cave and six miles of trails through a beautiful forest.

On September 11, I drove south to Medford and westward toward the Pacific. Upon arrival at Oregon Caves, I moved into a trailer located near the cave entrance. During the next two weeks I was free to wander the area, so long as I was on call for whatever emergencies might arise. None did!

ing squirrel working its way down the burning tree. As it came closer, I could see that it was carrying a baby in its mouth. It made steady progress from limb to limb and down the lower trunk to where it finally reached the ground, some of which was burning. I then watched the mother flying squirrel leap over the low flames from clear spot to clear spot until it reached the perimeter of the burning area. It continued another hundred yards or so where it climbed up another tree and disappeared into the up-

I found the cave to be intriguing, but I was most interested in the bats and the area's birdlife. I recorded 67 bird species during my stay. Mountain quail were abundant along the slopes, and during a hike on the Mt. Elijah Trail I encountered a family of northern goshawks. These large accipiters seemed unafraid, even when I approached to within a couple hundred yards. However, when I got closer to obtain a photograph, they soared off across the valley.

On the same hike I also found several mountain beavers. This large rodent, sometimes called "aplodontia" or "sewellel," is not at all like beavers found in wetlands throughout North America. About a quarter the size of a regular beaver, and with an extremely short tail instead of a flat leathery one, this mountain species is confined to the coastal ranges from British Columbia south to northern California, including the Cascades and Sierras as far south as Sequoia National Park.

Once I saw a few of these mammals, I began looking for their telltale "hay stacks" and found two with little trouble. Both were low mounds of cut grasses and leaves that had been laid out on the open, rocky ground. Apparently, mountain beavers put out these piles to wilt and dry. They later carry the materials underground into their burrows to use as food during the cold winter months. They do not hibernate, as so many other rodents do, but are quite active all winter, feeding on their cache as well as bark and twigs that they find by tunneling under the snow.

Transition

I returned to Crater Lake on September 27, and until my employment ended on October 17, I worked at road patrol and had some South Entrance Station duty. Snow comes early at Crater Lake, and long before leaving, I experienced a beautiful fantasyland, so much different from the summer greenery.

Although my seasonal employment at Crater Lake came to an end, I already knew that I wanted to continue working for the National Park Service, preferably as an interpreter rather than in law enforcement. No job openings were available at the time, and the folks at Crater Lake suggested that I consider applying for a cave guide position at Carlsbad Caverns, which could lead to a permanent job in the Park Service. I did look into that option, but before anything was settled, Superintendent Williams informed me that he had talked to Superintendent Binnewies at Death Valley, and a seasonal naturalist position was available there. Was I interested? I, of course, chose the Death Valley position.

Leaving Crater Lake was not easy, even though another job was waiting for me. I had

Annie Springs Entrance Station, Crater Lake National Park, October 1957

My Wild Life

fallen in love with Crater Lake and all the surrounding country, and I thought at the time that I would someday return, perhaps even retire in the area. Crater Lake was my first park! It had become a very special place to me.

Post-retirement Visits

I was to visit Crater Lake several additional times during the later years. Sisters Helene and husband, David, and Aleta and husband, Pat, eventually settled in Medford and Salem, Oregon, respectively. And in 1990, my father and stepmother also moved to Medford to be closer to the girls. It was only natural, therefore, that Betty and I made trips to Oregon often. On most of those visits we would drive up to Crater Lake for the day, usually picnicking in one of the many sites along the Rim or at lower elevations. Dad loved the outdoors! He passed away at ninety-six years of age in December 2004.

On my last visit to Oregon, in July 2009, Betty and I spent a day along the Rim, stopping at various overlooks for photographs and at flower areas for butterflies. All the time I had worked for the National Park Service, working and visiting many of America's most beautiful and wild landscapes, I had pretty well ignored the butterflies. But after retiring in 1989, my passion gradually shifted from birds to butterflies, so we spent much of our time observing and photographing those winged jewels whenever the opportunity arose.

On July 14, we drove the Rim Drive counterclockwise, stopping at a dozen or so sites where we thought we might find butterflies. The snow had not fully melted off the higher peaks and north-facing slopes, and the spring flower bloom had only just begun. Nevertheless, we photographed 14 butterfly species at patches of flowers or at muddy sites. We were surprised by the abundance of Edith's checkerspots and California tortoiseshells, but the spring whites, bramble green and alpine Sheridan's hairstreaks, and square-spotted blues were most welcome.

I enjoyed our return visit to Crater Lake, the butterflies, the gorgeous scenery, and some marvelous memories.

2
Death Valley National Monument, California and Nevada

I had never before spent much time in a desert environment, having been raised in Idaho and Wyoming and schooled in the greater San Francisco Bay Area. But I quickly fell in love with the desert. It can be the most peaceful environment on earth, and it can go from an arid, empty landscape to one filled with colorful wildflowers almost overnight. I discovered that every animal and plant was either new to me or was of special interest because of its ability to survive in such a hostile environment.

Death Valley, eventually designated as a national park in 1994, is one of the strangest places on earth. The valley is a 135-mile-long, north-south trough, containing the salty remains of ancient Lake Manly. The valley is bordered to the west by the Panamint Mountains that rise to Telescope Peak at an elevation of 11,049 feet and to the east by the Amargosa Range, which includes the Funeral and Black Mountains. The park contains the lowest place (Badwater at 282 feet below sea level) in North America. The 11,331-foot rise in elevation of Telescope Peak is the highest point in Death Valley National Park and the Panamint Range. In addition, the park contains a smorgasbord of ancient animal footprints; 14 square miles of sand dunes; Salt Creek, where endemic pupfish are able to live below ground in summer; Racetrack Playa with boulders that slide for no scientifically verified reason; and an explosion crater 800 feet in depth known as "Ubehebe."

My initial accommodation at Death Valley was a trailer at Cow Creek, the park's headquarters area at the time. A new visitor center was completed a few months after I arrived. It was a spacious structure that housed the Park Service offices as well as a large lobby, an exhibit room, a huge auditorium, and storage space for the abundant park collections. The new building was located at Furnace Creek Ranch, next to a date orchard and golf course, five miles

Badwater, Death Valley National Monument

south of Cow Creek. Housing for the majority of the park staff remained at Cow Creek; the houses were little more than refurbished CCC (Civilian Conservation Corps) buildings. But several "Mission 66" (a Park Service program to update employee accommodations) houses were already under construction when I arrived on November 3. Cow Creek also contained the park's maintenance area and a swimming pool,

a godsend in summer. According to the Park Service records, Death Valley's swimming pool was officially listed as a "fire reservoir." The federal bureaucracy frowned on such luxuries as a swimming pool.

My trailer, located at the entrance of the Cow Creek housing loop, was reasonably comfortable, at least during the wintertime. On warm days, however, which was most of the time, "air conditioning" depended on an ancient swamp cooler. As long as the cooler was working perfectly and continued to force moist cool air through the trailer, it was tolerable, although everything nearby could be wet. But when the cooler malfunctioned or the trailer lost power, which it did regularly when I used too much electricity at one time, it became a steamy hot box in very short order. Eventually, newly designed air-conditioning units were installed in all the new houses.

None of the park vehicles had air conditioning in 1957, although window swamp coolers were available. A few individuals utilized these wetting machines, but most of us preferred driving with our windows open an inch or two, allowing for air movement to keep things as comfortable as possible. After all, Death Valley is not only the hottest known place in North America but also one of the driest. The high-temperature record is based on an official reading of 134°F on July 10, 1913, along with five consecutive days that reached 129°F.

During the summer months, which lasted from late March through September, nighttime temperatures rarely dipped below 100°F in the valley. I got to the point that I could estimate the air temperature within one or two degrees when driving down the road, simply by holding my hand outside the vehicle. It was impossible to keep one's hand outside a moving vehicle for more than a few seconds once the temperatures reached 105. Fingernails began to burn almost immediately.

Wildlife, especially migrating birds, seemed to suffer the most. For example, the following paragraph was taken from the article "A Survey of the Birds of Death Valley," which I wrote for the *Condor*, an ornithological journal:

> Migrants arriving from cooler and higher regions are sometimes greatly affected by the high temperatures and aridity. Many Red-shafted Flickers are found dead each fall. Herons, warblers, and sparrows have a high death rate. During mid-summer, birds robin-size and smaller seldom decay when death occurs. They become dried carcasses within eight hours. I placed a dead Brown-headed Cowbird in the sun at 7:00 a.m. and by 6:00 p.m. it was mummified, dry enough to be stored out of a freezing unit. In late August, I found a Red-winged Blackbird attached to a shrub; its wings were open and it was mummified. Dehydration probably accounts for the greatest number of dead birds during the summer in the below-sea-level region of Death Valley.

I didn't know a soul when I arrived in Death Valley, although I had visited briefly with Superintendent Fred Binnewies about the job before leaving Crater Lake. I found Fred and his wife, Amy, to be extremely friendly and

My Wild Life

very gracious; everyone liked Fred and Amy. My direct supervisor—Chief Naturalist Meredith Ingram—was not as impressive. In fact, my initial conversation with Mert left me rather perplexed. Right off the bat, he said, "I am really glad to have someone working for me who knows something about natural history. I don't care about that; I'm more interested in administration."

As luck would have it, Mert transferred to Lake Mead a few months later and was replaced by Bill Bullard. Although Bill was not versed in natural history either, he was very well trained in all of the other facets of Park Service interpretation. He was especially knowledgeable about curatorial methods, and Death Valley had a huge collection of artifacts and specimens that needed attention. Thousands of items, ranging from archeological and historical artifacts to specimens of birds and mammals that had been left in boxes and scattered about, needed to be properly curated once space became available in the new visitor center. I spent considerable time in that endeavor under Bill's expert tutelage.

The Job

My initial position at Death Valley was as a seasonal naturalist, but eventually, after passing the Federal Service Entrance Exam (in Barstow on November 16, 1957), I obtained permanent status on February 25, 1958. That first full-time position was not the ordinary kind but a dual-park position, six months in Death Valley and six months in Pinnacles National Monument, a small park on the Pacific Coast near Salinas.

While I was a seasonal park interpreter those first few months, my duties included a large dose of information desk responsibilities; presentation of talks, walks, and auto tours; and a variety of other activities. Once the new visitor center opened with its huge auditorium and state-of-the-art audiovisual equipment, I found that I thoroughly enjoyed giving programs. I worked up talks on the Death Valley birdlife and its backcountry. Although I had given a few talks to small audiences in the past, the Death Valley talks often were given to audiences of several hundred. I was nervous at first, but I discovered that if I opened my talks with a few comments and a story, it helped me to relax. My favorite story, especially when giving a talk on the backcountry, included the following:

Have you ever tried to go someplace no one else has even been? That is something that I have tried to do on numerous occasions. One day I drove a long way into the backcountry, left my four-wheel-drive vehicle, and started hiking. I camped out overnight, and the next morning continued hiking. An hour or two later I stopped to eat a snack. Sitting in the canyon, I felt kind of proud of myself, because maybe here was a place no one else had ever been. Just about then I smelled coffee.

I immediately continued up the canyon. In another quarter mile, right in the middle of the canyon, was an old prospector, sitting by a fire brewing up some coffee. But it wasn't the prospector or his coffee that caught my attention, but lying alongside the campfire was a coyote. And this was one of the shaggiest, oldest mutts I had ever seen. A really poor example of a wild coyote.

The prospector invited me to have a cup of his coffee, which I did, while eyeing the old coyote all the time. In a little while I started back down the canyon; I had to be at work the next day. As I hiked down the canyon, I just happened to look back, and I discovered that the coyote was following me. Now, let me tell you, as a naturalist, I have had lots of coyote experiences. But never before had I had one come after me. I continued on, trying to ignore it, but it began to close in on me. So I stopped, right in the middle of the canyon and waited. That coyote—now you won't believe this—walked right up to me. It stopped a few feet away, sat down, and said, "You saw me by the fire back there, and I could see that you thought I was an old, worn-out coyote. But let me tell you, when I was a young coyote, I could catch any rabbit in these hills in three jumps."

Well, I didn't care if that coyote could catch a rabbit in one jump. But here was a talking coyote. And it was the very first talking coyote I had ever encountered. I was obviously excited! I ran back up the canyon to the prospector. But by the time I got there, I was totally out of breath. As I approached the fire, the prospector held out his hand to stop me. Then he said, "Now wait a minute, son, before you start, let me tell you the truth. That coyote never could catch a rabbit in three jumps."

Some of my responsibilities during the first few months were law enforcement oriented. In December 1957 on an unusually cold night, while I was still living in my trailer at Cow Creek, someone knocked on the trailer door in the early evening. When I opened the door, I found a gentleman who was obviously upset. He immediately asked me, "Are you a ranger?" I answered that I was and asked him if he needed help. He then told me that he had been leading a group of Boy Scouts on an all-day hike in the Funeral Mountains and that one of the boys had become lost. After some additional discussion, I contacted District Ranger Don Spaulding and told him about the situation.

Don immediately took over, and within the hour we met at the Cow Creek headquarters where Don described a plan of action. Park Rangers Bob Sellers and Lee Shackleton and I were to drive to the Chloride Cliff area, where the hikers had begun, and to retrace their route down the steep slope to the Keane Wonder Mill. Don, Park Ranger Howard Parr, and the Scout leader would drive to Keane Wonder Mill and hike up the trail.

It took us almost two hours to reach the Chloride Cliff area; by that time it was close to midnight. The road, little more than a track, ran to a parking area where the trail to Keane Wonder Mill began. Just before reaching the parking area, I suddenly detected a fire far down the slope. I yelled, "Stop! Back up a little!" We backed up to the spot but could see nothing. But I was sure. Bob thought we were almost directly above one of the historic mines. We decided to leave the vehicle there and hike down the trail. Although Bob radioed Don about the location, they could not detect anything upslope from their location at the Keane Wonder Mill site.

The night was unbelievably cold. A dry wind seemed to cut into my very soul. That was in spite of a jacket, a pack on my back, and a blanket, primarily for an emergency, that I wrapped around me. It took us another couple of hours to negotiate the steep trail. The moon that night was full or nearly so and provided adequate light for a slow and careful descent. Finally, we reached one of the old mine sites, evident by a jumble of tin sheets and other debris. As we approached the area, one of us shouted, "Is anyone here?" Nothing. We shouted again, "Hello, is anyone here?" Suddenly, one of the tin sheets was thrown aside and a boy literally

exploded into the open. His first comment was, "Oh, thank you for finding me. I am so cold!"

He was dressed for a daytime hike, without adequate nighttime clothing. He had built a fire on top of one of the tin sheets and crawled below to keep warm. But when the fire went out, he had no way of keeping warm. Bob examined him first to make sure he was not injured, although he was shaking from either cold or fear. Bob then radioed Don to tell him we had found the boy and he was okay. I gave the boy the blanket, and it seemed to help him calm down, but it left me colder than before. I had brought some snacks, including apples that we ate on-site. Bob had asked Don if we should continue down the trail or if it might be faster to hike back up to our vehicle. Don said we were more than halfway down the cliff and it would be faster to continue downhill to the Keane Wonder Mill, where they were waiting.

About halfway to the meeting place, the boy's attitude changed from being cold and frightened to belligerent. He informed us that he had no idea why we had come to find him: "I planned to do this all on my own." By the time we reached Don and the others, we were wishing that we had left him where we found him under the pile of tin. It was almost daylight. Don walked over and said something like, "I hope you know, young man, that you have kept eight men out all night without sleep to rescue you." That was when the boy stated that he had followed the right trail, but the rest of the group had taken the wrong trail, and we had all wasted our time. Don suddenly grabbed the boy by the arm and led him into the cab of his truck for a brief discussion. We were not privy to what was said, but the boy did not say another word all the way back to Furnace Creek.

Death Valley, because of its unique qualities, is a magnet to innumerable scientists. I was extremely fortunate during my tenure to have the opportunity not only to meet many of these individuals but also to spend quality field time

Nelson's bighorn ram, Death Valley National Monument

with a few. Although not part of my official job, I spent many hours with wildlife biologist Lowell Sumner; herpetologists Robert Stebbins and Frederick Turner; ornithologist Ned Johnson; mammalogist Charles Douglas; geologists Donald Curry and Charlie Hunt; and archeologist Alice Hunt.

For example, Frederick Turner and I drove the roads after dark looking for snakes, and we eventually wrote a paper, "A Survey of the Herpetofauna of the Death Valley Area," that was published in the *Great Basin Naturalist*. I accompanied Charlie Hunt as he surveyed the alluvial fans by helicopter, mapping the geological terrain based upon the vegetation zones that I helped identify from the air. And I spent several field days with Alice Hunt on various archeological digs.

Also, one of the park residents—Ralph Welles—was studying bighorn sheep. Ralph had taught drama at a little theater near Stanford but had come to Death Valley to photograph desert bighorn. He was an excellent photographer and a marvelous speaker. A talk about bighorn sheep by Ralph Welles convinced listeners that not only was Ralph the world's foremost authority on bighorn but, from his theatrics, he was their closest relative. He could make combat between two bighorn rams seem as if it were happening right there and then.

My Wild Life

Lowell Sumner, regional biologist for the Park Service and Ralph's mentor, had visited with me about Ralph's project and had encouraged me to get acquainted with Ralph and his wife, Buddy. Upon meeting the Welleses at the post office on my second or third day in the park, I received little encouragement when I asked to go into the field with them. In fact, Ralph was downright rude. Thinking that maybe it was just a bad day, I decided to try again later. But a second attempt a few days later was no better. Again at the post office and after a friendly greeting, I broached with Ralph the idea of spending some time with him in the field, to learn about bighorn. His response was no different from the previous two. But this time, I said, "Ralph, I don't understand your attitude. Mutual friends have encouraged me to get acquainted with you and to spend some field time together. I am extremely interested in bighorn. But if you don't care, I will stop bothering you." And I turned and walked away. But this time, Ralph followed me outside, and before I reached my vehicle, he called my name and said, "Ro, I didn't realize you really cared. How about coming up for dinner tonight?" And that is how I got involved with the Welleses and their bighorn sheep project.

Over the next few years I spent considerable time with Ralph and Buddy, both in the field and in their trailer. When their book *The Bighorn of Death Valley* appeared in 1961, it included a photograph I contributed that shows bighorn and wild burros sharing the same water hole, a situation that many biologists had previously doubted would occur.

A rather interesting part of the Welles's trailer life was their parakeet that Ralph had taught an amazing number of theatrical and other phrases. His bird could clearly say, "To be or not to be; that is the question." But it had trouble tying logical phrases together. So, it might just as well say, "To be or not to be," but instead of completing that Shakespearean phrase, it might add, "What's up, Doc?" And if someone knocked on the trailer door when the Welleses were not at home, Ralph had taught the bird to say, "Help, Ranger, let me out of here."

Besides the outings with the Welleses, I constantly documented my sightings of bighorn on all of my backcountry trips and in 1964 published the article "The Unpredictable Nelson Bighorn" in *National Parks Magazine*. To emphasize its unpredictability, I wrote:

A band may be seen grazing golden primroses on the Death Valley Buttes one day, and be far into the Chloride Cliff area the next. You might find several bighorns feeding in Death Valley's Furnace Creek Wash—perhaps only a few feet off the road—and be able to approach within a hundred feet or so. Another band might dash off across the barren slopes before you have had time for a casual glance from a mile away.

My major emphasis was to point out the numerous threats to the bighorn, in Death Valley and throughout their range. I continued:

> Severe competition for food with wild burros is a major factor in bighorn decline. The descendants of abandoned miner's [sic] burros befoul waterholes, compete with bighorn for the desert's sparse and slow-growing vegetation, and otherwise make it nearly impossible for the wild sheep to survive in any great numbers.

Friends, Colleagues, and Life at Death Valley

My closest friend in the park was Leroy Rutledge (purchasing agent), a West Texan with whom I shared many after-hours adventures. We both were hard-core baseball enthusiasts, except that he was a die-hard New York Yankees fan and I was a San Francisco Giants fan. There were times when we would leave the park on a Friday evening, drive to Los Angeles, and take in three or four ball games (depending on whether the Dodgers were playing a doubleheader or not) over the weekend. We would drive back to Death Valley after the last Sunday afternoon game and be at work on Monday morning.

Both of us were bachelors at the time, and when a new two-bedroom house became available, we joined forces and moved in together. New houses were in great demand, but because of our two full-time positions we qualified. Leroy was pure Texan. He had a marvelous Texas vocabulary, calling cigarettes "coffin nails," youngsters "buttons," and agitated people as having a "wall-eyed fit." As for beer, nothing came close to matching Lone Star for Leroy. One night around midnight, on returning from a visit home to Texas, he woke me up so I could try some of his favorite brew. He beamed as he handed me a can. I found it extremely hard to hide my disappointment.

I developed strong friendships with several additional park employees during my tenure. Dan Danielson, Boots and Nellie Dott, Warren and Mary Hill, Bill Hoy, Bill Lukens, Jim and Mary Mardis, Howard Parr, Joe Rockwell, Chuck Rowe, Matt and Rosemary Ryan, and Ray Smith were my favorites.

I also became friends with a number of concession employees, one of whom was Sandy

Hall. Sandy and I were married on February 22, 1959, in Reno, Nevada. Our daughter Rebecca Sue (Becky) was born on July 27, 1961, in Las Vegas while we still lived in Death Valley, and Katrina Ann (Trina) was born on May 28, 1963, in St. George, Utah, after we moved to Zion National Park. Sandy and I were divorced in 1965 while I was still at Zion.

All during my tenure in Death Valley it was necessary to drive out of the park to Las Vegas (140 miles) or Beatty (60 miles) for groceries and entertainment. I most enjoyed my visits to Vegas, as there was plenty of inexpensive entertainment at the lounges of the various casinos. There was no charge for spending an evening drinking a few beers and listening to some excellent music. A few years later, however, the better-known entertainers played only the high-priced shows, and the secondary entertainers played the lounges; there was even a charge for these shows. I never gambled, so my sole expense in Vegas was limited to a few beers. A couple of my favorite lounge shows during those early years included those by Earl Grant and Mahalia Jackson.

During the late 1950s, atom bomb testing was under way in an open desert area northeast of Death Valley, about halfway between the park and Las Vegas. On a few occasions, I was awakened in the middle of the night by a rumbling sound and the outdoors lighting up like midday. Although the park never got involved in any way with the tests, we were involved with an abundance of questions following each episode.

Death Valley Birdlife

Death Valley's wildlife was even more confounding. How the many species have been able to adapt to the hot, arid conditions is truly astounding. One of the best examples is the well-known house sparrow, the same sparrow that is so abundant in our cities and towns all across North America. In Death Valley, colonies of this little nonnative bird were scattered throughout, wherever there were patches of mesquites. This bird interested ornithologists Bob Selander and Richard Johnston, and I helped Bob collect a fairly large sample of this species. They planned to compare them with samples taken all across the country, from east to west and north to south. Their report, eventually published in 1964 in the journal *Science*, suggested that the species was already showing characteristics leading to subspecific diversity, meaning that the species could possibly be split into two or more subspecies. Bob later wrote me, "The Death Valley birds are much paler than any others we have examined and in a way

Author camping at Wilson Spring, Panamint Mountains, 1959

that sample . . . is the most valuable we have."

The common raven was another of the park's adaptable birds, but it was a native species that occurred at all elevations. It was just as likely to be soaring over Telescope Peak as walking along the salty shore of Badwater. Year-round, ravens could be found along the highways, flying these routes every morning checking for roadkill. In summer, ravens congregated at Furnace Creek Ranch, spending considerable time at shady areas. I found as many as sixty individuals there at one time. Yet many of the spring sites in the surrounding mountains, where I surveyed birds year-round, were devoid of ravens.

Unlike most of the Valley birds that moved to higher, cooler areas for the summer, ravens apparently congregated at Furnace Creek to loaf around the golf course. And on July 9, 1961, a day with a temperature of 122°F, I recorded an albino raven at Furnace Creek Ranch; it was not seen again.

Great horned owls were commonplace throughout most of the park, including the Valley proper, where they resided in the Furnace Creek date orchard. For five years in a row, a pair used the same nest in a date palm in the center of the orchard. And what was most remarkable was that every year the first egg, of a three-egg clutch, hatched on March 17 (Saint Patrick's Day). I was able to climb to the nest with one of the very tall ladders used to pick dates, and I obtained several good photographs, including some that included the snow-white chicks. The Death Valley Natural History Association had postcards made from one of my slides.

The Panamint Mountains backcountry contains reasonably good access via a few very long and very rough roadways. I found that my 1949 Mercury, relatively high centered for an automobile, could negotiate many of these tracts. I spent considerable time visiting the various springs that were situated in a long line at an elevation of about four thousand feet along the eastern slope. I followed feral burro trails from spring to spring, documenting the birdlife along

My Wild Life

the way. I eventually published my findings in "Ecological Distribution of the Birds of the Panamint Mountains, California" in the *Condor* (1964). The summary statement reads:

> Of 144 species reported for the Panamint Mountains, 75 are considered to be breeding. Three species nest in the valley alluvial fans, 16 species nest in the lower canyons, 11 species nest in the open sage flats and valleys, 41 species nest in the pinyon-juniper woodlands, 19 species nest in the limber pine association, and 8 species nest in the bristlecone pine association. Only one species, the Rock Wren, was found to nest in all of the associations. Forty-three species were found to nest in only one association.

Another bird, besides the ubiquitous rock wren, that could be expected anywhere in the park, was the prairie falcon. Although they were never as abundant as the raven, I found prairie falcon populations with very little fluctuation throughout the year at all elevations. These are highly successful predators, able to take a wide range of prey. One incident stands out. On an April morning near the Grapevine Ranger Station, I observed a red-breasted merganser (a migrant) under attack by a prairie falcon. I stopped my vehicle in time to watch the falcon actually force the merganser out of the air onto the ground, where it jumped up and down trying to finish it off. When I approached the birds, the falcon flew off and perched on a hill a hundred yards away and watched me. Checking the merganser, I found it too badly injured to fly off. I photographed the bird and then left it for the falcon.

In February, while exploring Bebbia Canyon in Death Valley Buttes, Bill Hoy and I discovered a copulating pair of prairie falcons about 50 feet from a nest, located on a narrow ledge about 150 feet up the side of a limestone cliff. I was able to climb to the nest, which was constructed of feathers, sticks, and bits of debris

Rock wren, Death Valley National Monument

and lined with soft feathers and pieces of plants. After examining the nest, we moved back down the canyon so as not to disturb the birds. We ate lunch in the canyon bottom beside one of several potholes, small basins of water. Noticing movement in the water, I looked closer to find numerous fairy shrimp, tiny crustaceans swimming about with a wavelike motion. I collected a number of these creatures and later sent them to the Smithsonian Institution for identification, where they were identified as *Eulimnadia texana*. The following January, I again visited the same potholes and collected additional specimens. However, that series of fairy shrimp were identified as *Branchinecta coloradensis*, an additional species from the same site. Fairy shrimp live for short periods only in vernal pools. Females carry their eggs in a sac on their abdomen. The eggs are either dropped to the pool bottom or remain in the brood sac until she dies and sinks. The eggs remain in the bottom of the pool when it dries up until the next rainy season; they then hatch and develop rapidly into adults.

My most-wanted Death Valley bird was the Le Conte's thrasher, a grayish-brown, rather nondescript bird with tawny undertail coverts and a long curved bill. I discovered that, in spite of its being a fairly common and reasonably large bird, it was not easy to find and to see well. In winter it frequented patches of mesquite along the edge of the salt pan, but it moved to slightly higher elevations for the hotter months. I found that it could best be seen by driving along the West Side Road, watching the tops of the mesquites some distance ahead, and stopping immediately when a bird was spotted. Unless I was already too close, I could then set up a spotting scope and get a decent look. If I was too close, it would drop from view, fly a distance, and then run to the next patch of mesquites. Another method of seeing one of these birds was to sit quietly among or near mesquites and simply wait for a bird to appear.

Snakes and Other Herps (Herpetofauna)

Deserts are often synonymous with snakes, but Death Valley does not possess a high diversity of these reptiles. Only two are venomous: sidewinder and Panamint rattlesnake. I had personal encounters with both. The most startling was with a sidewinder at the Mesquite Flat Sand Dunes. One day while searching for active badger dens, I was down on all fours looking into a recently excavated den when I suddenly detected a flickering tongue of a curled sidewinder within inches of my face. My backward movement was automatic and incredibly swift; I found myself five feet away sprawled out on my back in the sand in a split second.

Panamint rattlesnakes, very red forms of the

speckled rattlesnake, do not normally occur on the Valley floor but prefer the higher slopes. I found it most common at mountain springs. On one occasion I actually stepped on a coiled individual on a very cold morning. I was birding, and, without watching my step as I should have, I assumed that the reddish spot was a stone. That snake was too cold to react, except to give a short rattle, but its large size, about three feet, could have been real trouble for me, alone and so far away from help.

Although the California lyre snake is not known as one of the venomous snakes, it does possess sufficient poison to kill prey. It was known only from the mountain slopes in extreme southern California until I recorded one on Daylight Pass during the morning of June 26, 1962. And Warren Hill added a roadkill from Furnace Creek Wash on July 1. Those records were included in Robert Stebbins's 1966 book, *A Field Guide to Western Reptiles and Amphibians.* Our specimens also were discussed in a 1963 article, "A Survey of the Herpetofauna of the Death Valley," that I coauthored with Frederick Turner.

In many ways, the most interesting Death Valley herp was the chuckwalla, a huge lizard that lives in rocky areas and actually feeds on creosotebush leaves. This lizard is able to inflate its body by gulping air and wedging itself between rocks to escape predators. My first

Sidewinder close-up, Death Valley National Monument

observation of one of these large, rather flat lizards occurred in Titus Canyon. I decided I wanted to photograph it. I was able to grab one just as it began to wedge itself between some boulders; I found its loose skin to have a sandpaper texture, better for wedging. And when I tried to pull it out for a closer examination, it continued to wedge itself further in. I gave up shortly, deciding that I would probably need a crowbar to extract it from its hold.

Death Valley Tales

Death Valley seemed to have a way of bringing

out the craziness in people. Maybe it was the name, but I experienced more strange happenings there than anywhere else I ever worked. For instance, one day while I was manning the visitor center information desk, a gentleman walked in and announced that he had just killed his wife and her body was outside in their vehicle. Sure enough, she was dead, shot through the head. We later learned that this couple had a death pact; they had agreed that one would kill the other and then take his or her own life. The wife won (lost?) and was first to die. But when it was his turn, he chickened out.

One day as I was returning from Beatty, after a long day of hiking the eastern slopes of the Amargosa Range, I noticed someone camping at Daylight Pass. Since camping was not permitted there, I stopped to tell the camper that he had to move to the campground. I found a very old man lying on a mattress next to the spring. He was extremely weak and hallucinating, but he was able to tell me that he was a retired preacher who had come there to "get closer to God." Although water was readily available, and he had a six-pack of Cokes sitting next to the mattress, he would not drink anything, saying that it was his way to reach God. I could not persuade him to drink. I called the ambulance, but he died on the way to the hospital.

Another even more bizarre incident also began on Daylight Pass. Several of us had been out most of the day searching for someone, reported lost, who had last been seen in that area. Late in the afternoon, we finally gave up our search and decided to go into Beatty for dinner. Just as we were finishing our dinners at the Beatty Club, a gentleman suddenly ran into the club, calling for a policeman. Someone in our group immediately identified us as park employees and offered to help. He rapidly explained that he had been forced at gunpoint to drive a guy from Las Vegas to Beatty. When they arrived in Beatty, the vehicle was overheating and in need of gasoline, so they stopped at a service station just down the street from the Beatty Club. While filling the gas tank, this gentleman grabbed a tire iron and smashed the kidnapper over the head and knocked him to the ground. When the kidnapper started to get up, the gentleman ran off down the street and happened to come into the Beatty Club.

Just about then, he pointed out the front window at his vehicle, which was speeding out of town toward Daylight Pass and Death Valley. Immediately we all started out the door to give chase. District Ranger Matt Ryan and I (passenger) got away first, heading west some five miles or so behind the kidnapper. We later learned that the kidnapper had killed his wife in Los Angeles and forced another individual to drive him to Las Vegas. At Las Vegas he kicked the man out of the vehicle, and the man then reported the incident to the police. The next day, as this man was walking around town, he suddenly saw the thief driving his vehicle down the street. When the owner ran after him, shouting, the thief deserted the vehicle and ran. That was when he kidnapped the man in Las Vegas and forced him to drive to Beatty.

As we sped down the highway, Matt radioed his wife, Rosemary, at Emigrant Ranger Station (his duty station) and informed her of the situation. He warned her not to open the door in case the kidnapper stopped there. As they were talking, Rosemary saw the vehicle very slowly passing the station. She said it appeared to be overheated. In another fifteen minutes we passed the station and started to take the Towne Pass road that continues west to Lone Pine. As we passed the Emigrant Canyon Road Junction, I saw the vehicle we were pursuing pulled off the road a half mile away with the kidnapper leaning on the outside of the vehicle. Even at a distance it was obvious the guy was injured; his head looked bloody. Matt turned around, and we pulled up a quarter mile behind the guy and radioed the others coming behind us. Then the kidnapper got back into the vehicle, and we heard a gunshot. Within ten more minutes, backed up by others, we approached the stolen vehicle to find that the man had shot himself.

Then there was the summer day that I discovered a man, completely naked and holding his clothes high above his head, walking down the center of the road near Badwater. The day was considerably above 100°F. He told me that he was wading and did not want to get his clothes wet. He survived.

On another day at the Sand Dunes I found a pitched tent in a noncamping zone. I stopped to tell the camper to move and found a lovely brunette sitting nearby meditating. When I explained that she would have to move her campsite to the nearby campground, she told me she had been told to meet her party at this particular site, and she intended to wait for their arrival. I tried to convince her that her friend probably had meant the main campground instead. After some discussion she explained that her expected party was arriving by flying saucer, and they had instructed her to wait right there. It took me some time to explain that if she did not move to the campground, one of the rangers might arrest her and then she would not be able to make contact with her associates. She finally agreed, and I helped move her belongings into her vehicle. I encountered her again four nights later at the Furnace Creek store. When I asked her if her friends had arrived, she told me that soon after she had moved, she received a second message to go to the store and wait there for further instructions. That was what she apparently was doing.

Mesquite Flat Sand Dunes, Death Valley National Monument

My Wild Life

Scotty's Castle, Death Valley National Monument, 1960

I will end this discourse with one additional experience pertaining to summer temperatures. One July day, when the temperature ranged around 120°F, Bill Bullard and I drove the Ubehebe Crater Road, working on a manuscript that would evolve into a road guide. We had stopped at various spots that would be included and were en route back when our vehicle suddenly died. We could not get it restarted. And then we discovered that our radio was not working, and we knew that the Grapevine ranger, Howard Parr, was out of the park. Since we were reasonably close to the Grapevine Canyon turnoff to Scotty's Castle, we decided to walk the approximately four miles to Scotty's Castle, a huge structure built in 1924 by an eccentric miner, Walter Scott, and his financial backer, A. M. Johnson, that was open to visitors year-round.

Each of us had approximately a quart of water. We started walking, thinking there was a good chance that someone would come along and pick us up once we passed the junction. No one did! We decided to ration our water, drink a little bit every few hundred feet, so that we would have a final drink once in sight of the castle. That is exactly the way it worked out. And when we reached the castle, we were taken in like long-lost sons and immediately provided with plenty of refreshments. I can remember that the fresh tomatoes that day tasted better than any I had ever before eaten. I cannot think back on that day without salivating for fresh tomatoes.

Transition

Although I loved the desert, and Death Valley will always be a good memory for me, I eventually decided it was time to move on. I was eager to experience another park area, summers had become more difficult for me, and my various projects had been completed. So, when I received a call from my friend Bill Lukens, a park ranger at Zion National Park, about an open naturalist position at Zion, I was interested. Bill had worked at Death Valley prior to transferring to Zion, and he encouraged me to "put in" for the vacancy.

When the Zion position was announced, I applied. And I eventually received a telephone call from Chief Park Naturalist Carl Jepson, who offered me the position. I accepted, and my "effective date" was set for March 22, 1962, coincidentally my birthday.

3
Pinnacles National Monument, California

My first permanent position at Death Valley was a dual one that included a six-month assignment at Pinnacles. I had not even heard of the area before then, in spite of the park being located less than one hundred miles south of where I had gone to college at San Jose State. But soon after I arrived there, I discovered it to be an outstanding natural area. Although only about sixteen thousand acres in size, located in the Gabilan Mountains of California's Coast Range, Pinnacles was more a hiker's park (thirty-two miles of trails) than one that attracted hordes of sightseers. It fit my interests perfectly.

The Job

I was housed in a small cabin along Bear Gulch, within easy walking distance of the tiny headquarters building. I discovered that I was the park's first full-time naturalist, and Superintendent Russ Mahan and Chief Ranger Bob Ramstad gave me (practically) free rein to do whatever I thought was necessary. Although I spent some time at the headquarters information desk and occasionally in the entrance station, the majority of my time was spent in the field, walking the trails, taking pictures, and making wildlife observations. I soon developed a slide talk on the area, which I presented each weekend at the small amphitheater in the campground. My other duties consisted of curating a small collection of natural and historical objects and also building a collection of slides as well as specimens of plants, mammals, birds, reptiles, and amphibians that could be used for interpretive talks. Being the first naturalist on-site had its benefits.

In fact, I actually wrote an article, "Pinnacles of Wilderness," which ran in the *Soledad Bee*,

Pinnacles National Monument headquarters and author's car and cabin beyond, 1958

the local Salinas newspaper on May 22, 1958, that emphasized the wilderness character of the Pinnacles. It was my first newspaper article.

Russ Mahan and his wife, Mamie, were very special people. Although Russ looked big and rough, he was one of the kindest individuals I encountered in any of the parks. And Mamie was a great cook. I was invited to their home for dinner on numerous occasions. And a few years later, after the Mahans had transferred to

Waputki National Monument in Arizona, they were just as kind when I visited them there.

Pinnacles Birdlife

My field activities at Pinnacles, usually including both my workdays and my days off, were largely spent wandering the area, especially documenting the birdlife. The park was not known as a great birding park, mainly because it did not contain a specialty bird, one that could not be found elsewhere. But I discovered that the area was a microcosm of the Pacific Slope where all of the western California species could be found with little effort. Examples included the California quail, Nuttall's woodpecker, Pacific-slope flycatcher, yellow-billed magpie, wrentit, California thrasher, California towhee, and Lawrence's goldfinch. Years earlier, California condors also flew overhead, thus the name of Condor Gulch, a key landmark in the park.

I was especially interested in what bird species were present in each of the area's principal biotic communities, so I spent considerable time birding each of the park's five communities. I eventually prepared a written report, "The Ecological Distribution of the Birds of the Pinnacles," on my findings. It listed 111 species, of which 61 were found to nest. I recorded 43 species nesting in the riparian zone, 42 in the woodlands, 31 in the grasslands, 25 in the chaparral, and 12 on cliffs and rocky slopes. Several species were found utilizing more than one habitat.

What surprised me most was the high number of nesting raptors within such a small park. They included white-tailed kite; sharp-shinned, Cooper's, red-tailed, and red-shouldered hawks; golden eagle; peregrine and prairie falcons; American kestrel; barn, great horned, and long-

California quail

eared owls; northern pygmy-owl; and western screech-owl. The raptor diversity was ample evidence that the area was a relatively undisturbed natural system with minimal outside impacts. I found that the majority of the cliff nesters could be found by hiking either the High Peaks or North Wilderness Trails.

The most abundant of all the raptors was the American kestrel, which nested on the high cliffs as well as on trees in the lowlands. One day I discovered a pair attending a nest on a tall digger pine along Chalone Creek. They were feeding nestlings; I could hear their anxious cries each time an adult arrived with food. I sat on a rock maybe one hundred yards away for several hours, watching as the adults hunted along the mostly dry creek bed. It was obvious that insects, grasshoppers in particular, were the principal prey that day. Kestrels are sometimes known as "grasshopper falcons" because they take so many grasshoppers. The few hours that I spent with the family of kestrels were rather special to me; I have had a long, unique relationship with this little falcon.

My earliest memory of the American kestrel was while growing up in Idaho, living near a large vacant lot with a few old trees that housed kestrels during the breeding season. I learned to appreciate the "killy-killy" calls at a very young age. And years later, during one summer in college, I acquired a wounded kestrel male that I "nursed" back to health. That summer, while working at Summer Home Park on the Russian River in northern California, where I ran the little café and taught birding classes to the numerous youngsters, I was presented the kestrel by one of my students. He explained that he had found the bird on the roadside, apparently hit by a vehicle.

After examining the bird and finding nothing obviously wrong, I constructed a large wood and wire cage, complete with a perch, which I placed on the back porch of the café, and put the kestrel inside. By then it had regained its voice but still seemed unable to fly. I placed a dish of water inside the cage, along with pieces of chicken that I had appropriated from the café refrigerator. Although it ignored both of these offerings, it quickly accepted a house mouse that I trapped overnight, making a quick meal of that small rodent. And before the day was over, my birding class had captured several dozen grasshoppers that were also accepted.

In about a week my captive, which appeared much stronger, seemed to demand its release; its almost constant "killy-killy" was hard to ignore. I simply opened the little door, and the kestrel, after hesitating a few seconds only, flew away. It seemed not at all injured or damaged by its captivity but as good as new. It called loudly as it circled once and then disappeared from sight.

On September 10, I discovered a barn owl nest in a crevice near the base of the cliff along the Rim Trail. It contained several fresh pellets and many old ones. I collected a large number of the pellets, took them back to the office, and over the next several days removed the tiny bones in an attempt to identify the prey species. Eventually, I concluded that the pellets held the remains of nine deer mice, five wood rats, five

Hiking trail in Pinnacles National Monument

harvest mice, a lone kangaroo rat, and a passerine bird.

The most obvious and most abundant of all the large raptorlike birds at Pinnacles were the turkey vultures, which possess a keen sense of smell that aids them in finding dead meat. I had long heard of their ability to find decaying meat, even when it was not readily visible to a soaring bird. So, because of the abundance of these scavengers, I did my own experiment one day along Chalone Creek. I had already collected a good number of road-killed ground squirrels a few days earlier and had tagged them on the dates collected. I then placed the various carcasses out on the ground, some of them covered with either light brush or newspaper, and then sat back at a considerable distance and waited for a response. I didn't have long to wait.

Cruising turkey vultures very soon alighted next to the two- or three-day-old carcasses but

Turkey vultures, Pinnacles National Monument

My Wild Life

ignored the very fresh and even the one-day-old carcasses. I also discovered that the older carcasses, four or more days old, were not as highly prized. Covered two- and three-day-old carcasses received the same attention as did those left uncovered. I was convinced that turkey vultures see smell. They possess a truly unique olfactory sense. The vultures obviously preferred those carcasses that were beginning to ripen, not those that were extremely fresh or so old that they had already built up microbial toxins. Later studies by several ornithologists produced similar results.

In many ways, the most interesting of Pinnacles' birds was the yellow-billed magpie, not only because of its limited range on the Pacific Slope but also because of its fascinating behavior. A member of the Corvidae family, along with ravens, crows, and jays, it readily learns to take advantage of campers and picnickers. It is a true opportunist, utilizing everything from doughnuts and steak to carrion that it might find along the roadways. During the early-morning hours, I found it patrolling the entrance roads, along with common ravens, searching for the previous night's roadkills not already appropriated by the night shift of coyotes, gray foxes, and raccoons.

In addition, these black-and-white, long-tailed corvids utilize a communal nesting regime. Although they rarely entered the canyons and were seldom found in the highlands, they frequented the lower portions of the park, such as along Chalone Creek. In May I found three nests within a hundred feet of one another, each two to three feet in diameter, constructed of sticks, with a side entrance. While I was watching the nests from a distance, a pair of passing common ravens apparently ventured too close. One pair of magpies immediately took after the ravens, and their loud calls attracted two additional birds from the other nests, and the four birds chased the ravens until they all were out of sight. What impressed me most was the chase capability of the magpies, able not only to keep up with the ravens but also to maneuver just as well in flight. This action for a bird most often seen cruising along at a slow and steady pace, almost like it is floating, was surprising.

Bobcats and Foxes

Even the mammals at Pinnacles sometimes acted uncharacteristically. The best example of this was the bobcat that liked to stretch out on a ledge directly in front of the headquarters building, just across the roadway. One time it climbed a small tree and sat on a branch in plain sight for half an hour. Jim Alfsen, seasonal ranger that summer, observed three bobcat kittens in a tree outside his cabin one evening in August. It was not unusual to find a bobcat, presumably the same individual that liked to lie on the ledge, sauntering along the road past the residences in Bear Gulch. Bobcats were common at Pinnacles, but finding one so tolerant of humans was truly unusual.

I had two additional bobcat experiences years later while working at Big Bend National Park. The first was at my residence at Panther Junction. I had gone home from the visitor center for lunch and on arrival had first walked into my backyard to unfurl a mist net used for catching birds to band. A few minutes later, while eating lunch at a table situated where I could see the backyard, I discovered a bobcat lying less than a dozen feet away, right where I had unfurled my net less than ten minutes earlier. It remained there while I ate lunch, seemingly ignoring my presence. It undoubtedly could see me looking at it through the window. Then, for no obvious reason, it simply got up and walked away.

On another occasion, while hiking to Boot Spring via the Laguna Meadows Trail, I discovered a bobcat and kitten along a steep, rocky slope maybe five hundred yards away. She apparently was teaching her kitten to hunt. I watched through binoculars for twenty to thirty minutes as they slowly wandered back and forth along the slope, now and then running ahead a little, as if spotting prey. The following paragraph, from my book *For All Seasons: A Big Bend Journal*, further describes the action:

At one stop, the adult suddenly sprang forward, back arched somewhat like a house cat, and extracted a small rodent from a patch of grass. I watched as it turned and gave the limp rodent to the kitten, which took it, dropped it to the side, and then pounced on it in an inexperienced way. Then it picked it up and swallowed it whole. A second later they continued up the slope and soon disappeared from view.

Gray foxes were commonplace in the Monument. They were seen daily near the entrance station, chasing each other and rolling about in a nearby sandy area. On a couple of occasions there were four individuals, an adult and three youngsters. They eventually would wander off to the east up a small draw. Although I searched that area for a den, I was unsuccessful. In addition, a lone gray fox passed my residence in Bear Gulch almost every evening. It seemed unafraid even when I stepped out the door for a closer look. I suppose it had become accustomed to my presence.

Gray fox, Pinnacles National Monument

Deer

Black-tailed deer were commonplace throughout the Pinnacles area, and because of my earlier academic interest—a degree in wildlife management—I paid particular interest to the local population. During my last year at San Jose State, as a senior class project, classmate Joe Livingston and I had worked at the Coe Memorial Park, a large (12,500 acres) private ranch in Santa Clara County, where we had made a vegetation type map and surveyed the wildlife. Black-tailed deer were censused on each trip, and we paid particular attention to their available food supply and physical condition.

On the morning of April 16, 1957, while mapping the slopes near Soda Springs, we actually watched a coyote dragging down a young buck deer. We were standing on the hillside about five hundred yards above East Fork Creek when we detected the coyote slowly approaching a deer feeding along the creek. Apparently, the deer did not detect the coyote until it was too late. We watched through binoculars as the coyote rushed the deer, grabbed it by the throat, and flipped it to the ground. It then began gnawing through the neck. Apparently, in our excitement at seeing such a thing, one of us must have made a noise, because the coyote suddenly looked up and saw us. But instead of immediately running away, it was hesitant to leave, remaining with its prey until we were much closer. The coyote did not leave its prey until we were within a hundred feet or so.

It took us maybe ten minutes to work our way down the hill to where we were standing over the deer. On close examination, we found that the jugular vein had been severed in as many as five places. Two- to three-inch streaks showed along the side of the neck, and there was a gash on the temple and teeth marks on the left shoulder. My on-site field notes from that day state: "Very young buck, knobs on head ¼ inch. Deer still alive and kicking. Coyote weighed about 55-65 lbs. Coyote in excellent shape, fat and shaggy. Took two pictures of it before it ran up the hill. Estimate deer to weigh 65 lbs. finished slitting its throat. It took about 10 more minutes to die after throat slit. The jugular vein had already been severed by the coyote. The deer's overall appearance was that of stunted growth. It was lean, but not skinny."

Joe and I dissected the deer on-site. I wrote: "reddish-violet globules like masses inside of body cavity along vertebrae. These were very numerous and extended from neck all the way to rump area. They followed the central nervous system, and where the sciatic nerves extended into legs. The globules were suspended by tissue, not truly attached to the vertebrae." We collected some of the globules, placed them in alcohol, and they were later examined in the lab. Sometime later I learned that the globules were caused by parasitic meningeal worms derived from terrestrial snails or slugs that can be ingested when feeding. It often results in neurologic disease and mortality.

During my stay at Pinnacles, I weekly censused the deer along the five-mile roadway between the Monument headquarters and the Hollister Highway. Right after dark, Jim would slowly drive a pickup along the highway with me standing in the bed and holding a high-beam searchlight and a clicker. From spring to early summer, we recorded only 2 or 3 animals each time. But by midsummer deer populations began to increase, and on August 1, I tallied a high of 75 individuals. The reason for the increase related to the normal drying conditions throughout the area. The decline of the more nutritious shrubs and grasses forced the deer to the roadsides to take advantage of the grasses and herbs maintained by minimal runoff from the road surface and the moisture below the pavement. In spite of the high numbers of deer, I did not detect any that were considered unhealthy, like the Coe Ranch buck. All of the Pinnacles deer seemed in good shape.

Jackrabbits

One of the most numerous mammals in and around the park was the black-tailed jackrabbit. Night or day, several jacks could always be found along the roads. During the early spring and summer months they were more abundant than during the later part of the summer. On one occasion, driving between Paicines to the Monument entrance (twenty-eight miles), I counted 87 jackrabbits. And on September 12, driving the same road, only 24 were seen. On any early-morning drive one could find several roadkills; these usually were already claimed by one or several common ravens.

Herps

Reptiles and amphibians had always been one of my interests, so during the 1958 summer I recorded all of my observations and collected an occasional specimen for the park. I found the following species: western pond turtles along the stream in Bear Gulch; coast horned, western fence, side-blotched, and desert night lizards; California whiptails, and gopher snakes at numerous locations; several western yellow-bellied racers and common garter snakes; and one or two sightings of the spotted night and long-nosed snakes, and common kingsnake and western coachwhip. In addition, I encountered six western rattlesnakes during the summer.

Western Regional Office

Toward the end of my Pinnacles assignment, I spent a week in San Francisco in the Western Regional Office, writing a natural history handbook for the park. My material became the first draft of this document, which took several years and a number of rewrites by several Park Service employees before it was finally published in 1969. My week in the regional office, getting acquainted with a number of the employees there, probably benefited my career to a degree. But frankly, I mostly enjoyed the opportunities to eat at a number of superb restaurants.

My assignment at Pinnacles ran out on November 1, and I returned to Death Valley. Before the next six-month period ended, when I was to return to Pinnacles for another six-month tour in 1959, I accepted a full-time position at Death Valley.

4
Yosemite National Park, California

In December 1958, I was selected to attend the Albright Training Center, starting on February 9, 1959. This was a three-month "intake" training program held in Yosemite National Park; the program was later moved to the South Rim of Grand Canyon National Park. My official invitation letter was signed by the program director, Frank F. Kowski, who had developed the program and served as its first director for several years. His assistant in Yosemite was Bob McIntyre.

I later worked for Frank in the Southwest Regional Office when he was regional director. Everyone liked Frank, and following his death the annual Park Service golf tournament was named for him. I was not a golfer, but I traveled with him on several occasions. And wherever we went, he was welcomed with open arms. He kept a little "black book" with the names of all family members of all his employees and other associates. He would enter a park and immediately ask about everyone's family. In one instance, while I was visiting with him in his Santa Fe office, he excused himself to take a call his secretary had placed to a secretary at one of the parks; he had called to wish her happy birthday and ask about her family. Frank was an amazing individual.

The intake training program was designed to introduce new uniformed employees to the National Park Service and to provide training on a whole array of information and responsibilities, ranging from the history of the National Park Service to various activities from law enforcement, such as patrolling and search and rescue, wildland and structural fire control, to basic interpretation. Although a good deal of the training was redundant to my previous experiences, it was in greater depth. And perhaps more important, the large number of handouts on every covered topic provided a wonderful set of references; they became a valuable asset on returning to our various parks. Even more important were the numerous contacts made, both with fellow participants and the instructors brought in from the National Park Service and various other agencies.

All twenty-six participants stayed at the park's Ranger Club located in the center of the valley. I developed strong friendships with several individuals, especially Jim "Snoopy" Dempsey, Walt Hellman, Jim McKown, and Armund "Herbie" Sansum. And I crossed paths with several others during my Park Service career: Dave Butts, Art Graham, Jerry Hammond, Emory "Smoky" Lehnert, Dick Moeller, Vernon Smith, and Jerry Wagers.

Jim McKown was the park historian at Pipe Springs National Monument in Arizona, not too far from Zion National Park. During the years that I worked at Zion, I visited with him on several occasions, including initiating Christmas Bird Counts centered at Pipe Springs.

Herbie Sansum and I were both interested in photography, and we spent a lot of our free time taking pictures. On two occasions we drove to lower elevations out of the park to take pictures of spring wildflowers. And with Ansel Adams's studio very near the training center, I was able to visit his studio on a couple of occasions. In fact, I got acquainted with someone

Ranger Dorm, Yosemite National Park, 1959

who worked for him at the studio, and one night he took me into his back room so I could see firsthand where the great man actually worked. I was impressed!

Jerry Wagers and I got involved with the Venezuelan equine encephalitis (VEE) project in South Texas in July 1971 (see the chapter on Big Bend National Park for details). But Jerry became the first human being to come down with a case of VEE during the two-week project near Brownsville.

Albright Training Center itself was located in Yosemite Valley, in about the center of that incredibly beautiful valley, surrounded by steep granite walls, topped with dark green conifers, and in view of marvelous Yosemite Falls. Winter conditions, present much of the three months, however, were not quite as pleasant for me, by now a true "desert rat." The trainees from the mountain parks, including Jack Hughes from Yellowstone, John Fonda from Grand Teton, and Jerry Hammond from Rocky Mountain, spent every free hour on skis after each snowfall.

I did walk the valley roadways, once they were plowed enough, and I was able to take some outstanding photographs of the scenery and the wildlife. Deer were especially abundant in the open meadows, in places where they could find grasses below the snow. But my most exciting find was a great gray owl sitting on a low snag one hundred feet or so off the roadway. I was able to take a few photographs, but because I was using only a 60mm lens, the owl was little more than dots on the processed slides.

On February 28, I discovered an American dipper along the Merced River. I watched it for several minutes as it searched for insects along the icy banks. It actually dove below the icy waters on several occasions, even under the ice-crusted fringes. Through binoculars I could see it literally "flying" below the surface, using strong wing beats to propel itself along the river bottom in its search for food. The American dipper is our only truly aquatic songbird.

Perhaps my most memorable sighting during my time in Yosemite was of a bald eagle near Indian Flat, below the valley. On February 23, when driving back from a visit with my folks in Santa Rosa, I suddenly saw a mature bald eagle, bright white head and tail, flying right over the roadway coming in my direction. I was so surprised to see it that I craned my neck to watch it pass overhead. A second later, when my attention was again focused on the road ahead, I discovered a California highway patrol vehicle coming my way; I was halfway over the white line. At the same time, the red lights began flashing on the cruiser. I immediately pulled off on the right side of the road, and the patrolman parked across the road in another pull-off.

I quickly jumped out of my vehicle, binoculars in hand and looking skyward, and yelled at the officer, "Did you see the bald eagle?" He immediately responded, "No, where?" He seemed as excited as I was. He grabbed his own binoculars, and we spent the next ten minutes trying to relocate the bird. We did not, but apparently he believed me. We then spent another fifteen minutes or so introducing ourselves and talked about birding and my participation in the training program. As we parted, almost in passing, he got serious, and said, "Ro, by the way, next time you see a bald eagle over the roadway, be more careful."

Birders, who spend so much time in the out-

El Capitan,
Yosemite National Park

doors in a wide variety of settings, occasionally have those kinds of experiences. An earlier encounter with the police was back at San Jose, while I was involved with a bird survey of Williams Creek Park for my ornithology class. On each trip, I would walk along a roadway near the creek, watching for birds in the adjacent vegetation and in the surrounding terrain. Beyond the creek was a group of homes, mostly high-priced houses that overlooked the park. One day as I wandered along the roadway, a police car approached, stopped directly in front of me, and two officers got out to question me about what I was doing. It took me several minutes to convince them that I was birding, not looking at the houses across the way. My field notes helped to convince them of my purpose. They eventually decided I was for real and over the next several weeks, whenever they saw me in the park, would tell me where the California quail were feeding in the park.

I had visited Yosemite on several earlier occasions; the park was only a half-day's drive from Petaluma and Santa Rosa, where I had gone to high school and junior college. On one early-spring camping trip with friends from Santa Rosa, we had awakened in the morning with several inches of snow on the ground. Breakfast that morning was not a pleasant affair.

In addition, I had taken plant taxonomy from Dr. Carl Sharsmith, known as "Doc Sharsmith"

in Yosemite. He had worked in the park, particularly at Tuolumne Meadows, every summer for many years. Even after retiring from teaching, Dr. Sharsmith worked as a seasonal naturalist, continuing into his nineties.

Just about the time that spring began to creep into the valley, it was time to leave, to head back to our home parks. I went back to summer, after spending three months in winter conditions. I remember that the day after returning, with a temperature exceeding 100°F, was the first time I was glad that a good part of my workday could be spent in an air-conditioned building.

My Wild Life

5
Zion National Park, Utah

Zion had been one of my favorite national parks since I was a youngster; it was one of the parks I visited with my parents on several occasions. However, Grand Teton was my father's favorite, and while we lived in Idaho Falls, Idaho, until I was fourteen, we visited that nearby park often. But we made annual or bi-annual trips to Zion and Grand Canyon's North Rim. So, I felt like I knew a little about Zion. It is one of the original "crown jewels" of the National Park Service. In addition, my mother and stepfather were living in Salt Lake City, only about three hundred miles to the north, so a move to Zion would provide me with an opportunity to visit with them more often.

I discovered that Zion National Park was all that I had expected. I felt extremely fortunate to be working and living in what undoubtedly is one of the most spectacular of the national parks. I decided that it was also the most inti-mate of the parks. Driving up Zion Canyon, past the Court of the Patriarchs, Angels Landing, the Great White Throne, and into the Temple of Si-nawava was a spiritual experience every time. One could fully understand why the Mormon pioneers named the canyon "Zion." And walk-ing into The Narrows, at the end of the road, was an experience unlike anywhere else.

The Job

Because I was Zion's supervisory park natural-ist, my family (wife Sandy, daughter Becky, and I; a second daughter, Trina, was born while at Zion) was given a three-bedroom house in the Oak Creek area behind the visitor center, below the high red cliffs of the Towers of the Virgin. The site was the most spectacular setting of any of my housing locations within the parks. It also was close enough to walk to my office at

Wauer house below the Towers of the Virgin, Zion National Park, 1963

Visitor Center, Zion National Park, 1963

the visitor center, yet it was isolated from park visitors to the degree that it received traffic only from a few people living in the small Oak Creek subdivision.

My immediate supervisor, Carl Jepson, had previously been a naturalist at Grand Teton National Park. Although I remembered him from my many visits there—I had actually gone on some of his nature walks—he did not remember me. I discovered that Carl spent the majority of his time with activities relating to the Zion Natural History Association, the cooperative association responsible for sales of books, postcards, slides, and so on at the visitor center. My primary responsibility was management of the park's interpretive program, scheduling information desk duties and the abundant talks and walks. I also was responsible for the park's archives and library, as well as all contacts with the various scientists working in the park. Gradually this activity took more and more of my time.

Evening talks have always been an important part of a park's interpretive program; many park visitors attend evening programs but never participate in any of the other interpretive activities. I personally gave at least one talk weekly throughout the visitor season, generally from May through September. I gave two different talks: "Birds of Zion National Park" and "Zion's Backcountry." Although talk attendance

at Death Valley often included as many as five hundred people, attendance was only about one-third that at Zion.

Friends, Colleagues, and Life at Zion

All of the park employees got along very well, and I developed strong friendships with several. Dennis Carter, Alan and Claudette Hagood, Bruce Moorhead, and Dick and Judy Robertson became good friends. And I was exceptionally impressed with Superintendent Frank Oberhansley. He not only cared about the people who worked under him but, unlike so many superintendents whose principal concern is their next promotion, he loved the park and its natural values. He seemed to pay particular attention to me, constantly asking about my field trips and projects. I was invited to his home for dinner on several occasions, and each time I left with the feeling that he wished he were younger and had less responsibility so he could wander the backcountry with me. I would have liked that!

Most of the folks in and around the park were kind and considerate, although Springdale, the nearest town to the park headquarters and residential areas, was a Mormon community with people who did not always welcome "gentiles." But I found minimum animosity. I joined the local Lion's Club, and I also coached the

Springdale little league baseball team during my tenure at Zion. In addition, I taught a weekly ornithology night class at the College of Southern Utah in Cedar City; I was given an appointment there as associate in research that allowed me to receive minimal compensation.

Zion's Birdlife

Zion Canyon, with its abundant side canyons and deep niches, is the epitome of a place where one should be able to find cliff nesters. One can't spent any time at all in those hallowed halls without experiencing the high-pitched shrieks of white-throated swifts and the descending whistle calls of canyon wrens. And these same cliffs also supported a pair of peregrine falcons and an unknown number, at least during my tenure, of spotted owls.

A pair of peregrines had claimed an aerie site on Angels Landing long before I arrived in the park. Park visitors sitting on the lawn at the Zion Lodge could watch, even without binoculars, these amazing birds dive and tumble. Although I did find peregrines at several additional locations within the park, the total number of active peregrines was not determined until National Park Service biologist David Stinson recorded 13 active territories in an extensive survey in the 1990s.

I encountered spotted owls on two occasions. My first sighting, in the early morning of November 9, 1963, was of a lone bird perched in a low tree just below the visitor center. When I tried to photograph it, the owl flew across the river toward the Watchman Residential Area. In spite of searching, with the help of several local residents, for that bird for more than an hour, we were unsuccessful. My second sighting was while hiking the West Rim Trail, just below Scout Lookout on March 31, 1965. I came around a corner on the trail, and there, not more than six feet away, sitting on a ledge in a little slot canyon, was a spotted owl. For a good thirty to forty seconds we just stared at each other; I was afraid to move in case it would fly off. Then, when it seemed that it figured I was not a threat, I very slowly lowered my pack to retrieve my camera. It remained still, watching me intently with its large, all-brown eyes. But just as I began to raise my camera to see through the viewfinder, it suddenly flew up, almost vertically up the little canyon, and disappeared.

Although Zion National Park was not one of the most highly regarded birding parks, especially in comparison with Big Bend and the Everglades, the park still attracted an occasional birder throughout the year. So, Dennis Carter (my assistant) and I decided to write a Zion bird book. Actually, since I had also been spending considerable time studying the park's herpetofauna, we agreed that I would write a herp book and he would write the initial draft of the bird book; I would be second author. As it worked out, however, I completed my project, and Dennis had not written any of the bird book manuscript. So I went ahead and wrote that book, too; Dennis became coauthor. Both books were published by the Zion Natural History Association: the herp book, *Reptiles and Amphibians of Zion National Park*, in 1964; and the bird book, *Birds of Zion National Park and Vicinity*, the following year. Howard Rollin, a friend of Dennis's from Weldona, Colorado, painted six watercolors for the bird book: canyon wren for the cover, an American dipper, and four large habitat scenes for the desert, riparian woodland, pinyon-juniper woodland, and high country. The four habitat scenes were also enlarged and printed for sale in the visitor center.

Many years later, in 1995, I was asked by Vic Vieira, Zion Park's chief of resource management and research, to update the bird book. I readily agreed and spent two weeks back in the park revisiting numerous sites. I was also able to take advantage of the abundance of more recent records accumulated by local birder Jerome Gifford. That second edition, which I dedicated to Jerome, who had passed away in 1988, was published by Utah State University Press in 1997. The same four habitat scene paintings by Rollins were included, and Mimi Hoppe Wolf, wildlife artist friend, added thirty-four marvelous pen-and-ink bird sketches, each in suitable habitat. The 1965 book included 233 species, while the 1997 edition (same title as the earlier book) included 287, an addition of 54 species.

Bird Banding

My backyard was a perfect place to feed and band birds. Within a few days after moving in, I had established a feeding station and placed mist nets in suitable places so that they would catch birds coming and going. During the three and one-half years that I lived there, I managed to band more than 5,400 birds of 100 species. The majority of those were captured in my backyard, although I also established a banding station at the Springdale Ponds, along the Virgin River just below the park entrance. And I also banded birds at a few additional locations in the park at intervals during the year.

It was at the Springdale Ponds where a great horned owl, after becoming caught in one of my mist nets, grabbed hold of Clyde Harden's thumb and would not let go. Clyde, who was helping me band, was a large, robust man with huge hands. One of the claws went completely through his thumb. It took considerable time and effort to extract the claw from the thumb.

Dark-eyed juncos, both gray-headed and Oregon forms, were the most numerous species banded, a total of 1,905 individuals. One of my juncos, captured on February 17, 1966, had initially been banded at Salt Lake City on February 16, 1964. I discovered that wintering juncos tended to move up and down the slopes with the snow line. I was actually able to find banded birds during mild winter weather farther up the slope rather than in my backyard. But with the onset of each storm, they returned to lower areas.

Three state records were recorded while banding birds at Zion and the immediate area. A rufous-crowned sparrow was captured in my backyard, and an eastern phoebe and a rose-breasted grosbeak were captured at the Springdale Ponds. Other significant records resulting from my banding operations included flammulated owls in May, a tree sparrow in November, and a swamp sparrow in March. The flammulated owls arrived during a late snowstorm. I published a short note on this occurrence in the *Condor* in 1966. It included the following paragraph:

> The first weeks of May in 1964 were cold and overcast in southern Utah, and snow fell during the nights of 6-7 May. Upon checking my mist nets at a banding station in Oak Creek Canyon (elevation 4100 feet) on the morning of 8 May 1964 I discovered a single Flammulated Owl in the net. It was then banded, photographed, and released. Upon my arrival at the Visitor Center, I was told of a "small owl in front of a house in the Watchman Residential Area." It was perched on a willow at shoulder height, and I was able to grasp it from behind while another person attracted its attention from the front. This bird, too, was banded and released. A third Flammulated Owl was found dead a short distance up Zion Canyon four days later. . . . The fourth owl was found on 27 May 1964, by the author and Andrew Kurie in the Taylor Creek part of Zion Park.
>
> On 7 May 1965 a fifth Flammulated Owl was discovered in a mist net at Springdale, two miles from the first 1964 finding. . . . Taken together these records suggest the possibility of a regular annual assemblage of the species.

It was obvious to me that finding so many flammulated owls in early May, associated with a late snowstorm, indicated that the birds were migrants. However, the first draft of my note sent to the *Condor* editor Ned Johnson was returned for a rewrite. It was his opinion that this owl was a full-time resident and not a migrant. I was required to use the final sentence above. But since then, flammulated owls have been proven to migrate.

Later, when I queried my colleague Dr. Allan Phillips about similar records in Arizona, he

Flammulated owl with band, Zion National Park, 1964

(red-shafted) flickers in my backyard. I was initially attracted to the scene by their loud and insistent calls. On checking my nets, I discovered a female flicker in the lower strand of a net. The male, standing on the ground directly below the female, had hold of her bill, apparently trying to pull her free. When that didn't work, he jumped onto her body and began pecking the strands, all the time calling in a loud manner typical of an annoyed flicker. He then jumped back onto the ground and again clasped the female's bill with his and began backing away, wings beating all the while, trying to pull the female free of the net. He suddenly released his hold and flew at the net. He again jumped upon her body and began a vigorous pecking at the net strands. Just as suddenly he jumped back on the ground and began the tugging process again.

answered on August 21, 1964: "My records of Flammulated Owls are common in the lowland of Ariz., + your data is probably close to those of N. Ariz. + S. Nevada. But to find four is most extraordinary!!"

On November 14, 1964, I observed a fascinating interaction between two northern

I watched these actions for several minutes from inside the house. Then, noticing that there was blood from an apparent cut near the female's bill, I went outside to release the captured bird. The male then flew only a short distance away to a scrub oak, where he began a "chuur-ing" call and bobbed up and down in a manner I have seen woodpeckers do when they are excited. I banded and then released the female. She immediately flew to a rock about forty feet up the slope from the male and began a constant calling. The male responded with like calling. Within thirty seconds he flew to her,

My Wild Life

and they both flew up the canyon together and disappeared. This information was included in a note published in the *Wilson Bulletin* in 1965.

Because of the importance of the Springdale Ponds as excellent habitat for birds, I talked to the local landowners about providing the area greater protection by establishing a "Lions Club Refuge." Six months later, the refuge became a reality. The dedication, by club president Earl Manson, created considerable interest in the area's birdlife and the importance of habitat protection. Clyde and Lois Harden and I had already banded 78 species of birds at the ponds. I wrote a short article about this project for the *Lions Magazine*.

Beaver Dam Wash

I discovered early on that the birdlife of Utah's Virgin River and its side streams, such as Beaver Dam Wash—a major drainage in the extreme southwestern corner of the state—had received only minimal study. I was made additionally aware of the importance of the Beaver Dam Wash area when I received a call from Joe Carithers, coordinator of the Natural Landmark Program in the Southwest Region, asking me to visit the area to assess its natural values. I was able to spend several days in the area, primarily on the Lytle Ranch. Although the principal reason for the evaluation was that the area rep-

resented Utah's only example of Mojave Desert habitat, complete with a major stand of Joshua trees, I also found Utah agaves and barrel and cottontop cacti. The area also supported desert bighorn, desert tortoises, gila monsters, and Mohave rattlesnakes, all species at the northern edge of their range. My report to Joe, "Evaluation of Joshua Tree Natural Area, Washington County, Utah, for Eligibility for Registered Natural Landmark," was submitted in August 1966. The area eventually received Natural Landmark status.

The birdlife in Beaver Dam Wash and all of the Virgin River area was enticing, and I applied for a National Science Foundation grant to survey the birdlife, especially migration patterns, of the Virgin River drainages in Utah and adjacent Nevada, above where the river flowed into Lake Mead. My proposal was funded, and I

Gila monster in Beaver Dam Wash, Utah, 1965

made eighty-nine trips to select study sites from 1964 through the summer of 1966. An eventual 1969 publication in the *Condor* summarized my findings. Breeding range extensions in that paper and others included those for the common gallinule, common ground-dove, lesser night-hawk, Wied's (brown-crested) flycatcher, summer tanager, and black-chinned and rufous-crowned sparrows. Reported sightings and/or specimens representing first, second, or third state records included common black-hawk, mountain plover, semipalmated sandpiper, Vaux's swift, painted redstart, rose-breasted grosbeak, and golden-crowned and swamp sparrows.

Herps

The reptile/amphibian book was the result of numerous surveys that I had undertaken at all elevations in the park, especially in the Coalpits Wash lowlands with its desert environment. In addition, I had spent considerable time driving the roadways after dark looking for snakes, and I also set out a series of can traps in key locations. Can traps are most useful for trapping small snakes and lizards as well as some frogs and toads. Each series of cans (large coffee cans or larger) was dug into the earth to ground level, behind a twenty- to forty-foot-long, low fence positioned to direct herps toward the cans. This method worked extremely well in most cases, but large specimens simply crawled out of the can and disappeared. Catching herps in this way also allowed me to photograph the captured individuals before turning them loose. I was able to photograph 32 of the 33 species included in my book; the exception was a tiger salamander photo that I acquired from Myrl Walker.

One unexpected product of the can traps was the capture of a desert shrew adjacent to my yard on November 1, 1963. This discovery represented a new mammal genus and species for Utah, extending its range approximately 250 miles eastward from the nearest locality in Nevada. I prepared a short note on my find that was published in the *Journal of Mammalogy* in 1965.

Deer and Elk

The larger fauna, especially mule deer and elk, received much greater visitor attention than did the birds and herps. Deer and elk were also of interest to the park staff. These large ungulates moved in and out of the park on a regular basis, and the Park Service participated with the State of Utah in establishing annual hunting limits in the counties along the park boundary. The park ranger staff, under Chief Ranger Del Armstrong, was responsible for monitoring the park herds and patrolling the boundaries during hunting seasons. The ranger most involved with this activity was Bruce Moorhead, who lived only two houses away from me; we became good friends.

I participated in several of Bruce's surveys and also a research project that included placing radio transmitters on a few elk. These transmitters were secured as collars and adjusted to send signals to a receiver that could be carried in the field. The biggest surprise for me, resulting from an animal with a transmitter, occurred the first day of hunting season in 1964. Bruce and I were located on a hill just inside the park's east entrance at dawn. We could see hunters at a distance outside the park boundary, waiting to shoot any elk that might leave the park. Then we noticed two individuals inside the park walking toward the boundary; their idea was to drive elk out of the park so they could be shot once they crossed the boundary. They were unaware that we were watching. Bruce had his receiver with him, and we had detected one bull elk wearing a transmitter directly below our hill. It was somewhere between the drivers and the shooters. But the two individuals continued on to the park boundary without detecting or frightening the elk into making a break for it. After the unsuccessful drivers reached the park boundary, and the hunters moved elsewhere, Bruce and I decided to locate the individual elk

Bruce Moorhead and collared elk, Zion National Park, 1964

Kolob Canyons, Zion National Park

My Wild Life

that we knew was nearby. Using the receiver, we were able to walk right up to it; we found it literally lying in a little gully in the sagebrush flat, with its antlers laid flat so it was well hidden. We were convinced it was aware of the hunting season, and it was wise enough to remain within the protection of the park.

Deer populations were studied in two ways. I initiated a deer census in January 1963, utilizing the pellet count method as I had done at Crater Lake. Bruce and I laid out 200 plots within five habitat types in Zion Canyon: 88 in evergreen woodlands, 76 in deciduous woodlands, 14 in oak woodlands, 11 in sage flats, and 11 in grasslands. Thirty-five days later, I recorded 76 pellet groups within the 200 established plots. Using the formula I had been taught at San Jose State, I estimated the 2,475-acre canyon population at 2,066 individual deer, or 0.835 deer per acre. This estimate was probably reasonably close to the actual number residing within the eight-mile-long canyon. Bruce and I also ran nighttime deer counts between the Watchman Residential Area and the Temple of Sinawava, again as I had done at Pinnacles. One May night we detected a high count of 230 individuals.

Mountain Lions

Mountain lions were reasonably common at Zion, especially in the Kolob and at a few other backcountry areas. Sightings in the main canyon were few and far between, although lion tracks were regularly found in the side canyons. This included the area right outside my house in Oak Creek Canyon. Although I did not see a lion while working at Zion, I did have one rather unusual mountain lion experience. Assistant Superintendent Russ Dickinson (who later became director of the National Park Service) and I spent considerable time exploring the Kolob Canyons area on the western edge of the park that was slated for a road and minor development. We actually walked the proposed road right-of-way, mapping out potential pull-offs for interpretive signs as well as flagging environmentally sensitive areas that should not be disturbed. The route eventually became the Kolob Canyons Road, which ends at spectacular Timber Creek Overlook.

On one trip we hiked to the end of South Fork, to a point where we could not continue farther. A quarter mile or so into the canyon we began to find very fresh mountain lion tracks in the wet sand, and we realized that a lion was not far ahead of us. By the time we arrived at the head of the canyon, we were so close to the lion that water was seeping into its very recent paw prints. And when we stopped because we could not go any farther, small rocks and debris rained down on us from above; we knew that the debris was the result of our lion escaping up the very steep slope, undoubtedly only a few dozen feet away.

On another hike into Parunuweap Canyon with Russ to check on this historic site, we continued beyond the old rock houses to the head of the canyon. Parunuweap Canyon contained the remains of an old Mormon settlement that was visited by Major John Wesley Powell in 1871. We worked our way above the canyon to take some photographs and then decided to circle around the head of the canyon and descend on the opposite side. We were following an old animal trail that was barely evident at the upper end and mostly of loose rocks. It dropped off almost a hundred feet. As I edged around the end I realized that if I did begin to slide that I could always catch myself on a huge pricklypear cactus growing at the edge of the drop-off. That is exactly what happened! I did begin to slide, right into the cactus and the hundreds of sharp spines. As I clambered back onto the trail, I discovered that my left side and jacket were filled with cactus spines. It took hours to extract all of the spines from my body, and I was finding spines in my jacket for months afterward.

Zion National Park is a hiker's park, although the vast majority of the summer visitors rarely leave Zion Canyon or stray far from the various overlooks. But the park's trail system offers an amazing variety of routes, ranging from riverside trails to a marvelous network of high-country trails. I was able to hike all the park trails, and I wrote a twenty-eight-page brochure, *A Guide to the Trails of Zion National Park*, published by the Zion Natural History Association. I had three favorite trails: the easy Emerald Pools Trail in the center of Zion Canyon; the more extensive West Rim Trail through Refrigerator Canyon and onto the western highlands; and The Narrows.

The Narrows Trail begins outside the park, not far from the park's East Entrance, and follows the bed of the Virgin River for sixteen miles; much of the route requires wading. Few routes compare with this unique hike from the headwaters of the North Fork to the Temple of Sinawava. There is one place where the walls are only ten feet apart and rise more than twenty-five hundred feet to the rim of the plateau. I was so impressed with The Narrows that I wrote an article on one Narrows hike that was published by *Summit Magazine* in March 1965. The following two paragraphs are from that article:

> The sky was completely blue, as seen only along the Utah-Arizona border. . . . I began to try to follow the winding streamcourse as far as possible without giving in and begin wading. This I only succeeded in doing for about a mile before the banks became too steep and

the rocky streamsides became too few. It was then that I became aware of a strange sensation. It had something to do with the knowledge that once committed to this downward plunge with the river, it is best to go forward rather than retreat. It also has something to do with the little sign posted at the Temple of Sinawava, "a sudden flash flood drowned five hikers in the Narrows." . . . You become amazingly aware of the blue sky, and each shadow along the waterway seems to predict a searching glance upward. Yet even this is forgotten as the first narrow passageway is approached.

I was somewhat surprised at the lack of wildlife within the upper Narrows, but once Goose Creek was reached it changed considerably. The quantity of deer tracks was evidence enough to indicate that the North Fork and Goose Creek is a heavily used deer-route in and out of Zion Canyon. The common bird was the Dipper. Bruce and I watched it feeding upon insects that it found below the surface of the water, and I followed one to a nest of mud and moss built in a rock crevice not far above the waterline. Wading forward for a closer examination, I became aware of the thin squeaks of young birds from the nest. The adult suddenly appeared and flew down canyon, probably in search for food for her tiny offspring.

Narrows of the Virgin River, Zion National Park

Cave Valley, Zion National Park

My Wild Life

Interpretive Training

In March and April 1964, I attended the Stephen T. Mather Interpretive Training and Research Center at Harpers Ferry, West Virginia. It was my first time on the East Coast. Center Director Russ Grater had been an acquaintance for several years, and one of the most dedicated interpreters I had ever encountered. Thirty trainees were involved, and I became good friends with at least two individuals: Doug Evans from Big Bend and Dick Burns from Sequoia. Perhaps the most significant part of that program was the field trips to a variety of historic sites along the Mid-Atlantic Seaboard. Visits to Antietam, C&O Canal, and Fort McHenry in Maryland; Gettysburg in Pennsylvania; and Colonial Fredericksburg, Jamestown, and Williamsburg in Virginia provided me for the first time with a true appreciation of our American history. However, by the end of the course, I was anxious to get back to my red-rock canyons.

Cave Valley

Like all avid birders, I occasionally found myself on private property, trying to see some especially interesting species. One day while driving the North Creek Road through Cave Valley, en route to Lava Point and other high-country sites, I discovered a pair of courting prairie falcons just above the roadway. I stopped to watch those acrobatic raptors, but they soon flew across the fenced field and disappeared into a cleft in a cliff about a half mile off the road. Assuming the birds had a nest that needed documentation, I parked off the roadway, climbed over the fence, and walked across the open field to investigate. When I got to where the birds had disappeared, they were not in sight, nor could I see anyplace that might harbor a nest.

Nearby, however, was the mouth of a cave at the top of a steep slope about 150 feet above the valley floor. I decided to check it out. Although the cave extended only about 85 feet deep, about 40 feet high, and 30 feet wide, the walls were literally covered with pictographs, rock paintings by early peoples. And even without a flashlight I could make out an amazing variety of symbols and animals, including birds and mammals, all done in a variety of colors. Since I planned to bird the high country beyond Cave Valley that day and the next, and since I had no way of adequately seeing all the pictographs without a flashlight, I returned to my vehicle and continued on to Lava Point. But I immediately began to plan my next visit to Cave Valley.

Two weeks later I was back with an adequate flashlight and a camera with flash. The cave was even more interesting than I had first imagined. All of the walls were covered with carbon and pictographs, evidence of previous

Back wall with pictographs, Cave Valley

sects, mammals, snakes, and various ones that were unidentifiable.

Some of the mammalian figures were the most interesting. One was an animal with three toes on each foot, a short tail, large ears, and a large mouth, which appears to be ready to swallow a snake. Others represented deer, with forked antlers and a short tail, a bearlike image, one that I named "the crazy rabbit," and near the ceiling was a figure that looked very much like a mastodon.

My efforts in documenting the Cave Valley pictograph site had two results. I made a presentation on the site to the Utah Archeological Society at the University of Utah on April 17, 1965, and I also prepared a well-illustrated paper that was published by the University of Utah in its Anthropological Papers series in June 1965. I wrote that the Cave Valley pictographs "probably do not date further back than A.D. 1-55, and many may have been done by the modern Shoshonean. If the figure in Fig. 2 is truly a mastodon, it could possibly present evidence which would lead to an older determination, although it may have been copied from earlier paintings by the Cave Valley artist." The last mastodons died out about six thousand years ago; a mastodon petroglyph does exist in a cave near Moab, Utah.

Cave Valley was the private property of Evan Lee, grandson of Mormon pioneer John D. Lee of Mountain Meadows massacre fame.

occupation. The rear wall contained an amazing assortment of images, including a large human figure with a white-dotted crest that stood out over the rest. The side walls contained the largest number of figures and the greatest variety. I counted about eighty images in all, including groups of birds, concentric circles, crosses, dots, hands, human and kachina-like figures, in-

Side wall with pictographs, Cave Valley

Kachina pictograph, Cave Valley

My visits to Cave Valley were on the sly; I could only imagine what his response might be to find a government employee on his land. On my photographic visit, I had parked my private vehicle a hundred yards or so beyond his property and walked back. On returning to my vehicle late that afternoon, I found a handwritten note on my windshield: "No Trespassing With Out Permission" and signed "Evan S. Lee." I still have that note so many years later.

New Awareness

During my various trips into the Taylor Creek area, I began to wonder if the habitats that existed on top of the high, isolated, flat-topped peaks and plateaus were any different from similar but more accessible sites that had constant human visitation. One of my job responsibilities was to work with the various scientists in the park. I coordinated the permits for research within the park for the serious scientists; final approval rested with the superintendent. Although the park rangers generally acted as resource managers in regard to deer and elk, the rest of the park's resources were usually ignored. So I began making occasional trips to universities, visiting with biologists about possible studies in the park, especially in disciplines we knew very little about.

On a trip to Logan, while visiting with Dr. Neil West, plant ecologist at Utah State University, I brought up the idea of surveying Zion's isolated plateaus. He became very interested, and a year later, after obtaining a grant for the research and a park permit, he began to systematically visit various isolated sites by helicopter. This project produced not only several new plants for the park but, more important, a much better perspective of the park's wild habitats not already impacted by human presence.

It was during this period in my career that I began to realize how little new scientific information about a park actually becomes part of the basic understanding of a park. Scientific information was seldom used in management decisions or even in interpretation, primarily because the parks lacked anyone with the responsibility to translate new data into a useful form. I found myself spending more and more time involved with such endeavors.

On a personal note, Sandy and I were divorced a year after moving to Zion; she moved to her mother's home in Vallejo, California, with the two girls. I spent even more time in the field, birding the park and the Virgin River Valley. A year later I was introduced to Sharon Stephenson at the College of Southern Utah, where she taught. We were married in Rexburg, Idaho, in 1966.

Transition

Superintendent Oberhansley retired in 1965, and Warren Hamilton replaced him. He, too, seemed very interested in the park, and he eventually retired to Springdale. A few months after Superintendent Hamilton arrived, he called me into his office one day for a talk. During the 1960s and 1970s, the National Park Service required all uniformed personnel to update their "Employee Background and Skills" form at least every three years. This was the form that the regional office sent to a park that was filling a vacant position. Superintendent Hamilton explained that the regional office had informed him that the only uniformed Zion employee who had not submitted a form was Wauer and that I was expected to complete my form promptly.

I attempted to explain to him that I was happy at Zion, I had a number of projects under way that I hoped to complete, and I did not really want to go elsewhere. I remember him looking somewhat surprised at my comments, and then he asked me what park, if I had my way, would I consider. Without thinking too much about it, I said, "There is only one park I would be interested in, Big Bend National Park in Texas." When he asked me why, I explained it was the number-one birding national park and that it was close to Mexico, a country I would love to explore.

The timing of my visit with Superintendent Hamilton was rather interesting because just that spring—March 12 to 22—several friends and I had taken a super birding trip to Mexico. Dennis, Dennis's friend Allerga Collister, my longtime birding friend Mike Parmeter, and Al Walent, a seasonal naturalist at Zion, had taken the train from Nogales to Tepic, Sinaloa. We then traveled to a number of key birding sites in that area via taxi. It had been a marvelous first adventure in Mexico, and I wanted more.

I, of course, completed my form, and it went to the regional office to become one of many hundreds. I had completely forgotten it when, less than two months later, Superintendent Hamilton called me into his office again. With little fanfare, he said, "Ro, it looks like you are going to get your wish. Expect a call later today from Superintendent Parry Brown of Big Bend. He will offer you the chief naturalist position."

6
Big Bend National Park, Texas

fell in love with the Big Bend country on my very first visit in 1963, four years before moving there as chief park naturalist. And even now, half a century later, when people ask me about a favorite park, without any hesitation I tell them it is Big Bend. There are several reasons for this. First, Big Bend National Park is one of our few truly wilderness parks. Only a fraction of the 800,000-plus acres contains any development. Second, Big Bend is unquestionably the finest biological park in the National Park System. More birds (450+), more reptiles (56), and more butterflies (190+) have been recorded there than in any of the other national parks. The park also boasts of more than 1,000 plant species. And because of its position along the Mexican border, many of its plants and animals are not found elsewhere in the United States.

In addition, the majority of the park visitors to Big Bend go there really to see and enjoy Big Bend, not just to stick it on their checklist of national parks visited. This is in spite of the park being a long way from a major highway; it is not readily accessible. National Park Service statistics claim that the average stay at Big Bend is 4.5 days, twice as long as for most of the other major parks like Yosemite, Grand Canyon, and Great Smoky Mountains.

The Job

There is still another although coincidental reason why I enjoyed my assignment at Big Bend so very much. My arrival there in late July 1966 followed a period when my predecessor (Doug Evans) had already completed the park's interpretive prospectus and related documents, activities that required considerable in-office paperwork. Much of my responsibility during my

Chisos Basin from Emory Peak, Big Bend National Park

tenure was implementing the interpretive prospectus. That required a considerable amount of field time, including the preparation of road and trail guides, waysides, checklists, and other informational materials. I felt that I had found my true calling.

My principal responsibilities, according to my position description, included the coordination of the park's interpretive activities, such as talks and walks, and managing the park library, collections, and the Big Bend Natural History Association. I gave at least one weekly talk during the visitor season throughout my residency. In addition, I was responsible for contacts with all visiting scientists.

The park's visitor center and most of the em-

Big Bend National Park visitor center

My Wild Life

ployee housing were located at Panther Junction, or PJ, as it is known to most of the staff. PJ is centrally located and at midelevation (3,750 feet) in the park. It is nine miles from the Chisos Basin, twenty miles from Rio Grande Village (located along the eastern edge), and thirty-five miles from Castolon and Cottonwood Campground on the western edge of the park; Santa Elena Canyon is only eight miles beyond.

The Chisos Basin in 1966 contained the Chisos Mountains Lodge, a number of cottages that had been constructed by the CCC, and an equally ancient store operated by the National Park Concessions. NPS presence in the Basin was limited to a small ranger station. A major trailhead for the mountain trails was located along the western edge of the Basin. The lower Basin contained a campground and adjacent amphitheater, a few houses for Park Service and concession employees, and the Chisos Remuda, a horse concession operated by "Buck" Newsome, a wrangler of the old school.

The majority of the Park Service employees lived at PJ, up the hill behind the visitor center. Houses were situated along a double-loop roadway, and my residence was located on the outer edge of the upper loop. While we lived there, Sharon and I adopted two children: Susan in 1969 and Stephen in 1971. Although my front door faced north and a neighbor's house just across the driveway, my backyard provided a marvelous, unobstructed view of Panther Peak and Wright Mountain, the northeastern corner of the Chisos Mountains. The little arroyo directly behind my house led to Mouse Canyon, a little isolated canyon where I eventually spent considerable time.

My office at the visitor center was located behind the lobby and information desk; the small but excellent park library was just beyond. The park collections, preparation room, and a darkroom were located across a closed patio.

Friends and Colleagues

I never got to know Superintendent Parry Brown, who hired me, very well because he retired soon after I arrived. He was replaced by Luther Peterson, who had a Park Service background in maintenance but little understanding of ecology or wildlife. Peterson had a rigid demeanor, expecting his employees to do it his way or else. However, he and his wife, Betty, were wonderful hosts when they invited folks into their home.

Besides the superintendent, several other employees retired or transferred soon after I arrived. They were replaced by people who soon became good friends. My favorites included (alphabetically) Bob and Carol Barbee, Jim and Virginia Court, Paul and Maryann Gerrish,

Banding station at Panther Junction

reacquainted when I worked at the Santa Fe Regional Office. We were married in 1976. In retrospect, she is another reason that Big Bend is my favorite park.

Big Bend's Birdlife

Almost before I had completely settled into my new residence, I started a bird feeding station in my backyard that was intended to be my principal banding site in the park. But before I could begin banding, I first had to request a Texas permit and also renew my federal permit to include Big Bend National Park. These were not received until late September. My first bird banded in Big Bend was a cactus wren on October 1, 1966, and during my six-year residency at Big Bend, I banded 3,003 individual birds of 104 species. I had 129 returns during the six years. These were banded birds that returned a second or third time, proving that many individuals that nested elsewhere returned to the park for the winter months. Of special interest was a white-throated sparrow banded at PJ on January 26, 1967, that was captured at Hot Springs, South Dakota, in May 1967.

Banding provided me with a better understanding of Big Bend's bird density and distribution as well as racial determinations. For example, I discovered that the breeding population of brown-headed cowbirds belonged to the

Dean and Donna Hatfield, Bill and Mur Jensen, Jay and Ruth Jessen, and Roger Siglin. Non-NPS favorites living in the PJ area included Larry and Sue Claybaugh and Judge Charlie Shannon. Larry was the Texas agricultural inspector ("river rider"), and Sue became my secretary.

Bill Jensen was chief of maintenance, and in January 1968, he hired a new secretary, a pretty young woman named Betty. She worked at Big Bend for three years, transferring to LBJ National Historical Park, then Ft. Davis National Historic Site, and then Bandelier National Monument, near Santa Fe, where we got

My Wild Life

small subspecies *obscurus*, often referred to as "dwarf cowbird." I found that dwarf cowbirds leave the park by midsummer and are replaced by a larger brown-headed cowbird of the subspecies *artemisae*. The larger birds remain only a few months before moving south for the winter months, but there is an intermingling of the two forms during September and October.

By banding at various park locations, I discovered that breeding cowbirds above an elevation of approximately twenty-five hundred feet consisted of one large flock; birds banded at PJ were just as likely to be found in the Chisos Basin. But the population at Rio Grande Village formed a separate population, not intermingling with the Chisos Mountain population. The Rio Grande Village population of breeding cowbirds spent much of their time across the river in the Mexican village of Boquillas.

Banding also provided insight into the abundance of some species that was not evident purely by sight observations. For instance, the number of migrating northern waterthrushes banded on a particular day at Rio Grande Village was three times greater than that otherwise observed during the same time period.

Big Bend National Park already had a reputation as a choice birding park, primarily because it is the only place in the United States where one could find the Colima warbler, a Mexican species that barely reached the United States and only during the nesting season. It arrives in the park by late March and remains until July to early September, before returning to its wintering grounds in the southwestern Mexican states of Jalisco and Colima. Its name was derived from Colima, where it was first collected.

In addition to the Colima warbler, the park is the best North American location to find the Lucifer hummingbird and varied bunting, two additional Mexican species barely reaching the United States. Some of the other high-priority species for birders include zone-tailed hawk; peregrine falcon; elf and flammulated owls; blue-throated hummingbird; vermilion flycatcher; Bell's, black-capped, and gray vireos; Mexican jay; crissal thrasher; hepatic tanager; black-chinned sparrow; and pyrrhuloxia.

Bird study at Big Bend before my arrival already had a long and fascinating history, going back to the United States Biological Survey in 1901 when Harry C. Oberholser, Vernon Bailey, and Louis Agassiz Fuertes did extensive fieldwork throughout the area. Some of the other better-known ornithologists who had visited the park area during the first half of the century included Frank A. Armstrong, Herbert Brandt, Frederick Gaige, George Miksch Sutton, Josselyn Van Tyne, and Walter Weber. The first park-specific checklist, which included 236

Rio Grande Village and distant Chisos Mountains, Big Bend National Park

species, was developed in 1960 by the park's first chief naturalist, Harold Brodrick. Philip Allen and Anne LeSassier revised Brodrick's checklist in 1966, bringing the list to 241 species. My revised checklist in 1973 included 357 species, and my book published in 1973, *Birds of Big Bend National Park and Vicinity*, included 385 species; 26 of those were hypothetical only.

My full-time residency within the park al-lowed me to visit regularly all of the key bird-ing sites, specifically Rio Grande Village, Chisos Basin, Cottonwood Campground, the Window Trail, and Boot Canyon, more or less in that order of significance. Other productive birding sites that I visited regularly included lower Blue Creek Canyon, Laguna Meadow, the Pinnacles Trail, and Pine Canyon.

During my six-year residency in the park,

I had numerous truly marvelous birding experiences. Perhaps the most memorable was finding the first North American records of the black-vented oriole, earlier known as Wagler's oriole. I first observed one at Rio Grande Village on September 27, 1968, but that individual almost immediately left the area and I was unable to document its occurrence properly. The following spring (April 28, 1969) I found it again less than three hundred feet from the first sighting, and this individual remained in the vicinity at least until September 19, almost a full year after the original date of discovery. The 1969 bird was seen and photographed by numerous birders. I later (1970) published a note on its occurrence in the ornithological journal *Auk*.

Banded black-vented oriole, first US record, 1969

I decided to net the 1969 bird to examine it for possible breeding and also to determine its racial identification. My description of that effort, from *Birds of Big Bend National Park and Vicinity*, included the following:

I made several attempts to net it between June 28 and July 4. On July 1, I placed a mounted Great Horned Owl, a species that occurs commonly in the immediately vicinity, on the ground next to a mist net. *I. wagleri* perched ten feet above the stuffed bird and watched while a pair of Mockingbirds launched attack after attack on the owl until both Mockers were caught in the netting. I even drew a

Wagler's Oriole on paper, colored it with the proper colors, and mounted the drawing on a stick next to the net. This, too, was a failure. The only reaction obtained from *I. wagleri* was one of vague curiosity. Yet it did show interest in people on a number of occasions. Several times I observed it watching campers going about their routine camp duties, and on one occasion it flew into a tree above two children who were rolling a red rubber ball around on the ground. It sat there watching this action for about four minutes before flying off to another perch. On only two occasions did I observe it showing any aggression toward another bird, and then only two very short chases (fifteen to twenty feet) of a female Orchard Oriole. Although *I. wagleri* could usually be detected by a very low, rasping call, like that of a Yellow-breasted Chat or Scott's Oriole, a song was never heard.

Finally, by moving the nets each time *I. wagleri* changed positions, I succeeded in capturing it on July 4. Closer examination showed that it was in nonbreeding status; it clearly lacked evidence of a brood patch and had no cloacal protuberance. Close examination of the bill and cere showed no indication that the bird had been caged at any time. Close-up photographs of the chest were sent to Allan Phillips, who identified the bird racially as the *wagleri* form of eastern Mexico. The chest had a light chestnut tinge.

I recorded several other new park records during my residency. One of the earliest was a rufous-backed robin at Rio Grande Village on October 23, 1966. That was the first Texas sighting, and, although I saw it very briefly the next day, I was unable to obtain a photograph to document its occurrence fully. In 1967, my new park records included a purple gallinule at Rio Grande Village on April 20, a worm-eating warbler in upper Boot Canyon on May 4, a saw-whet owl at Boot Spring on November 3, and Kent Rylander and I found an Anna's hummingbird near Santa Elena Canyon on November 5;

we later published it as the second Texas record in the *Auk* (1968).

On May 21, 1968, I found nesting groove-billed anis at Rio Grande Village, representing new park and Trans-Pecos records. Also at Rio Grande Village were a least grebe and a swallow-tailed kite on August 5, 1969; a Lucy's warbler on April 8, 1970; and a mourning warbler on April 18, 1972. The kite represented only the second Trans-Pecos record.

I had several additional memorable birding experiences at Big Bend. For instance, on March 20, 1968, I discovered a roadrunner nest containing a single egg at Rio Grande Village. Three additional eggs were laid during the next several days, and I banded and photographed all four nestlings before they fledged two weeks later. The roadrunner is one of the park's best-known birds, probably because of its fictional cartoon image of outsmarting Wile E. Coyote. Although it is most numerous in the park's lowlands, I have also found it, especially during dry years, in the Chisos highlands, including along the South Rim.

On May 27, 1969, Donald Davis and I visited a cave about three hundred feet above the arid terrain along the eastern slope of Mariscal Mountain, a massive limestone anticlinal ridge that lies at the "bottom" of the Texas Big Bend. Don had found cave swallows nesting there a few weeks earlier, and I had hoped to document this species for the park. During our visit we located eighteen cave swallow nests within the cave, sixty to seventy feet back from the entrance; two nests contained young birds, and a third contained three eggs. But what was most interesting about the site was its dual use by both cave and cliff swallows: cliff swallows were nesting near the entrance, and cave swallows were nesting in the twilight portion of the cave. Our sightings were later published in the *Condor* (1973).

A fascinating interaction between a Harris's hawk and badger occurred on June 15, 1976, after I had moved to Santa Fe but was on a trip back to the park with John Egbert. While still in the ranching country north of the park, we discovered a Harris's hawk on the ground to the left of the roadway. We got out of the vehicle with our binoculars to watch the hawk. It was then that we saw the badger and watched as it methodically rooted under piles of cow dung and dug into the loose soil. By this time the hawk was standing near and watching the badger, which seemed to be ignoring the hawk completely. The badger moved from one dung pile to another, followed by the hawk, which examined the overturned dung piles as soon as the badger moved on. At one time the hawk was no farther than two feet from the badger. At another time the hawk flew to the top of a fence post directly above the busy mammal.

Roadrunner, Rio Grande Village, Big Bend National Park

Roadrunner chicks, Rio Grande Village, Big Bend National Park

Banded Colima warbler in hand,
Big Bend National Park

We watched these activities for approximately twelve minutes while the badger and hawk moved a distance of about eighty feet. Not once did the badger seem to be disturbed by the presence of either the hawk or us.

Afterward we examined the piles of cow dung overturned by the badger and others that had not been disturbed. We discovered several arthropods beneath undisturbed piles but none on the ground surface under the disturbed piles. Although we did not observe the hawk take any prey, we surmised that it searched for arthropods missed by the badger. The relationship between the Harris's hawk and the badger might be mutualism, in which both animals benefit from the association. However, unless the hawk acted as a lookout, it is doubtful that the badger received any benefit from the hawk. Opportunism is a more likely relationship. The Harris's hawk had learned to use the badger's feeding habits for its own benefit.

Another interesting experience occurred on the afternoon of April 27, 1971, when Forrest and Aline Romero came to the visitor center to report a prothonotary warbler in the Chisos Basin. Whoever was at the information desk at the time called me out so I, too, could listen to their report. Although Forrest and Aline seemed to know what they were talking about, there had never before been a prothonotary warbler reported for the park, and finding this species among the pinyon-juniper woodlands in the mountains seemed totally out of place. I listened politely but doubted their sighting. But just as they were leaving, one of them said that if their photo comes out, they would send me a copy to prove their sighting. I of course encouraged them to do so. And in a few weeks when their photo arrived, showing a prothonotary warbler perched in a Mexican pinyon, which is three-needled rather than two-needled, there was little doubt. I began to realize that almost anything could turn up in Big Bend National Park.

I spent more time and effort studying Colima warblers than any of the other Big Bend specialties. Not only did the Colima receive considerable attention from birders but some biologists had suggested that it should be considered for listing as an endangered species by Texas and also perhaps by the federal government. In order to get a better understanding about its abundance and distribution within the park, I initiated a Colima warbler census in 1967 that was repeated in 1968, 1969, and 1970. All locations where suitable habitats existed were searched. I discussed these counts in my 1973 bird book:

> Totals of 45 pairs of Colima Warblers were found in 1967, 65 in 1968, 83 in 1969, and 61 in 1970. In all instances it was associated with oak-pinyon-juniper or oak-maple-Arizona cypress environments. Approximately 85 percent of the birds counted were located along a narrow and relatively humid canyon, with considerable overstory of vegetation, and 15 percent were located on relatively open slopes or ridges. Some localities appeared to offer quite stable habitats, whereas others vary considerably. All the Boot Canyon drainages were heavily used every year, but considerable variation of populations occurs in fringe areas like Laguna Meadow and its canyons, Emory Peak, and upper Pine Canyon. In general, the distribution of breeding birds

appears to be determined by the precipitation during the months just prior to the nesting season. During wet spring months, as in 1968, Colimas were found nesting along the trail just below Laguna Meadow and in upper Pine Canyon. During the dry years, such as 1969, more were found in the higher canyons and fewer in such lower and drier canyons as Pine Canyon and below Laguna Meadow.

I also wrote an article about the 1967 count for *National Parks Magazine* that appeared in November of that year. I pointed out that John Galley and I had censused upper Boot Canyon, the East and South Rims, and the Emory Peak area. Francis Williams, Ann LeSassier, and Ted Jones searched along the Lost Mine Trail and the upper Basin to Laguna Meadow. Ned Fritz covered Kibby Spring and upper Green Gulch. Dick Nelson surveyed upper Blue Creek Canyon. Kent Rylander covered the upper Basin along the slope of Casa Grande south to the Pinnacles. And Jon Barlow and Jim Dick searched the lower Basin and the canyons along the southern slope of Pulliam Ridge.

I coordinated a fifth Colima warbler census in 1974 after I left the park; eight counters tallied 48 pairs. The park staff conducted duplicate counts in 1976, 1982, and 1984, tallying 52, 58, and 58 Colimas, respectively. In 1996 and 2000, I coordinated additional counts in which twenty-two participants tallied 68 Colimas in 1996, and twelve counters tallied 68 pairs in 2000. And in 2005 and 2010, Jim and Lynne Weber coordinated counts that produced 75 and 56 pairs, respectively. All the same sites were surveyed in all the later counts. Based upon those surveys, there is little doubt that the Big Bend population of Colima warblers is doing very well and does not need to be listed.

In addition to making numerous Colima warbler surveys and other observations over the years, I recruited John Egbert, a birding friend in Santa Fe at the time, to spend six weeks in the Chisos Mountains studying Colimas and their habitat. The intent was to obtain a better understanding of their habitat requirements. Although I spent several days on-site with John, he was on his own most of the time. Our joint report, "Preferred Habitat with Special Reference to Nest Site Selection and Density and Distribution of *Vermivora crissalis*," provided a much better understanding of Colima warbler habitat requirements in the Chisos Mountains. Years later in 1999, I also coauthored (with Robert C. Beason) "Colima Warbler (*Vermivora crissalis*)."

All during my residency, I spent as much time as possible in the Boot Canyon area, surveying the birdlife and banding at various locations in the highlands. The Boot Spring cabin was a convenient place to stay. It was available only to employees, and when it was not in use by the trail crew, I was able to stay overnight. The cabin contained a few bunks, table and chairs, stove for cooking, and water. During the first few years, Boot Spring itself, located in the drainage directly below the cabin, and flowing, was drinkable.

The cabin, however, was sometimes overrun with mice, not the nonnative house mouse but the native white-footed mouse. At times they became more than just a nuisance. One night I was awakened when one that apparently was exploring my bunk decided to cross my face; it stepped in my mouth. I remember that I exhaled so hard that it literally flew across the room hitting the wall; I could not find it the next morning. But in order to control their numbers, I tied a string across a bucket filled with water, and placed some peanut butter in the center to entice them onto the string. The following morning I found seventeen drowned mice in the bucket.

After retirement, I volunteered to study the park's breeding birds within six different communities during April and May 1990 to 1997. Sites selected included the Dugout Wells area to represent the lechuguilla-creosotebush-cactus community; Blue Creek Canyon, the arroyo-mesquite-acacia community; lower Green Gulch and lower Pine Canyon, the sotol-grasslands;

Boot cabin, Boot Spring,
Big Bend National Park, 1970

Oak Creek Canyon, the deciduous woodland community; upper Green Gulch and Juniper Flat, the pinyon-juniper-oak woodland community; and middle Pine Canyon, the mesic canyon community.

The abstract from my report, published in 2001 as *Breeding Avifaunal Baseline for Big Bend National Park, Texas*, included the following:

> A total of 50 surveys were completed on eight study plots representing six communities. . . . A total of 110 bird species were recorded, 74 of which are considered breeding. Oak Creek Canyon supported the greatest number of breeders (52), followed by Upper Green Gulch (49), Blue Creek Canyon (41), Middle Pine Canyon (37), Lower Pine Canyon (35), Lower Green Gulch (34), Dugout (32), and Juniper Flat (31). Individual numbers were highest on Dugout (355), followed by Lower Green Gulch (311), Upper Green Gulch (289), Blue Creek Canyon (286), Lower Pine Canyon (260), Oak Creek Canyon (252), Middle Pine Canyon (240), and Juniper Flat (188). All 74 breeders were classified as to their nesting and feeding guilds, and species diversity and evenness were computed for each study plot. The highest species diversity value occurred on the Oak Creek Canyon plot (3.67) and the lowest on Middle Pine Canyon (2.70); Upper Green Gulch ranked second with 3.54, followed by Blue Creek Canyon (3.38), Lower Pine Canyon (3.04), Dugout (3.01), Juniper Flat (2.92), and Lower Green Gulch (2.86).

My conclusions stated that the results "offer reference points that can be used to assess environmental changes. Increases suggest stability; declines suggest habitat deterioration. Species diversity and evenness values should increase as the communities continue to recover and the resources stabilize; values should decline with various perturbations such as clearing for development, fire (at least in the short-term), and other natural and unnatural changes that reduce or eliminate essential wildlife needs such as water, food, and cover."

. . . . .

Several years later I was asked by Tim Brush, an ornithological colleague, to prepare an article to be published by the Cooper Ornithological Society in an extension publication. I agreed and asked Mark Flippo, naturalist at Big Bend, to be junior author. Our article, "Avifaunal Changes in Big Bend National Park, Texas," appeared in 2008. Our abstract follows:

Population changes in the breeding avifauna of the Big Bend National Park, from 1901 through 2006 were recorded for 24 species. They included recent arrivals, increasing, declining or extirpated, apparently stable species, and species of uncertain status. Recent arrivals include Black-crowned Night-Heron, Eurasian Collared-Dove, Golden-fronted Woodpecker, Dusky-capped Flycatcher, Cave Swallow, Carolina Wren, and Lucy's Warbler. Increasing species include Mallard, Green Heron, Gray Hawk, Common Black-Hawk, Lucifer Hummingbird, Green Kingfisher, Painted Redstart, Great-tailed Grackle, and Bronzed Cowbird. Declining or extirpated species include Gambel's Quail, Montezuma Quail, Harris's Hawk, Golden Eagle, Prairie Falcon, Yellow Warbler, and Hooded Oriole. Apparently stable species include Peregrine Falcon, Loggerhead Shrike, Bell's Vireo, Black-capped Vireo, and Colima Warbler. Uncertain status applies only to Aplomado Falcon.

American Birding Association

One of the many birders who visited the park in 1969 to see the black-vented oriole was Jim Tucker, an avid longtime birder living in Austin. Jim and I became good friends and traveled together a good deal afterward. During Jim's 1969 visit, I gave him a copy of a two-page interpretive sheet, "You Asked about the Birds," that I had prepared to answer questions about Big Bend's birdlife. Jim liked my sheet and told me he was going to do something of the same sort for the Austin area. A week or two later he called to ask my permission to send my sheet along to a number of friends, saying that he was thinking about developing a more extensive newsletter or brochure that could be expanded into a national program. Jim's efforts evolved into the American Birding Association (ABA), an organization that began with about a dozen members and rapidly grew into an international one that by 2007 had more than twelve thousand members located in every state and more than one hundred foreign countries. The ABA magazine, *Birding*, has become one of the most respected birding magazines anywhere.

ABA's mission is principally to help its members find and identify birds. For that reason, I started a book sales operation out of my house at PJ. During the first couple of years I was able to handle all the sales by myself, but it became so popular that I (ABA) eventually hired Ruth Jessen to handle the sales. When I moved to Santa Fe in 1972, ABA sales moved with me. But because of the amount of traveling required by my new job, we moved the book sales to Jim's office in Austin in 1973. Eventually, ABA moved its office and the book sales to Colorado Springs, Colorado.

During the time that Jim and I were visiting and traveling together, we talked about starting our own publishing company. That eventually became a reality in 1972 when our Peregrine Productions published a brochure: *Traveler's List and Checklist for Birds of Mexico*. A year later we published a book, *Naturalist's Big Bend*, a manuscript I had written during the previous couple of years; retail cost was $3.50. Jim and I had each put $1,500 into that venture, and I had found a printer in Santa Fe and had 750 copies printed. We distributed it through ABA sales, along with outlets at Big Bend National Park. The book sold reasonably well, and a few years later when trying to fund a second printing, I found that the cost had increased so much that we decided we could not afford it.

I had sent a copy of the book to a number of libraries and a few publishers. In June 1976 I received a thank-you letter from Frank Wardlaw, director of Texas A&M University Press, telling me that "I think we should give strong consideration to the possibility of bringing out a new edition of this book in a better format and with added illustrations, some of them in color." I signed a contract in 1978, and the book (same title and format) was published with color in 1980. The book was reissued with significant additions, including a new chapter on butterflies, in 2002. This edition was updated by Carl Fleming, a recently retired natural resource specialist from Big Bend, who became the junior author and received equal royalties.

Big Bend Mammals

Mountain lions, black bears, and javelinas receive almost as much attention in the park as do Colima warblers, perhaps because these three mammals are full-time residents while Colimas are present in the United States for only a few months each year. Although I had experienced mountain lions, better known as "panthers" to most West Texans, before moving to Big Bend, I still had never seen one in the field. And during the 1960s Big Bend's lion population was reasonably low; sightings were few and far between. Yet everyone talked about them as if they could be expected around every corner. And many of the park landmarks were named for this large predator: Panther Junction, Panther Peak, Panther Pass, and Panther Spring. Even the park's athletic teams were known as the Pink Panthers. We had T-shirts dyed pink and, using a black marker, wrote "Pink Panthers" across the front. In retrospect, it was kind of corny but did give our team identity. We played baseball and basketball with several of the local communities; we won very few games but had fun times.

My first mountain lion sighting occurred one night while driving home after presenting a talk at the Chisos Basin Amphitheater. On August 3, 1972, at about 10:30 p.m. in upper Green Gulch, a lion suddenly crossed the roadway in front of my vehicle. I immediately came to a stop, just as the lion decided to sit down on the roadside; it apparently was far less excited than I. It just sat there, looking in my direction. I was able to grab my camera and a spotlight that I plugged into the cigarette lighter, and then I slowly got out of the vehicle. It simply sat there as I took several photographs. Even when it was spotlighted, it seemed more curious than concerned. After sitting for a short time, it simply got up and walked away into the darkness. I was elated! Yet that first mountain lion sighting was anticlimactic. It would have been so much better if my first panther sighting had been somewhere in the backcountry rather than on a well-traveled roadway.

Over the years that I worked at Big Bend, and afterward when I returned to present seminars and such, I have had a total of five mountain lion sightings, including at least one far in the backcountry. But a nonsighting experience stands out more than the others. I had hiked up to Boot Spring after work, planning on banding birds the next day. After leaving my gear in the cabin, I hiked to the South Rim to watch the sun set. It had rained that day, so the trail was wet enough to leave footprints in dirt areas. I sat on the Rim for an hour or so after sunset, enjoying the solitude and the night sounds. Then I began my walk back to the cabin. About halfway back, using a flashlight to light the trail so I wouldn't step on a rattlesnake, I suddenly realized I was walking in very fresh mountain lion tracks. Curious about its behavior, I retraced its route to discover that it had stepped in footprints that I had made earlier en route to the South Rim; it had actually followed me up the trail. I soon found where it had left the trail, presumably when it detected me coming back down the trail a few minutes earlier. As far as I knew, I had not previously been tracked by a giant cat!

Mountain lion numbers, of course, directly affect the deer population. During my years working at Big Bend, it was not unusual to count two to three dozen mule deer grazing each evening from the roadway between PJ and the Basin Junction. Mountain lion populations during that period were at an all-time low;

Black bear, Sam Nail Ranch, Big Bend National Park

Black bear blocking Boot Canyon Trail. Courtesy of Lynne Weber.

they had not yet recovered from prepark years when they were shot and aggressively trapped by area ranchers. But once they were no longer hunted, and with plenty of easy prey, their numbers gradually recovered. By the 1970s and 1980s, lion populations had increased significantly and deer populations had declined. They apparently had reached equilibrium.

The park's black bear population experienced a similar recovery. While I had not seen a bear during the period when I lived in the park,

after I retired and began to conduct seminars in the park each spring and fall, I recorded bears almost every year. My most exciting bear experience occurred on May 4, 1996, when my seminar group had a face-to-face encounter in Boot Canyon. We had been birding along the canyon for a couple of hours and were en route back to Boot Spring when a sow and her cub suddenly appeared on the path, barring our way. I included this incident in my book *For All Seasons: A Big Bend Journal*:

Knowing that black bears can be dangerous when accompanied by a cub, I immediately stopped to let the sow realize our mutual predicament. We were in her path to water, and she was in our route back to the Basin. The slight breeze was blowing toward us, and she at first seemed unaware of our presence. I purposefully shuffled my feet in the loose rocks to alert her to our presence. She stopped then, stared our way, and sniffed the air to detect the source of the noise. It was soon obvious that she was aware that her route to the water was blocked and that one of us had to give in.

She first made several strides toward us, expecting, I think, that we would retreat. I slowly advanced toward her, making considerable noise with my feet, and even picked up a large, flat rock and let it drop. It was then that she realized, apparently, that she might need to reconsider her attempt to get her own way, for she sent the cub up the steep rocky slope out of harm's way. But she continued to bluff her way toward us, even growling as she swung her bulky body toward us. Through binoculars, I could see her beady eyes focused on us.

I continued to move, step by step, ever so slowly toward her, making shuffling noises in the rocks. Finally, after about ten minutes, she began a slow retreat up the slope, following her cub. Not until she was a couple hundred feet above the canyon did we dare to pass. But we watched her carefully for any movement that she might make toward us. By then, I am sure she realized that we did not pose a danger but only wished safe passage down-canyon. She remained on the hill, sitting on her haunches, watching us disappear from view.

Although black bears and mountain lions are rarely seen by the majority of park visitors, javelinas are widespread and seen on a regular basis. Campers often find them grazing within Rio Grande Village and Cottonwood Campgrounds. Most people consider javelinas a potentially dangerous species; there are lots of stories about attacks on humans. However, from my experience they rarely if ever are dangerous. They do, however, bluff intruders when the occasion arises. Javelinas are extremely tough, able to survive very well in some of the most arid areas in the Southwest. In the Chihuahuan Desert they are able to feed on the succulent parts of lechuguilla leaves. That requires them to tear the lechuguilla plants apart to get to the basal leaves. I have tried unsuccessfully to tear leaves off the lechuguilla plants, but javelinas do it regularly.

On one occasion while hiking on Tornillo Flat, I suddenly found myself surrounded by a herd of javelinas. They apparently had been sleeping in a patch of low-growing mesquite, and my sudden appearance sent them scurrying off in all directions. The exception was an old boar that remained in place about fifty feet away, sniffing the air, snorting, and pawing the ground like an Andalusian bull. The hair on its neck stood straight up. I froze in place, waiting to see what it might do next. Rather than run off with the rest of the herd, it began to walk a circle around me, checking my scent as it progressed. Each time it got upwind and lost my scent it seemed to relax, but kept circling nevertheless. When it got downwind and caught my scent again, its hairs would again elevate and it would face me, snort loudly, and clack its teeth. I remained still and quiet, although I was able to take several photos. Javelina eyesight is extremely poor; they largely depend upon smell and hearing to detect danger. Finally, after four complete circles, it moved away, following the others across the desert and out of sight.

My javelina boar was undoubtedly an alpha male, the leader of the herd. According to John

Javelina boar on Tornillo Flat, Big Bend National Park

Bissonette, who was studying javelinas at the time for a PhD at the University of Michigan, groups hold their own territories with little or no overlap by adjacent groups. John wrote in a book published by the National Park Service (1982) that they mark "vegetation and rocks with scent gland excretions, and scat piles were observed scattered along boundary lines." Javelinas possess a very distinct odor that is not unlike the diluted smell of a skunk, and they rub against each other, head to rump, as part of the group's interactions.

On another occasion just outside my house, I decided to see just how dangerous javelinas might be; I actually walked between a sow and her baby. I was close enough to cover in case I had to make a fast retreat. Although she was obviously upset, growled, and raised her neck hairs, she did not attack or show any overly aggressive behavior.

There is yet another javelina incident that deserves telling. On the morning of March 7, 1968, I met a group of a dozen or so folks at the entrance to Rio Grande Village Campground for a birding nature walk. As we passed through the campground en route to the nature trail, a lady in an adjacent campsite asked if she and her little white poodle could join us. I invited her to come with us but explained that she would need to leave her poodle behind. She tied the poodle to a table leg and joined our group. In about two hours, after birding the nature trail and the

Trans-Pecos rat snake in hand, Big Bend National Park

outer edges of the campground, we returned to the start, walking past the lady's campsite. As we approached her campsite, instead of finding "Fifi" yapping at us, we discovered only its remains. A javelina was just completing a poodle dinner. The woman was hysterical. Although I felt sorry for her, the experience only confirmed my belief that pets and camping trips are not compatible.

Herps

Desert areas generally have a reputation, at least with many nonappreciative people, as being overrun with snakes, that rattlesnakes are present behind every shrub. Desert folks, full-time residents of desert areas, pay little attention to such stories. But those same individuals don't want to live in California because of earthquakes or along the southeastern coast because of hurricanes. At Big Bend I have hiked for days without seeing a single snake. They are never abundant, and most snakes are active only at night; very few venture out during the daytime. The coachwhip, a nonvenomous, reddish racer, however, is one of the few that is sometimes active at midday. Almost daily in summer the folks at the information desk are asked about "that red snake" seen crossing the highway.

My special interest in Big Bend's herps was partly due to the opportunity to spend time with herpetologist Roger Conant, who spent several weeks in the park in 1966 and 1967, capturing snakes, lizards, and amphibians that his wife, Isabelle, photographed the following day. Roger was in the process of gathering information on Big Bend's herps to be utilized in the revision of his book, *A Field Guide to Reptiles and Amphibians of Eastern North America*, published in 1958. The revised book appeared in 1975. I was able to accompany Roger by driving the roads after dark and hiking to various locations to find species to be included in his book. I discovered that Roger and Isabelle were some of the kindest and most helpful of all the scientists I got to know during my tenure in Big Bend.

One of the very popular interpretive activities I started during my time in the park was

Texas alligator lizard on Lost Mine Trail. Courtesy of Betty Wauer.

a summer afternoon reptile talk in the cool auditorium at the visitor center. It included a discussion of snakes in general, their characteristics, and their importance in the natural environment. Afterward we allowed participants to touch one of the more docile snakes, and it undoubtedly helped many better appreciate reptiles.

Nineteen species of lizards are known for the park. A few, such as the spiny lizards, whiptails, and desert side-blotched lizard, are commonplace and usually can be found with little trouble. Others are less numerous or more secretive. One of my favorites is the Texas alligator lizard, a large alligator-like lizard that occurs only in the mountains and is rarely found except in late summer and fall. Although these lizards look slow as they crawl across the ground, on one occasion when I caught one to photograph, it quickly turned back and grabbed my finger in an amazingly strong grip. It actually drew blood.

On another occasion, on a July 4, 1972, visit to Boquillas, across the Rio Grande from Rio Grande Village, George Burdick and I discovered a number of Mediterranean geckos. Two individuals were collected from an outhouse wall, and five additional individuals were seen on adjacent buildings. One gecko was located in an adobe house, and four were in a little store that was selling fruit and vegetables. We eventually published our findings as "Range Extension of Mediterranean Gecko in Coahuila, Mexico," in the January 20, 1975, issue of *Southwestern Naturalist*. Our finding extended the known range of the species west for about 150 miles, and it has since become common throughout the Big Bend Country and much of Texas.

Although I handled numerous snakes during my years at Big Bend, only once did I have a close-up, potentially dangerous experience with a rattlesnake. In May 2000, while checking out the butterflies at Glenn Spring with friends Jim and Lynne Weber, I almost jumped in the middle of a coiled western diamondback. Walking along the little stream, I discovered a viceroy (butterfly) perched on a willow tree on the opposite side of the stream. Jim and Lynne were farther up the stream but within view. I decided to jump across the stream to get a photo of the viceroy, and without looking carefully where I would land, got halfway into my jump when I realized that the "bare" place where I was going to land was actually a huge coiled rattlesnake. Somehow I realized my error in time, like stopping in mid-jump. The rattlesnake uncoiled, rattled a few times, and crawled away into the brush.

Fish

Deserts and fish are seldom linked together in one's thinking, yet Big Bend has about three dozen fish species. One of those, the Big Bend gambusia, is endemic and listed as a federally endangered species. It was discovered in small springs at Rio Grande Village and described by Carl L. Hubbs as late as 1928. Son Clark Hubbs, ichthyologist at the University of Texas, worked with the newly established national park to give it protection during development of the campground, including establishing a small pond dedicated specifically to its protection. However, on the morning of January 18, 1968, I discovered a number of nonnative green sunfish swimming in the pond. These predatory sunfish, probably placed in the pond by well-meaning fishermen, would eventually eliminate the entire population of gambusias if ignored. I immediately set in motion a number of steps to save this fragile species. The following description of those steps was included in *For All Seasons*:

Within a couple days, park maintenance employees began to dry up an adjacent pond that also contained a number of exotics: goldfish, mosquito fish, bluegill, and green sunfish. Once that pond was dry and we were satisfied that it no longer contained any fish, we added filtered water and allowed it to stand for about two weeks so that a natural food supply could develop. At that stage, the gambusia pond was drained, and Roger Siglin and I spent several hours seining out as many of the Big Bend gambusias as we could. We were able to collect more than 250 individuals; 150 of these were released into the new pond, and the remainder were taken to park headquarters, where they were placed in an aquarium in my office.

Once the initial pond was completely dry, we added new filtered water and allowed a natural food supply to develop (this took about thirty days). I then released the approximately one hundred gambusias being held in my office into their new home. We also built a fence around the pond and erected a new sign that I had written: "Fish So Fragile—This pond contains the world's population of Gambusia gaigei. These minnow-sized fish have lived here since Mastodons. Unique and fragile, they survive only because man wants to make it so."

Clark Hubbs was a regular visitor to the park during my tenure, each time checking on the gambusia population. On one trip we decided to survey the fish fauna that can be found in Tornillo Creek at Hot Springs, where it flows into the Rio Grande. So, on eleven occasions from December 1967 to January 1970, we sampled the fish species present. The results were a collection of eleven species, all of which utilize the area of Tornillo Creek as a nursery area, although few or none were permanent residents there. Three of the species—Mexican stoneroller, Chihuahua shiner, and Rio Grande pupfish—were essentially unknown elsewhere in the United States. We wrote up our surveys and published a paper, "Seasonal Changes in the Fish Fauna of Tornillo Creek, Brewster County, Texas," for the January 1973 issue of *Southwestern Naturalist.*

Invertebrates

Even the invertebrates were of interest during my Big Bend residency. I tried to spend time with any biologists who visited the park and obtained a collecting permit. On August 27, 1967, I helped Dr. Willis J. Gertsch collect scorpions. He used a black light to locate these largely nocturnal creatures; they stood out like diamonds. In a little over two hours we located several specimens of what was later reported as a new park record but a widespread species, *Uroctonus apacheanus*. Gertsch and Michael Soleglad published several new species in 1972, including one that Gertsch and I had found in the Chisos Basin, that they named *Vejovis waueri*.

I also spent time with Lloyd Pratt while he was studying land snails in the park; he discovered one that resided in the debris of dead agave leaves that was new to science. Later, on June 9, 1968, when he needed additional specimens, I visited Laguna Meadow and dug through agave leaf debris in search of additional land snails. I collected four dead and a single live specimen during a two-hour search and mailed these to Lloyd. In 1971 he described these as a new species, the agave snail (*Humboldtiana agavophile*), stating that this unique species is found only in association with Big Bend's century plants, which are restricted to the uplifted block of Boquillas limestone at Laguna Meadow.

One additional but more serendipitous land snail experience occurred in March 1971, when I was able to hitch a helicopter ride with US Geological Survey (USGS) scientists to Sue Peaks, the highest area in the Deadhorse Mountains. I spent the entire day along the high ridge while the USGS team was mapping the Deadhorse and Mexico's Sierra del Carmen. The extremely isolated uplands of the Deadhorse Mountains are not generally accessible, primarily due to the distance from even the most remote roadway and the total lack of water. My interest in this area was to learn what birds might be present in such an arid environment. I found only seven species: red-tailed hawk, white-throated swift, Bewick's wren, spotted and canyon towhees, rufous-crowned sparrow, and dark-eyed junco. Only the junco was a nonbreeder.

I also collected a number of land snails from the rocky limestone terrain that day, and I later mailed my specimens to Lloyd Pratt at the Dallas Museum of Natural History. He eventually wrote that at least one of the three species was a "liptooth" of the genus *Polygyra*, representing a new species, and that he planned to name those specimens *Polygyra waueri*. Years later, in an August 1995 telephone conversation with Lloyd (then at the University of Nevada at Las Vegas), he informed me that my new *Polygyra* discovery had never been written up. He added that the two additional land snail species I had found that day included specimens of the distorted metastome (*Metastoma roemeri*), a fairly widespread land snail, and the Stockton Plateau three-band (*Humboldtiana texana*), representing the westernmost record of that species.

Cacti

Another area of interest was the park's amazing diversity of cacti. Early on I began to take pictures of all the species, but I discovered that none of the available references helped identify all of the plants. So I began sending my photos to various specialists for identification: Del Weniger in San Antonio, Dale Zimmerman in New Mexico, and Lyman Benson at Pomona College in California. But some of their determinations varied. I even sent a few specimens to Benson, and on one occasion I visited Benson

Chisos Mountain hedgehog, rare and endemic

in Pomona to discuss my findings. And when Benson's book *The Cacti of the United States and Canada* was published in 1972, it contained a dozen or more of my photographs.

I established eight transects at key locations in the park to document what species were present; this was primarily to establish a baseline to determine any later poaching that might occur. Transects were undertaken on upper Tornillo Flat, near Hot Springs, lower Green Gulch, Dodson Trail, Fresno Creek, above Sam Nail Ranch, Mariscal Mountain west of Solis, and along the Old Ore Road. The transects followed an unfortunate experience of giving a tour to several members of the Cactus Society of America. Later, when checking the same localities, I discovered some of the rarities that I had pointed out were missing. I had earlier written an article, "The Big Bend Country," that appeared in 1971 in the *Cactus and Succulent Journal.*

Other Activities

In spring and summer 1971, more than fifteen hundred horses died from Venezuelan equine encephalitis (VEE) in South Texas and adjacent Mexico. Scientists from the Centers for Disease Control and Prevention (CDC) were called in to monitor the epidemic, determine the vector, and identify host species. I was one of a handful of National Park Service employees sent to participate in the CDC project at a study site in the Boca Chica area along the mouth of the Rio Grande below Brownsville. For ten days in July, I netted birds, took blood for testing, and banded and released the captured individuals. Of the 148 birds of 27 species that I processed and were tested, none carried the virus. Only three vertebrates, besides horses, tested positive during the study, an opossum and two Texas tortoises.

An additional opportunity arose in September 1971 when I was invited to participate in a float trip on the Rio Grande, a recon trip for a study of the river for Rio Grande Wild and Scenic River status. I also participated in the official "study" in March 1972. The 1971 participants included Red Arnold, Bureau of Outdoor Recreation; John Baker, dentist from Dallas; Reagan Bradshaw, photographer for *Texas Parks & Wildlife Magazine*; Bob Burleson, attorney from Temple; Tom Cowden, attorney from Austin; Joe Friedkin, commissioner for the Internation-

Bleeding a rattlesnake at Boca Chica, Texas, 1971

My Wild Life

al Boundary & Water Commission; Ken and Ralph Jennings from New Mexico; Les Redman from New Mexico; David Riskind, Texas Parks and Wildlife Department; Bill Salmi from New Mexico; Tom Sedberry, attorney from Austin; Art Stewart, Bureau of Outdoor Recreation; John Supulski, US Fish and Wildlife Service; and me, from Big Bend National Park.

The official team on the 1972 trip included Al Kesterke and Bob McIntosh from the Bureau of Outdoor Recreation; Southwest Regional Archeologist Cal Cummings, Big Bend Chief Ranger Bob Morris, and me from the National Park Service; Harold Belisle, David Riskind, John Smith, and Ron Thuma of Texas Parks and Wildlife Department; Bob Clark, Texas Land Office; Dick McHenry, Texas Forest Service; and John Vandertulip, International Boundary and Water Commission. Guides and boatmen included John Baker, Bob Burleson, Dick Galland, Dick Phelan, Bob Sims, and Jim Underwood.

Both trips were most worthwhile. I thoroughly enjoyed the opportunity to see the Lower Canyons with such marvelous companions. We stopped on numerous occasions to hike into the adjacent canyons and onto the upper reaches. Three sites impressed me most: Hot Springs rapids, Asa Jones Waterworks, and Burro Bluff. Of course, I recorded all of the birds seen on each trip, 46 species in 1971 and 74 in 1972. I

Burro Bluff on the Lower Canyons of the Rio Grande (notice the person at the top)

later wrote a report on the birdlife, a document that was intended to become part of a comprehensive "Natural Areas Survey" publication on the natural resources of the Lower Canyons.

That publication never became a reality, although my chapter, "The Birds of the Lower Canyons of the Rio Grande," was completed and submitted. It included a discussion of the avifauna within the various habitats, from the waterway to the floodplain and cliffs, as well as an annotated list of 138 species.

The Lower Canyons were designated the "Rio Grande Wild and Scenic River" by Congress in 1978. The area includes a 196-mile strip of land on the US side of the river, managed by Big Bend National Park, containing "outstanding remarkable scenic, geologic, fish and wildlife, and recreational values," according to the General Management Plan. Much more recently, most of the Mexican side of the Lower Canyons has been purchased by Mexico's CEMEX for a preserve.

In addition, during the later part of my Big Bend residency, I become involved with the activities under way at the University of Texas in Austin in preparing the huge Harry C. Oberholser manuscript for eventual publication of the two-volume *The Bird Life of Texas* (1974). Edgar Kincaid and his two principal assistants, Suzanna Winckler and John Rowlett, had asked me about several Big Bend records as well as permission to use a number of my habitat photographs. I had also spent a few days with Edgar, helping on the Mesa de las Tables Christmas Bird Count in Mexico that he coordinated. Ed-

gar was one of the few birders I had ever met who went into the field fully dressed in coat and tie, which were always part of his field attire. As a result of our association, he began calling me "Kingbird," after the first Texas record of a thick-billed kingbird that I had published on a few years earlier. Acquiring a Kincaid moniker did not impress me at the time, but over the years it has become some sort of status symbol with those in the know.

Maderas del Carmen

The high peaks to the south of the Rio Grande in Mexico seemed to beckon me soon after arriving in Big Bend. But it was not until July 1967 that I was able to arrange a trip into the Maderas highlands. Señor Padilla of Boquillas drove our small group south across the desert to where an old road climbed upward to the Los Cohos Mine. From there we hiked a couple of miles on a very steep trail to a small spring, where we camped for four nights. We daily hiked farther up into the forest to explore the deep canyons and rocky precipices. We discovered a very different world from that in the Chisos. The highest peak—Loomis Peak at an elevation of ninety-six hundred feet—rose above the mantle of conifers on the east but dropped off steeply on the western face. From the summit, the Chisos Mountains were visible fifty miles to the north-

View south from Loomis Peak, Maderas del Carmen, Mexico

west. And we found that many of the canyons to the east of the high cliffs were filled with clear, running streams.

The birdlife was similar to that in the Chisos, but the higher and more extensive forest of the Maderas supported an additional eight breeding species: northern pygmy-owl, saw-whet owl, hairy woodpecker, pygmy nuthatch, brown-throated wren, western bluebird, olive warbler, and yellow-eyed junco.

We also found an active logging operation in the highlands on that first trip. Several loggers were actively cutting the forest and dragging the logs down the steep slopes, cutting deep gashes into the forested hillsides. Once the logs were dragged to lower elevations, they were trucked south to Musquiz. And we also encountered a couple of bear hunters; one proudly showed us a fresh bearskin.

Between 1967 and 1976 I was able to visit the Maderas highlands on eight occasions. On each trip I was able to hike to new areas in search of birds and other wildlife. On one occasion I surprised a mountain lion stalking a deer. On another morning I was awakened by the low whistles (a descending call like that of a hypothetical canyon wren/screech-owl hybrid) of Montezuma quail. In total, we recorded 73 bird species on the eight trips.

Years later, after retirement, I was again able to visit the Maderas del Carmen on the invitation of Bonnie McKinney. She and husband, Billy Pat, were the managers of the newly established El Carmen Preserve. The Mexican cement company CEMEX had acquired more than one hundred thousand acres of the Maderas, stopped all logging and hunting, and was in the process of establishing natural order to the area. The change in management and the protection of all wildlife were most impressive.

Butterflies

For some odd reason, during all of the years that I lived in the park I paid little attention to butterflies. It wasn't until after retirement, in the mid-1990s, that my major interest shifted from birds to butterflies. Someone made the statement that a butterfly enthusiast is only a bored birder. That may be true to an extent, but my interest in Big Bend's birds, mammals, and herps remained high. But when I made trips to the park to conduct seminars and for other reasons, I also began to list all the butterflies found. By early May 1997, I had developed a database on all my sightings as well as valid records from others, including those of longtime lepidopterist Roy Kendall. Roy had been visiting the park for butterflies long before I went to work there, and we got well acquainted during his visits. But even then I did not get involved with butterflies.

Once I did get involved, I began making

Plate 1: Grand Teton National Park

Plate 2: Crater Lake National Park. Courtesy of Betty Wauer.

Plate 3: Clark's nutcracker on Rim, Crater Lake National Park

Plate 4: Panamint Mountains from Dante's View, Death Valley National Monument

Plate 5: Pinnacles National Monument

Plate 6: Yosemite National Park

Plate 7: Great White Throne, Zion National Park

Plate 8: Zion Canyon from Lady Mountain, Zion National Park

Plate 9: Chisos Mountains from Grapevine Hills, Big Bend National Park

Plate 10: Green Gulch in Big Bend National Park. Courtesy of Betty Wauer.

Plate 11: Sotol Vista,
Big Bend National Park

Plate 12: Santa
Elena Canyon, Big
Bend National Park

Plate 13: Santa Fe Baldy near Santa Fe, New Mexico

Plate 14: Frijoles Canyon, Bandelier National Monument

Plate 15: Guadalupe Peak,
Guadalupe Mountains
National Park

Plate 16: US Capitol, Washington, D.C. Courtesy of Betty Wauer.

Plate 17: Washington Monument and cherry blossoms, Washington, D.C.

Plate 18: Mount McKinley, Denali National Park

Plate 19: Reid Glacier and boat (in far left center), Glacier Bay National Park

Plate 20: Great Smoky Mountains National Park from Clingmans Dome

Plate 21: Cades Cove, Great Smoky Mountains National Park

Plate 22: View from East End to Buck Island, St. Croix

Plate 23: Maho Bay on St. John, Virgin Islands National Park

Plate 24: Salt River Bay National Historical Park and Ecological Preserve

trips to the park to cover periods of time when there had been no reports. This eventually led to a *Butterfly Checklist: Big Bend National Park, Texas*, published by the Big Bend Natural History Association in 2000; a revised checklist that included 183 species was published in 2006. But almost immediately after the revised checklist was published, I added three more species to the Big Bend butterfly list: white peacock, hammock skipper, and white-patched skipper. I wrote a short note on these new species for *Southern Lepidopterists' News*.

Perhaps my two most exciting butterfly records occurred in September 1999. On September 1, I photographed a very worn metalmark in Mouse Canyon that I was unable to identify. A few months later I sent my image to Ed Knudson for identification. Ed reported that my metalmark was a zela metalmark, representing a brand-new butterfly for the state. We (Ed, Charles Bordelon, and I) then published a short note, "Zela Metalmark (*Emesis zela*): A New Record for Texas," in the spring 2001 issue of *News of the Lepidopterists' Society*.

On September 9 I photographed a hairstreak in upper Green Gulch that I was unable to identify. Although I understood that it represented a new park record, it wasn't until a few weeks later that I showed my photograph to Chris Durden, who claimed it also was the first US record, a species he had collected in the Burro

Orange-crescent groundstreak, first US record, 1999

Mountains of Coahuila, Mexico. Chris told me that he was calling his Burro Mountains specimens "brown burro hairstreak" of the genera *Fixsenia* and he planned to describe it as a new species. However, before he could publish, additional specimens were taken by a couple of other lepidopterists, including Nick Grisham on

May 28, 2004. Nick soon published his records as mountain groundstreak (*Ziegleria guzunta*). But when this butterfly appeared in the new field guides, it was included as orange-crescent groundstreak. Since my original photo, it has been found in the park a dozen or more times.

In late 2000, Jeff Glassberg asked me to write an article for *American Butterflies* magazine on the butterflies of the park. I asked Ed Knudson to collaborate on this article, and our "Definitive Destination: Big Bend National Park, Texas" appeared in the magazine in the spring 2001 issue.

Also in 2000, while visiting with Noel Parsons, natural history editor at Texas A&M University Press, we talked about doing a book on some of my West Texas butterfly findings. We reached an agreement on a little book that would include Big Bend National Park, the Davis Mountains, and Guadalupe Mountains National Park. However, before a contract was written, Noel moved to Texas Tech University Press as editor. I then moved my book to Texas Tech, and *Butterflies of West Texas Parks and Preserves* was published in 2001.

In spring 2008 I received a call from Joe Sirotnak, botanist/ecologist at Big Bend, inquiring if I would be interested in conducting a butterfly survey in the area near Santa Elena Canyon. The park was introducing exotic beetles (*Diorhabda elongate*) in that area in an attempt to control nonnative salt cedar, and Joe asked if I would develop a butterfly population baseline on the site. The project would be funded by the World Wildlife Fund (WWF), where my contact was Mark Briggs. I agreed and very soon had prepared a proposal that included Betty as my assistant to survey dual sites on three occasions during fall 2008 and spring 2009 and 2010. We would stay at either Castolon or the K-Bar research station near PJ on each seven-day visit.

My final report, *Butterfly Richness and Abundance on the Rio Grande Floodplain*, in June 2010 included the following abstract:

Forty butterfly species were recorded during the three survey periods in fall 2008 and spring 2010. Thirty-six species were considered residents, utilizing vegetation within the study site for nectaring and egg-laying. Nine species—Checkered White, Lyside and Dainty Sulphurs, Western Pygmy-Blue, Fatal Metalmark, Painted Crescent, Empress Leilia, and Common/White Checkered-Skipper—are identified as indicator species for later comparisons.

Transition

While still working at Big Bend, I had discussed the idea of vacating my chief naturalist position and moving into a management biologist slot. Although such a position did not exist in Big Bend, I had solicited letters from a number of scientists about the need for such a position. Letters from such well-known biologists as Roger Conant, Clark Hubbs, Marshall Johnston, James Scudday, and Barton Warnock were sent to both Big Bend Superintendent Joe Carithers (he had replaced Peterson in 1971) and Regional Director Frank Kowski. And in October 1971, Superintendent Carithers wrote a letter to Chief Scientist Robert Lynn that was endorsed by Regional Director Kowski, requesting his help in establishing a biologist position at Big Bend.

In early June 1972, I was asked to attend a meeting of NPS scientists at the regional office in Santa Fe. The purpose of the meeting was to discuss ways for the Park Service better to address the science needs in the parks. One of the results of that meeting was the decision to decentralize the Washington Office science program by establishing a regional chief scientist position in each of the ten regions. The meeting also provided me an opportunity to meet all of the current NPS scientists, including Lynne and his two assistants, Ted Sudia and Al Greene.

Toward the end of the meeting, Frank Kowski invited me into his office for a chat. Frank told me that he would like me to move to Santa Fe to be his regional chief scientist. I answered that I would rather stay in the field, that I would prefer staying at Big Bend in a park biologist position. He then told me that if I agreed to transfer into the new chief scientist position for two years, that at the end of that time if I still was interested in returning to Big Bend, he would establish a position for me. He told me to discuss such a move with my family and let him know within a few days.

It was an offer that was difficult to ignore. It was a way to get into the science program, along with a rather significant grade increase. And I had completed a master's degree in biology at Sul Ross State University at Alpine, using my bird research as a thesis, as additional support for a move into the science program. My major professor at Sul Ross was Jim Scudday, who had recently completed his PhD at Texas A&M in ecology. Jim was up-to-date and a good friend.

In spite of my reluctance to move from the field into a regional office, I accepted the offer. My change of duty station from Big Bend to Santa Fe did not take place until the following summer, providing time to complete a number of ongoing projects. I was able to complete the *Hiker's Guide to the Developed Trails and Primitive Routes*, which was published in 1971. This guide was the last of three guides that I wrote: *Road Guide* and *Guide to the Backcountry Roads and the River* had appeared in 1970.

I also had been involved with attempts to reintroduce Montezuma quail into the park and made two trips into the Davis Mountains, in 1968 and 1969, to capture sufficient birds. Neither attempt was successful, but plans were under way to capture enough birds in Arizona in spring 1973. Pertinent permits were being requested and contacts were being developed. This story is included in the Southwest Regional Office chapter.

Another project under way was the coordination of a spring 1972 meeting of the Texas Ornithological Society (TOS) in the park. It went off without a hitch. And one of the evening sessions was a panel discussion that I moderated. Participants included Drs. George Newman and Richard Albert, representing TOS; Drs. Keith Arnold and Charles Dean Fisher, representing professional ornithology; Roland Clement, vice-president of the National Audubon Society; and Jim Tucker, representing the ABA. I taped the panel discussion and later transcribed the material, which was published in December 1972 as "Birds, Bird Study, and Conservation of Birds in Texas: A Panel Discussion," in *Bulletin of the Texas Ornithological Society*.

I left Big Bend with considerable excitement about the new job and the opportunities such a position provided. I knew that I would miss the quiet atmosphere and scenery of Big Bend, but I also knew that my new assignment would allow for a regular visit, and that seemed to help with the transition. And over the years I have told many folks that the two things I miss most about the park are the songs of the coyotes and scent of creosotebush after each rain.

7

Southwest Regional Office

My new assignment as regional chief scientist did not become effective until July 23, 1972. An August 24 press release, issued by the National Park Service, summarized my principal responsibilities thus: "Mr. Wauer . . . will be responsible for the Natural Resources Management and Scientific Studies program for the Southwest Region . . . will work with regional park superintendents to determine the studies needed, then provide liaison between the field areas and colleges or other institutions involved with research."

It was an exciting opportunity for me, as I was involved with natural science programs in seventeen park units throughout the states of Texas, New Mexico, Louisiana, Arkansas, Oklahoma, and portions of Arizona, and with colleges and universities throughout the Southwest and Southeast. Very few of the park areas had previously undertaken an assessment of their research and resource management needs, although several of the areas had previously submitted funding requests for natural science projects. Although all of those projects were of high priority locally, few had been ranked high enough on a regional basis for funding. Natural science projects generally went unfunded because they did not have an advocate at the level where such decisions were made. That was now one of my responsibilities.

The Southwest Regional Office, located on Canyon Road in historic Santa Fe, New Mexico, was a huge adobe structure, complete with a patio, and located within picturesque woodland of pinyons and junipers. It was a unique setting! My office was located off the patio, while Regional Director Kowski's office was in a second-story portion of the adobe near the

Regional Director Frank Kowski, author, and NPS Director Russ Dickinson

I realized that my office needed additional personnel. Within a few months I was able to hire Milford Fletcher as my deputy and Keith Yarborough to address air- and water-quality issues. I later hired Hank LaSalle to help address fire-management issues.

I soon began to visit park areas within the region, to meet the park superintendents, and to assess their natural resource needs. I felt good about my visits, and the word spread fast that there now was someone at the regional level who cared about their natural resource issues. Kowski soon was getting calls asking for my visit. I discovered that when I identified an issue that could be addressed with minor funding, I could make myself a hero immediately; my office had a small amount of available funds. However, for larger, more expensive projects, it was still necessary to seek specific funds.

entrance. A downstairs coffee room, where the majority of the staff met twice daily, provided a good place to keep up with what was going on throughout the region. All in all, it was a comfortable place to work, and I felt immediately accepted and a vital member of the regional office staff.

Because my office was a new one without an adequate staff, it was necessary to hire a few key assistants early on. Although I was fortunate to have an excellent secretary, Fran Dean,

Padre Island National Seashore

One of my earliest trips took me to Padre Island in Texas. Although I had worked in Texas for several years and visited the Lower Rio Grande Valley and South Padre Island for birds, I had somehow missed the national seashore that represents the longest natural seashore on the Gulf Coast. Superintendent Jack Turney was glad to see me, and the first day on-site he drove me the entire length of the national

Padre Island National Seashore

seashore. I was impressed with the wilderness character. Although we did see a lone peregrine falcon that day, it was too late in the year to see the abundant peregrines that spend their winter months within the national seashore. John told me that the area supports the largest concentration of peregrines during migration and through the winter months than anywhere else in North America.

Another topic that came up during my visit was Kemp's ridley sea turtles, a sea turtle that once nested on Padre Island but no longer occurs there. I visited with Bob Whistler, Padre's chief naturalist, who seemed to be very knowledgeable about ridley turtles. This was an endangered species that was considered the most threatened of all the sea turtles. I was to become very involved with ridley turtles at a later time.

Guadalupe Mountains

The other park that required my early attention was Guadalupe Mountains National Park, an area that had been established by the US Congress on September 30, 1972. The enabling legislation included a political agreement for a tramway to be constructed to the very top of Guadalupe Peak, an action that most environmentally sensitive people knew would create considerable impact to that wilderness area.

And when Sierra Club friends John Baker and Bob Burleson contacted me about their concern, I realized that I was most responsible for any action to stop such a project. I already was aware of the extremely strong winds that blow in the general vicinity, and I recognized that any tramway would require more than the average construction. With this in mind, I spent several days in the park to acquire a more personal understanding of the topography and natural resources. In June 1973, I hiked the Bear Canyon Trail to get closer to the high point itself, and I even camped out two nights in the Bowl. I found a small herd of Roosevelt elk (nonnative) that had been previously introduced into the Guadalupes. Also during my visit, I talked with several of the park staff, who at that time were headquartered in Carlsbad, New Mexico. I came away with the impression that I would need to find better evidence than currently existed about the high winds if the tramway was to be stopped.

During the next few weeks I traveled to Lubbock, where I visited with several professors at Texas Tech University about various studies that should be undertaken within the newly established national park. Few good studies on various natural resource issues had been undertaken in the past. By the end of my visit I had been promised several proposals for studies in the Guadalupes. Eventually, I was able to fund

Guadalupe Peak, Guadalupe Mountains National Park

a number of projects, including an "Analysis of Wind Data for Planning and Design of a Tramway in Guadalupe Mountains National Park." The result of that study provided the necessary data that convinced any potential tramway contractors that such a project would not be feasible.

Some of the additional studies that were initiated from my Texas Tech visit included a vascular plant survey by David Northington; fire ecology by Gary Ahlstrand; mammal surveys by Robert Baker, Hugh Genoways, and Robert Packard; ecology and population of elk by David Simpson; insect survey by David Foster; and watershed and land classification by Ernest Fish.

Pine Canyon release site for Montezuma quail restoration

Two holdover projects from Big Bend also required attention: the restoration of Montezuma quail and the Chihuahuan Desert Symposium. Montezuma quail, a very attractive native grassland quail, had once been commonplace in the Chisos Mountains but had disappeared during the 1940s, probably as a result of overgrazing before the park was established. So Walt Kittams, biologist at Carlsbad Caverns and Guadalupe Mountains National Parks, and I un-

successfully attempted to capture a number of birds in the Davis Mountains in 1968. Although we did net three birds over an eight-hour period, knowing that would not be sufficient and concerned about their survival if we held them too long, we released the birds and left the site.

I later made contact with Dave Brown of the Arizona Fish and Game Department, who was very knowledgeable about Montezuma quail, their needs, and how to capture them. I arranged for Dave to visit the park and access the habitat prior to making a commitment. We decided that Pine Canyon would be an appropriate release site; it contained adequate habitat and was sufficiently isolated from traffic and any developments. In January 1973, Dave and I captured twenty-six Montezuma quail near Nogales, Arizona. We used Dave's dog to locate the quail, and then we captured them by throwing a net over the birds and placing them in a holding cage. I drove them overnight to their new home in Big Bend National Park.

There was a serious hitch in the release plan, however, as an ice storm had hit the Chisos that very same night, so I held them in their cages in the visitor center auditorium for several hours until the sun appeared and the day began to warm. Concerned about their long confinement without food, that morning I collected large handfuls of *Oxalis*, a key food plant, and placed small amounts in each cage. By midafternoon, when the ice had melted away, I drove the birds to the mouth of Pine Canyon and released them. All seemed in good health, and they immediately flew into the lower drainage and disappeared. The success of that release was uncertain. Although an occasional bird was reported through May 1983, there were no more reports until 2004.

In April 2004, Dave Holderman, Texas Parks and Wildlife Department biologist, while hiking along the South Rim found small scrapes in the soil that he believed to be made by Montezuma quail. He told coworker Junie Sarola about his discovery, and on May 14, while hiking the South Rim Trail, Junie was able to call a male Montezuma quail within thirty feet. That sighting led to another visit to the area by Sarola, Holderman, and Big Bend's Wildlife Specialist Raymond Skiles. They were then able to photograph at least three individuals, final proof that Montezuma quail is indeed part of the Big Bend avifauna. I am assuming that the 2004 and 2005 birds are the result of my 1973 release.

Chihuahuan Desert Symposium

David Riskind, resource specialist for Texas Parks and Wildlife Department, and I had started planning a symposium on the biological resources of the Chihuahuan Desert in 1973. That meeting finally came to fruition on October 17 and 18, 1974, at Sul Ross State University in Alpine. Unlike most symposia, where participants meet only in their select disciplines, we planned for everyone to participate in every session in a truly collegial setting. Six sessions were included, each of which ended with a summarization: quaternary environment, summarized by Edward Meyer; mammalogy, by Rollin Baker; botany, by Marshall Johnston; ichthyofauna, by Clark Hubbs; herpetofauna, by William Degenhardt; and avifauna, by Allan Phillips. I presented two papers in the avifaunal session:

"Changes in the Breeding Avifauna within the Chisos Mountains System" and "Distributional Relations of Breeding Avifauna of Four Southwestern Mountain Ranges"; the latter paper was coauthored by J. David Ligon.

Two keynote addresses were included, by Bernardo Villa Ramirez, a Mexican wildlife biologist, and Bob Burleson. The symposium ended with a panel discussion among W. Frank Blair, Horacio Gallegos, John Henneberger, Robert Lynn, Bob McIntosh, and Myron Sutton (moderator). The entire symposium was published by the National Park Service as *Transactions of the Symposium on the Biological Resources of the Chihuahuan Desert Region, United States and Mexico* in 1977.

One of my most pressing responsibilities as regional chief scientist was the development of Natural Resource Management Plans for all the Southwestern parks. These plans, generated at the park level, were designed to document the area's resource management activities and, when additional information was required, to document the necessary research.

Because Bandelier National Monument was located very near Santa Fe, and Superintendent John Hunter was in agreement, I decided to work with that park early on to help with the completion of their Natural Resources Management Plan. There was no single individual at the park involved with resource management planning, so I talked to Superintendent Hunter about utilizing one of his rangers—John Lissoway—for this project and actually placing Lissoway into the new position of resource management specialist, with this and other related duties. It wasn't too difficult, especially when my office was able to provide partial funds for Lissoway's salary and all of his eventual training activities. The park and regional office then prepared a training program (an IDP or Individual Development Plan) for Lissoway that included numerous requirements for his new role, a principal one being development of the area's Natural Resource Management Plan. Lissoway was the right guy at the right time!

Bandelier's most important natural resource issue at the time was the impact of wild burros on the natural environment and the area's very significant archeological sites. The Natural Resource Management Plan called for a burro impact assessment and a separate burro management plan that could be reviewed by the public.

Bandelier's Birdlife

Because of my ornithological expertise, I initiated a study on the impacts of burros on the park's breeding birds in May and June 1977. I surveyed two comparable mesas within the

Upper Frijoles area, Bandelier National Monument

park: Frijoles Mesa (control site) was free of burros, and adjacent Frijolitos Mesa possessed burros. After selecting comparable locations, marking each with flagging that divided the one-mile-long transect into 52 intervals (an area comprising 100 acres), I surveyed the birdlife in each area early in the mornings on eight occasions. I recorded 46 breeding bird species on Frijoles Mesa and 32 on Frijolitos Mesa.

My report, a timely document for management, provided comparisons of both species' diversity and abundance. Frijoles Mesa supported a 31 percent higher avian population and significantly higher species diversity and biomass than Frijolitos Mesa. The difference was the presence of feral burros within the Frijolitos Mesa area and their absence within the Frijoles Mesa area. My report stated that "the environmental deterioration of the Frijolitos Mesa habitat was clearly a direct result of the influence of the feral Burros."

As a result of my research and public comment, burro reduction (shooting by park rangers) began in earnest in July 1977. My responsibilities at that stage were pretty well limited to an overview of the reduction activities and public relations, primarily visiting with reporters. I made an embarrassing mistake when talking to the press. In responding to a reporter who asked if shooting burros bothered the park rangers involved with the reduction, I answered that it may bother some, but they all were pro-

fessionals who understood the reason for such action but that none had a "Bambi complex." I meant that none of the shooters would consider the death of an animal more important than the reason for the reduction. But the press seized on that remark, and it made headlines in a number of western newspapers; Regional Director John Cook decided to call off the reduction program for a time.

In addition to the two transects established at Bandelier to demonstrate the impacts of burros on the area's breeding avifauna, I established five additional breeding-bird transects in the park. But very soon after initial surveys were completed, three of the survey sites—on Burnt and Escobas Mesas and Apache Spring—were burned by the fifteen thousand–acre La Mesa fire in mid-June 1977. Even before the fire was under control, I surveyed birds on each of the three burned areas, trying to document the fire's effects on the area's birdlife. And I duplicated the surveys during the breeding-bird seasons in 1978 and 1979; Terrell Johnson (a local birder) helped with the surveys during the latter two years. We recorded a grand total of 55 nesting bird species within the three study areas: 44 on Burnt Mesa, 47 on Escobas Mesa, and 43 on the Apache Spring transect.

I was later asked to participate in the La Mesa Fire Symposium that was sponsored and later published by the Los Alamos National Laboratory. My report, "La Mesa Fire Effects on Avifauna, Changes in Avian Population and Biomass," was coauthored by Johnson. I presented our paper at the October 6 and 7, 1984, symposium. Our summary and conclusions section stated:

La Mesa fire affected the avifauna in a number of ways. In general, populations and biomass values declined immediately after the fire on Burnt and Escobas mesas but exhibited increases on the higher, less severely burned Apache Spring unit. All three units displayed small to extensive increases in 1978, but exhibited minor to moderate declines, with a few exceptions, in 1979. In comparing 1979 data with prefire values, considerable variations are evident.

Species richness returned to the same values on Burnt and Escobas mesas as before the fire, but remained 12.5% higher at Apache Spring. Species density values declined 16% on the average; on Burnt and Escobas mesas, they declined 35% and 14%, respectively, but at Apache Spring, they increased by 2%. Species diversity increased on all three units: 2% on Burnt Mesa, 5% on Escobas Mesa, and 8.5% at Apache Spring. Evenness values increased on all three units as well: 1%, 5.5%, and 5% on Burnt and Escobas mesas and Apache Spring, respectively.

Biomass analysis reveals that middle-sized species (those of weight classes from 30.1 to 100 g) increased more than large species and considerably more than smaller species. Four of the 10 feeding guilds exhibited population increases between the prefire period and 1979, and 6 guilds exhibited declines. Timber-drilling-insect and foliage-nectar feeders received the greatest benefit, and timber-searching-insect, ground-predator, and air-perching-insect feeders were critically affected. Two of the four nesting guilds (parasitic and cavity-depression nesters) exhibited positive response, and two (ground and foliage nesters) exhibited negative responses.

Combined analysis of the avifauna before and after the fire suggests that middle-sized species that use the timber-drilling-insect guild (woodpeckers) and are either parasitic in nature or use cavities and depressions for nesting receive the greatest benefit from fire. Large species that use foliage-insect and ground-insect feeding guilds receive some benefit. All other combinations are casually or severely affected by fire.

Evidence accumulated from this study suggests that Bandelier's avifauna, particularly species diversity, which in itself is a foremost objective for a natural environment such as Bandelier, is increased by fire when the habitat received light to moderate fire. Of the three categories of fire, severe fire has the most drastic effect on avifauna and the longest period of time is required to adjust.

View from Capulin Mountain, New Mexico

My Wild Life

Severe burns also subject the environment to greater probabilities for other adverse effects such as erosion, overgrazing, and infestation. These in turn will affect the avifauna in a secondary way and extend the period of adjustment.

The three-year bird study at Bandelier essentially established an avian baseline for the park's various habitats, providing essential information for comparisons at a later date. And since a number of the Southwestern parks' Resource Management Plans called for similar baselines, I initiated a similar project at Capulin Mountain National Monument in eastern New Mexico. With the assistance of James Vukonich and Steve Cinnamon, local park employees, birds were censused in three habitats—grassland-savanna, scrub oak woodland, and pinyon-juniper woodland—from late April to early July in 1978 and 1979. We recorded 63 bird species on 69 surveys, including 261 individuals of 20 breeding species in the grassland-savanna habitat, 281 individuals of 29 breeding species in the scrub oak woodlands, and 339 individuals of 38 breeding species in the pinyon-juniper woodlands.

Our conclusions, written in a 1981 report, stated:

> Data presented in this paper indicate that the three vegetation communities differ significantly in avian diversity, population size, and biomass. Each provides habitat for a distinctive avifauna, but that of the grassland-savannah community is trended toward one of the other communities. If the National Park Service wants to retain grassland habitat as part of the Capulin Mountain environment it will need to either manipulate the woody vegetation or permit natural prescribed fires to reduce the trees and shrubs that seem to be invading this zone.

> Since birds are easily monitored, and long-term indices of the health and stability of the natural environment are best obtained by using the breeding avifauna, these transects should be read and compared with these baseline data at least every four years. Differentials greater than 15% should suggest a change in the breeding avifauna that is likely to be influenced by some kind of negative impact.

All during my Regional Office tenure, I encouraged all of the Southwest Region parks, especially those containing significant natural resources, to hire a natural resource specialist, an individual who would take the lead on natural resource issues and could interface with scientists, just as we had at Bandelier. Several other park superintendents soon realized the value of such an individual on their staff, and within the next few years we provided resource management training to employees at seven priority areas. Two of those trainees were new hires, at Buffalo National River and Padre Island National Seashore.

Big Thicket National Preserve

Big Thicket National Preserve was authorized by Congress on October 11, 1974, although no funds for operations were approved for a number of years. I had been casually involved with the Big Thicket area for a number of years, even before moving to the Regional Office. My first association with the area was about 1971 when I attended a meeting of Big Thicket supporters in one of the areas later to become one of the park units. The main speaker that day was US Senator Ralph Yarborough, who supported the concept of a national park. I had flown from Midland to Houston with Big Bend Superintendent Peterson, and I was at the meeting in uniform to hold an ivory-billed woodpecker mount. I felt a little silly at the time, but I also realized that the establishment of a national park might help protect the essential habitat of the endangered ivory-bill.

On another trip to the Big Thicket area, I met up with Ned Fritz, an attorney from Dallas who was a staunch advocate for the national park, and Geraldine Watson, a local botanist who was also fighting for a park. That evening we met with a local birder, and we took a rowboat into one of the bayous. The birder actually called a pair of barred owls to within a few yards of our boat. His hooting was identical to the deep calls of the owls that sat on tree branches over our heads hooting back.

Once the park was funded and staffed, I visited the new preserve on a number of occasions. Although the original Big Thicket covered about 3.5 million acres from Louisiana west to what is now Houston, and from the coastal plain north to the upper watersheds of the Trinity, Neches, and Sabine Rivers, only about 300,000 acres of the thicket remained in 1974. Only 96,757 acres, scattered in twelve units, are protected in the national preserve.

A few of those later visits included morning bird walks into various units. I was able to find all of the representative bird species: anhinga, red-headed and pileated woodpeckers, fish crow, chuck-will's-widow, brown-headed nuthatch, and Bachman's sparrow.

Years later, after retirement, Betty and I continue to visit some of the Big Thicket units. Perhaps our favorite is the Pitcher Plant Trail in the Hickory Creek Savannah Unit. On an April 2008 visit we recorded five swallowtail species—zebra, black, eastern tiger, spicebush, and palamedes—as well as Georgia satyr, a lifer for us both.

Pitcher plant bog in Big Thicket National Preserve. Courtesy of Betty Wauer.

Ridley Turtles

One of the projects documented in Padre Island's Resource Management Plan was the restoration of Kemp's ridley sea turtles. Although it had not been seen at Padre Island for many years, it still did occur to the south on at least one beach in Tamaulipas, Mexico. During an unrelated trip with Clyde Jones of the US Fish and Wildlife Service to Mexico's Tiburon Island, Clyde and I talked about ridleys and their disappearance from Padre Island, and we jointly decided to initiate a restoration program. We were aware that ridley turtles still nested at Mexico's Rancho Nuevo beach, where forty thousand individuals had been photographed in 1947 by Dr. Henry Hildebrand. That 1947 congregation (known as an *arribada*) was the first and last of its kind to be documented for the Kemp's ridley sea turtle. Henry eventually showed his film at a meeting of the American Society of Ichthyologists and Herpetologists in 1961, proving for the first time that the Kemp's ridley is a valid species, is a daytime nester, and nests in huge *arribadas*. By 1961, however, ridley populations had declined by 90 percent, in spite of being listed as an endangered species. Furthermore, in 1968 the International Union for the Conservation of Nature declared it the "most endangered" of all endangered species.

Step one of our Padre Island restoration project was a feasibility study undertaken by Dr. Howard "Duke" Campbell, US Fish and Wildlife Service biologist. Duke's very positive report was followed by establishing an advisory group that, besides Clyde, Duke, and me, included Drs. Archie Carr and Henry Hildebrand of the United States, and Mexican biologist Rene Marquez, who had already been working with ridleys in Mexico. In October 1977, Duke and I, along with John Smith of the Texas Parks and Wildlife Department, made a presentation on this project to the National Park Service Advisory Board, which was meeting at Padre Island. We received their unanimous support. I then prepared an Action Plan, dated January 1978, that was reviewed and approved by the advisory group members as well as acting Southwest Regional Director Ted Thompson. That plan was designed to increase protection of Kemp's ridleys at Rancho Nuevo by focusing attention on the area during the nesting season and to move some of the eggs from the natal beach to Padre Island for hatching and imprinting. It also involved the Texas Parks and Wildlife Department and the National Marine Fisheries Service.

In May 1978, I traveled to Rancho Nuevo to participate in the egg-gathering project on-site. I had flown to Tampico, where I met USFWS Biologist Bruce Bury, who had driven down with several Styrofoam boxes filled with Padre

Island sand. We then drove back northward to Aldama and east for thirteen miles on an unpaved road to Rancho Nuevo. We arrived in the evening, and by the time I had met the half-dozen volunteers, Rene Marquez and a couple of Mexican marines, and put up my tent, it was dark.

I was awakened the very next morning by a sharp breeze on my tent, and by 8:00 a.m. it had increased to twenty-five miles per hour, suggesting that this would be the day when ridleys would suddenly appear on the beach to dig a shallow pit and lay eggs. They apparently evolved this behavior to reduce the chances of detection of their tracks and nests by predators. Our timing was perfect! We collected almost 15,000 eggs that day. And, although I left Rancho Nuevo after an eight-day visit, almost 85,000 eggs were collected by July.

In a November 1978 article I wrote for *National Parks & Conservation Magazine*, I explained:

> Two thousand of the eggs collected in May were given special handling. They were taken directly from the turtles as they were being dropped, immediately placed in bags containing sand brought from Padre Island, then placed in Styrofoam containers filled with Padre Island sand.
>
> Biologists generally believe that young

La Coma, Kemp's ridley sea turtle camp at Rancho Nuevo, Mexico, 1978

Ridley turtle digging nest at Rancho Nuevo, 1978

Ridley turtle eggs at Rancho Nuevo, 1978

Ridley turtle hatchling at Padre Island National Seashore

turtles imprint on their hatching beach. We were taking no chances on their imprinting on the beach at Rancho Nuevo, so we permitted the eggs and hatchlings to touch only Padre Island sand. We stored the Styrofoam containers at Rancho Nuevo for forty days, until the eggs were far enough along in their development to be safely moved. Then they were flown to Padre Island to complete incubation there. On the fiftieth day the eggs began to hatch.

Each morning for five days the hatchlings of the previous day were released at the high-tide line at Malaquite Beach, a portion of Padre Island National Seashore where oversand vehicles are not permitted. As the sun warmed their tiny bodies (about the size of a silver dollar), they began their trek to the sea. We let the hatchlings scamper down the beach to the surf on their own. This probably is when imprinting occurs. All two thousand hatchlings headed directly for sun, apparently an instinctive move toward a "guiding light." They reached the surf within an hour. No hatchlings were lost to gulls or other predators. Without human escort, this form of predation occurs extensively in the wild.

As the hatchlings reached the surf, we permitted them only a few moments' time in the water before we scooped them up in nets and placed them in holding cages. . . . Daily litters were flown . . . to Galveston, Texas. There they were placed in a "head start" program operated by the National Marine Fisheries Service. The little turtles will be kept in special tanks constructed for them. They will be fed a carefully selected diet of shrimp and fish pellets until just before release. Then, at about one year of age, they will be released.

A total of 1,900 baby turtles survived the hatching and imprinting stage that first year. And the program was repeated every year for ten years, until approximately 22,000 ridley eggs were collected in Mexico, transferred to Padre Island to be hatched, then flown to Galveston to be raised by National Marine Fisheries personnel. Eventually the young sea turtles were returned to Padre Island, where they were released fifteen miles offshore.

The success of the restoration program was not realized, however, until late spring of 1994, when a female Kemp's ridley crawled onto the Padre Island beach and laid eggs. Since 1994, ridley nests found on Padre Island and adjacent South Texas beaches have gradually increased: 4 in 1995, 6 in 1996, 9 in 1997, 13 in 1998, 16 in 1999, 12 in 2000, 8 in 2001, 38 in 2002, 19 in 2003, 32 in 2004, 51 in 2005, and 102 in 2006.

Avian Population Survey

Also during my two-week stay at Rancho Nuevo, I established five transects that I walked one to five times each, recording all of the birds detected, along with notes on whether they were breeding or in migration. The transects were located in five distinct habitats: a littoral zone with both littoral scrub and mangrove habitats; thorn scrub with either dense vegetation or open in places where grazing occurred; thorn forest where larger trees and shrubs were dominant; and riparian habitat that was more luxuriant and dense due to the continuous presence of ground water.

I recorded 147 bird species within the five habitats: 82 (56%) were nesting and 65 (44%) were migrants. On two censuses in the littoral scrub habitat, 29 species were recorded; 36 species on one census of the mangroves; 66 species on four censuses in thorn scrub; 92 species on five censuses in thorn forest; and 90 species on three censuses in riparian habitat. The thorn forest and riparian habitats supported the highest number of nesting and transient birds: 57 nesting species in the thorn forest and 43 in the riparian, and 35 and 47 migrants, respectively.

Only 6 of the 82 breeding birds were found to nest in all five habitats: red-billed pigeon, groove-billed ani, ladder-backed woodpecker, Couch's kingbird, olive sparrow, and Altamira

Thorn forest transect, Rancho Nuevo, 1978

My Wild Life

oriole. Eleven species nested in four habitats, 10 in three, 23 in two, and 32 were exclusives, nesting in only one habitat. The exclusives provided a better understanding of their habitat preferences and also suggested a hierarchical ranking of the five habitats.

Thorn forest hosted the greatest number of nesting species as well as the highest number of exclusives (13), suggesting the greatest ecological integrity. The 13 exclusives were thicket tinamou, black vulture, hook-billed kite, crane hawk, wild turkey, squirrel cuckoo, mottled owl, blue-crowned motmot, smoky-brown woodpecker, ivory-billed woodcreeper, black-crested titmouse, crimson-collared grosbeak, and melodious blackbird.

Nine exclusives were recorded in the riparian habitat: least grebe, neotropical cormorant, bare-throated tiger-heron, boat-billed heron, olive-throated parakeet, green kingfisher, yellow-green vireo, yellow-throated euphonia, and brown-headed cowbird. Seven exclusives were recorded in the thorn scrub habitat: white-tailed kite, crested caracara, long-billed thrasher, loggerhead shrike, tropical parula, northern cardinal, and yellow-faced grassquit. Only one exclusive—gray-crowned yellowthroat—was found in the littoral scrub zone, and one exclusive—anhinga—was found in the mangroves.

All of my data were later written up for a report, eventually published as an article, "Avian Population Survey of a Tamaulipas Scrub Habitat," in the autumn 1999 issue of *Cotinga*. My conclusions included the following:

The above data assign the greatest importance to the thorn forest that supported the highest number of breeding birds. The thorn scrub habitat supported the second highest number of breeding avifauna as well as the greatest number of transients. These two communities, therefore, are subject to the greatest potential losses. It is paradoxical that these habitats are most susceptible to change. Human activities take the greatest toll on habitats with the tallest trees, and key ingredients are dependent upon the retention of these habitats. The loss of the thorn forest, thorn scrub and riparian habitats from the Tamaulipan ecosystem would eliminate not only approximately a third of the breeding avifauna, but would undoubtedly cause other losses that have not yet been analyzed or may never be understood.

Cooperative Studies

Starting about 1975, the US Fish and Wildlife Service and Mexico's sister agency, Fauna Silvestre, developed a working agreement to undertake joint studies of wildlife habitats in select areas in Mexico. The purposes of these projects were to identify environmental disturbances and to better understand the basic roles of the major components of the ecosystems. I became involved through a special request for my services by Clyde Jones, director of the Bird and Mammal Laboratory, US National Museum. The US Fish and Wildlife Service and National Park Service had a cooperative agreement to provide assistance to one another as needed.

My involvement included attending an initial meeting at Kino Bay, Sonora, on December 5 and 6, 1976; making a scouting trip on the mainland and on Tiburon Island from May 14 to 18, 1977; and conducting a breeding-bird population study on Tiburon, May 10 to 15, 1978.

Tiburon Island, the largest island (484 square miles) on the Pacific coast of North America south of Canada, is situated within the Sea of Cortez, directly west of Kino Bay, across an extensive channel from the Seri village of Punta Chueca. A Seri Indian provided us transportation across the channel in the vessel he used for fishing, a long, sleek, wooden boat with an outboard motor. In spite of Tiburon Island appearing to be only a short distance away, it took us a good part of an hour to negotiate the 1.2-mile passage across El Infiernillo (Little Hell) Strait.

As we neared the island, we could see four uniformed marines, automatic rifles in hand, watching our approach. Although we had informed the Seri boatman that we were expected, he took no chances and stopped well short of the beach. The Mexican marines looked very businesslike when they pointed their weapons toward us and warned us to leave. Two members of our party, Roberto Munoz and Mateo Aguayo, representatives of Fauna Silvestre, were soon recognized by the marines, and we were permitted to land. Once ashore we were treated with courtesy. And several days later, before we left the island, we enjoyed an excellent fish fry, with all the fresh fish we could eat, lots of fried potatoes, tortillas, excellent salsa, and tequila and lime drinks that we drank from fire-blackened cans. I have since cherished the memory of our farewell fish fry and the comradeship that we enjoyed on Tiburon.

The party of scientists involved with the 1978 study included Drs. Norm Scott (leader) and Tom Fritts, both USFWS employees, and three of my colleagues: Dick Russell and Roy and Lois Johnson. Norm and Tom intended to study the mammals and reptiles. The bird censuses that I had planned required at least four transects run in each habitat, and the assistance of my three friends was essential.

Our base camp during our stay was a rather comfortable bunkhouse, complete with running water, at Carcol. It had been built by Fauna Silvestre for housing Mexican scientists and other visitors like us. It provided an excellent base

Tiburon Island habitat, 1978

from where we could hike to various places in the center of the island, and except for one overnight in the cactus forest habitat along the northeastern coast, I was able to accomplish everything I wanted to do by foot.

We first established one-mile-long walking transects, each containing 100 acres, within five habitats: littoral scrub, desert scrub, cactus scrub, riparian, and thorn scrub. Birds were then censused as we walked the one-mile transect lines at about one-half mile per hour between 5:30 and 10:15 a.m. All avian species and their detected activities relating to breeding and feeding behavior were recorded on field sampling sheets. The data were later transferred to permanent summary sheets and still later divided into those species that breed in the area, that breed nearby, or that were transients.

A total of 105 bird species were recorded during the six-day survey: 38 (36%) were considered to be breeding. The remaining 67 species (64%) were either migrants or winter residents that had not yet departed. The most common bird recorded within the five habitats was the verdin. In fact, this tiny bird made up 12.6% of the total Tiburon Island breeding-bird population. The second most abundant species was the black-tailed gnatcatcher (9.3%), followed by black-throated sparrow (8.8%), white-winged dove (8.4%), ash-throated flycatcher (7.4%), Costa's hummingbird (5.9%), and cactus wren (5.9%). Those 7 birds made up 58.3% of Tiburon's total breeding-bird population.

It is interesting to speculate on total bird populations for the entire island. Exact estimates of this kind are next to impossible because they would entail a thorough analysis of all vegetation communities on the island. Since time did not permit that, I arrived at rough estimates for the whole island by converting known population data to perceived habitat units. I assumed that our twenty-square-mile study area was an adequate representation of Tiburon's full complement of plant communities. I then calculated total populations of the island's 7 most common species as follows: verdin, 101,852 individuals; black-tailed gnatcatcher,

79,255; ash-throated flycatcher, 54,551; white-winged dove, 58,413; Costa's hummingbird, 54,551; and cactus wren, 47,145.

As for the five communities censused, 7 bird species were found to breed in the littoral scrub community, 18 utilized the desert scrub, 21 utilized the cactus scrub, 20 were found in the riparian community, and 31 were found to breed in the thorn scrub.

On May 12, while Mateo, Tom, and I surveyed the extensive cactus forest, Mateo pointed out a tall cardon cactus that contained two stick nests being utilized by both ospreys and great blue herons. Both adult birds flew off their nests as we approached. The osprey circled the cardon, calling continuously. The heron flew several hundred yards away to another cardon, where it sat and watched as we examined the nests. We then retreated to about three hundred feet from the cardon, and the osprey returned to its nest almost immediately. The heron re-

Osprey and great blue heron nests on cardon, 1978

turned within a few minutes and attempted to alight on its nest. It made three attempts by approaching from above and passing over or alongside the osprey nest. In each case it was driven off by the osprey. On its fourth attempt it approached the nest from the front and below, apparently not disturbing the osprey, and was permitted to settle on its nest. Since I never before had heard of dual nesting for these species, I later prepared a short paper on the occurrence that was published in *Southwestern Naturalist* in January 1980.

On another morning on the desert, as I walked slowly along my transect line, carefully listening and watching for birds, I suddenly realized that I was not alone. A pair of coyotes were following me, some fifty to sixty feet away. As I continued the transect, I realized that my canid companions were keeping pace with my movements. They would move when I did but stop when I stopped to record a bird or to listen or look more carefully at one place or another. The male seemed most interested. When the female wandered off as if bored with the whole affair, he stayed. He sat or lay down when I stopped for a longer than usual time. And he seemed to be getting closer to me as I progressed along the transect. At first I ignored him completely, and that must have frustrated him or created even greater curiosity. Once he lay down, just like any other dog, within twenty feet of me.

Once or twice I even talked to him in a low voice. But then he began to lose interest in me, and suddenly he disappeared as mysteriously as he had appeared. I regarded the entire affair as curiosity on behalf of the coyote, but it did occur to me that I might have been the first human being that pair of coyotes had ever seen. Maybe, until I gave myself away by talking to him, I was just another item of curiosity in the natural world of Tiburon's desert environment.

Mule deer also were present in small numbers. I found fresh tracks each morning but saw only two individuals during six days. Their shyness may suggest that the island's wildlife continued to be hunted in spite of the area being classified as an official wildlife refuge. Also, each time I climbed onto the rocky ridges, I watched carefully for bighorn sheep but found none. Desert bighorn were introduced to Tiburon Island by Fauna Silvestre during the 1960s, and Mateo informed me that a few still occur on the upper slopes of Sierra Kunkaak. Several members of our party hiked into the area where bighorn had been seen most often, but to no avail.

The desert tortoise was also present on Tiburon and was one of the species listed within the USFWS agreement with Fauna Silvestre for study. Bruce Bury of USFWS and Sandalio Reyes studied this slow-moving animal on Tiburon in 1978 and 1979. They located 146 individuals and estimated tortoise density at 169 individuals per square mile. Tortoises dig shallow burrows in suitable places such as into stream banks, woodrat nests, and debris. In about half of the burrows examined, the investigators found two to four individuals together, suggesting greater communal habits than previously known. The tortoises feed on a wide variety of desert vegetation and are most active during the warmest time of the year, especially after late-summer rainstorms.

Tiburon Island is the only known area of the Sonoran Desert that has not been heavily grazed by domestic livestock. Only small numbers of cattle and goats lived there when the island was inhabited by the Seris. All have since been removed. It is most important that the island continue to be protected in its natural state. On August 2, 1978, President Lopez Portillo officially declared forty-seven islands in the Sea of Cortez, including Tiburon, as wildlife refuges.

The Seri Indians have been closely tied to Tiburon for all of its recorded history. They are known to have lived in the same general area for at least five hundred years, and on the island itself during the 1930s and until after World War II. Unlike the several other islands within the Sea of Cortez, Tiburon possesses several springs that provide fresh water during even the driest years. But in 1965, and confirmed in 1978, the Mexican government prohibited Seri residency and moved Mexican marines on the island to enforce the laws.

Today, the entire Seri population of approximately five thousand lives on the Sonoran mainland along a sixty-five-mile strip from the village of Punta Chueca north to Desemboque. The buildings at Punta Chueca were mostly crude or adobe structures, many with ocotillo walls; paper was stuffed in the walls or plastic woven into place to help keep out cold winter winds.

We also found two open structures that had been built on the Punta Chueca beach. One was a simple, thatch-covered, twenty-foot-square ramada that provided shade for anyone wishing to sit near the beach. A smaller pen was enclosed with chicken wire. In 1977, it was empty on my first observation, but it held two recently captured green sea turtles the next time I looked. Both had been either speared or shot in about the center of their shells. Although they were alive, it was obvious that their days were numbered. Three days later I found their guts and empty shells nearby on the beach. I assumed the meat had been utilized for soup or turtle steaks; it wasn't until the following year that I learned the rest of the story.

Sea turtles have long been part of the Seri livelihood and probably were a popular food even before the Seris deserted their more nomadic lifestyle for one of fishing and settlements. At least two sea turtle species have been recorded within this area, the Pacific ridley and green. Neither nests in the region, but both are known to occur there at any time of the year, even in winter. It is then that these reptiles are most susceptible to being taken by Seri fishermen. The sea turtles dig into the muddy bottom of the bay when the water temperature gets below 45°F and "hibernate" there with much-reduced respiration rates. It is then that the Seris can often see them, partially covered with mud, resting on the bottoms of the shallowest bays. These sleeping turtles are then speared, lifted into the boats, and brought home. They are kept alive in pens until eaten. The Seri have long understood this local sea turtle characteristic and taken advantage of it, but marine biologists learned these facts only recently.

One day I watched the Seri fishermen unload their day's catch on the Punta Chueca beach. There were a few mackerel, two fish species I did not recognize, and many, many sharks. One of the four boats being unloaded was so full of sharks that the fishermen had been forced to stand on the seat or sides. Unloading the day's catch was done simply by throwing all of the fish one by one onto the sandy beach. Then the fishermen, with questionable help from several children who had arrived to help beach the boats, began to gut the fish. The innards were thrown back into the bay, and within a very few minutes the water was stained with red. The slow but steady current soon spread the bloody water out along the beach. The other fish remains eventually became scattered as well. The shark population out there soon would be feeding on its cousins. The Seri had inadvertently developed an excellent system for recycling parts of their daily catch, a process that probably has existed for hundreds of years.

By the time the sharks were all eviscerated, it seemed the entire human population of Punta Chueca was present. Everyone there appeared to be involved in one way or another. Finally the men loaded the cleaned sharks into large washtubs, which they used to haul the day's catch to a small but functioning freezer plant built a few hundred feet inland from the beach. The frozen sharks were picked up daily and trucked to a cannery in Hermosillo, I was told. But I wasn't able to learn about the final product. I knew that shark is often used for dog food. I also knew that some restaurant-served "scallops" are only specially prepared shark. Ever since then, when eating scallops, I can't help wondering if I am eating shark from El Infiernillo Strait.

An additional cooperative project occurred in 1979 when I and five colleagues—Drs. Norman Scott, Tom Fritts, Bruce Bury, Cathy Blunt, and

Seris and sharks at Punta Chueca, Mexico, 1978

Jean Duke—visited Cedros Island for six days from June 19 to 24. We surveyed numerous localities, and I censused birds on three areas by transects, using a method similar to the one utilized on Tiburon Island. Cedros Island, however, is a very different kind of environment from that on Tiburon. Instead of being principally flat lowlands, it is exceedingly steep and rugged and contains six habitats that reminded me of those that occur in Southern California: pine forest, juniper woodland, chaparral, coastal sage scrub, maritime dune scrub, and desert scrub.

Cedros Island is situated fourteen miles off the Baja mainland and is considered part of Baja Norte. The island is 24 miles in length, north to south, and varies in width from 4 to 11 miles. The total landmass consists of approximately 134 square miles. The highest elevation is 3,950 feet at the summit of Cerro de Cedros.

The six of us flew from Guerrero Negro on the mainland across the sprawling, one hundred thousand–acre saltworks of salt pans and canals and Scammon's Lagoon and Vizcaino Bay to the little town of San Isidro. Scammon's Lagoon, a shallow, natural bay, has a saline content of 4 percent, and that of the open ocean is 3 percent. Because saltier water provides for greater buoyancy, it serves as excellent calving grounds for gray whales. And because so many gray whales frequent the area in winter, the area has become a popular location for whale watching. Therefore, the Mexican government has designated Scammon's Lagoon and much of Vizcaino Bay as a whale refuge. Parque Natural de la Ballena Gris is one of the first of its kind anywhere in the world.

Gray whales can reach forty-five feet in length but average only sixteen feet when they are born. Unlike other baleen whales, grays are bottom-feeders and scoop up mouthfuls of bottom materials that, in their northern habitat, are rich in crustaceans. The water and mud are filtered out through special baleen plates. But once they reach their southern wintering grounds, the adults will not feed again until they return to their northern territories; some scientists believe that they feed throughout the year. Adults migrate six thousand miles from Alaska to the southern Pacific waters each year,

the longest migration undertaken by any mammal. Newborn calves are nursed within the protected lagoons during the first two or three months of their lives. By springtime, when they are large and strong enough to travel, they head north for Alaska.

San Isidro, with about 120 buildings, was dominated by a salt-processing plant. The town was clustered around a cannery and dock, where seven or eight fishing boats were docked. Our party of biologists selected a camping site near a small spring on the south slope of Cerro de Cedros, about a mile above town. From there we had a great view of the town and surrounding waters.

I established three transects and ran each

Cedros Island and Scammon's Lagoon, Mexico, 1979

on three occasions, recording 13 bird species. But only 11 were considered to be breeding: red-tailed hawk, American kestrel, mourning dove, Costa's hummingbird, Say's phoebe, common raven, Bewick's and rock wrens, northern mockingbird, black-throated sparrow, and house finch. Two of these made up 53 percent of the population: black-throated sparrow and Bewick's wren.

I also spent portions of two days on a fishing boat along the coast, where I added an additional 13 species: black storm-petrel; brown pelican; double-crested, Brandt's, and pelagic cormorants; osprey; black oystercatcher; willet; marbled godwit; a large colony of western gulls; Hermann's gull; royal tern; and Cassin's auklet. Of greatest interest to me was the black storm-petrel, a pelagic species known to nest on islands off the Pacific coast of Baja California. This is a little (only nine inches long), all-dark bird with a fairly long, forked tail. Its flight is most distinctive: deep, vigorous, but graceful. These birds appear to actually walk on the water. Nests are located in burrows or among boulders. Although I observed up to 85 seabirds fishing off the northern end of the island, only one came close enough for identification. But I believe that the majority of the other birds were also black storm-petrels.

As we approached Punta Norte where the boat was to pick up a cargo of fish and abalo-nes, the four members of our team were rowed ashore to where we were going to camp and investigate this part of the island; we planned on returning to San Isidro the following day. On landing we were greeted by several gentlemen, including the village alcalde (mayor), who invited us to his house for dinner. We readily accepted his gracious offer, and we were escorted to the largest and nicest house in town, back from the beach a hundred feet or so. I was not sure whether it had been a spur-of-the-moment invitation or if he and his wife had discussed it beforehand, but we were welcomed with all sincerity, and even though we were strangers, she immediately set about preparing dinner for us.

Sitting in the corner of the main room where I could see into the kitchen, I watched as she took eight or ten abalones from a refrigerator and began to prepare them in two distinctly different ways. Several were cut into extremely thin slices and dumped into a bowl containing a liquid that I couldn't identify. She chopped a second group into tiny cubes, each less than a quarter of an inch, and put them into a preheated pan and fried them just like hamburger. When she was done, she added all of the ingredients that go into salsa, along with some additional things that I did not see, and then stirred all of that together. She then put that mixture back on the stove and cooked it some more.

In the meantime, we visited with the mayor

about the island, its history, the fishing industry, and the wildlife that we had already seen and that which we still hoped to find. He was most helpful, and we all were impressed with his knowledge about the topography, ways to reach certain inaccessible parts of the island, and his willingness to be of assistance. But the most remarkable event that afternoon was the dinner. I had eaten very little before the start of an early-morning transect count, and we had left port at about 11:00 after a lunch of some granola bars. So by the time we were called to eat, after watching the food being prepared, I was more than ready. And I was not disappointed. Everything was excellent! The bowl of abalone strips was served as a salad in the form of ceviche. The second abalone dish was chili. We made burritos by rolling tortillas filled with that incredible abalone chili. Cold cerveza helped to round out a unique and unforgettable meal.

Since we had yet to hike into a nearby canyon to find a campsite, we left after dinner. We managed to find an excellent campsite not more than a mile from Punta Norte, set up camp in the dwindling light, and then spent a couple of hours wandering along an adjacent canyon searching for whatever might crawl, run, or fly across our path. The only animal of interest was a horned lizard that someone found partly buried in a sandy arroyo. It was kept overnight,

and I photographed it the next day; it was one of the island's endemic species, the Cedros Island horned lizard.

My early-morning bird census along the canyon bottom produced the same species that I had already recorded on earlier censuses. By 10:00 a.m. I had finished my transect and was exploring the coastal area that forms a broad plain at the mouth of the canyon. That was where I discovered a hundred or more sea lions along the rocky beach. I crept up to a place where I could watch and photograph these marvelous creatures better and lay there on my belly for about an hour admiring their grace in the water. On land, they were awkward and lumbering. They either didn't see me or ignored me; I couldn't be sure.

By midafternoon the fishing boat returned. After a fond farewell to the mayor, we boarded the boat, along with another six cartons of fresh abalone and several sacks of fish, and headed back to San Isidro. Two days later, following another evening of abalone steaks, I boarded the same DC-3 that had brought us to Cedros and headed back across Vizcaino Bay to Guerrero Negro, where I caught an even smaller plane for a flight to the States and home.

On a personal note, I moved with Sharon and

Wauer house in winter, Bandelier National Monument

the two children to Santa Fe in 1972; in 1973, we were divorced, and Sharon and the children moved to Utah.

In the summer of 1975, I got reacquainted with Betty; she was the administrative officer at Bandelier. I had worked with her from 1968 to 1970 in Big Bend, and I knew her four sons: Bill, Brad, Brent, and Barry Nichols. Betty and I were married on August 27, 1976, in Taos, and we moved into one of the park houses on the mesa. It was a great location within a beautiful ponderosa pine forest and with a grand view across the park to the south.

We did have a major scare when the La Mesa fire got within one mile of our house. We evacuated the house in case the fire could not be stopped from reaching the six houses on the mesa. Loading choice materials into our two vehicles so they would not be lost if the fire reached the houses was upsetting, to say the least. We, of course, chose photographs and similar items that could not be replaced. After the fire was controlled and we returned home, the only evidence was the significant smoke smell that remained for many days.

The drive back and forth from home in Bandelier to my office in Santa Fe was less of a chore than one might think, because of my frequent travels and the magnificent scenery along the way. In fact, I enjoyed the drive, as it gave me the opportunity to concentrate on my various activities both at work and at home.

Transition

The National Park Service science program was restructured during the Carter administration. Assistant Secretary of Interior for Parks and Wildlife Bob Herbst initiated a significant push for improving the science program in the National Park Service. Ted Sudia and staff were given the task of developing recommendations on the reorganization. Ted was acting chief scientist at the time. Out of that effort evolved a new science and technology program that reported to an associate director for science and technology.

Ted had been impressed with some of the activities under way in the Southwest Region, and he asked me to become one of the eight new Washington Office division chiefs. So in 1978, I succumbed to the Washington Office offer and moved to the "puzzle palace" as chief of natural resource management.

La Mesa fire stopped just yards away from the house, Bandelier National Monument

8
Washington, D.C.

We moved to Washington with a good deal of trepidation. We had never before lived on the East Coast and in a large city, and the very idea of becoming a member of the Washington bureaucracy was totally against my nature. Yet both Betty and I discovered that we thoroughly enjoyed the area. Great history! Marvelous restaurants! Unique ambience! Plus, we were able to visit numerous places along the Eastern Seaboard, from Florida to Maine, many that we had not previously seen.

We bought a house just inside the Beltway in Springfield, Virginia, and I soon discovered that it was well situated near a variety of birding sites, many with reasonably good habitats. Some of my favorites included the old towpath along the C&O Canal; Great Falls Park; Hughes Hollow and the Turf Farm in Maryland; and Dykes Marsh, Roaches Run, Fort Belvoir, and

Huntley Meadows Park in Virginia. Shenandoah National Park was in easy driving distance, and the Atlantic coastal areas were also relatively accessible over a weekend.

My work environment, however, was something else, especially with the change of administration from Jimmy Carter to Ronald Reagan. Reagan brought in some of his old cronies, including G. Ray Arnett as assistant secretary for fish and wildlife and parks. Arnett had been Governor Reagan's director of California state parks, and his sole interest was hunting and fishing. He had little or no regard for the protection of natural systems, including endangered species, in spite of his position as the nation's principal guardian.

Secretary of Interior James Watt, previous member of the prestigious Heritage Foundation, was, on the other hand, a bright and articulate individual. The problem, from my per-

US Capitol, Washington, D.C.

Towpath along C&O Canal, Maryland

Director Bill Whalen was doing whatever he could to kill the new science thrust by creating as much animosity as he possibly could. He and his administrative officer, Nancy Garrett, also known in the Park Service as "the Dragon Lady," searched high and low for someone who would do their bidding. And I can state unequivocally that they succeeded when they hired Dick Briceland, an engineer instead of a natural resource scientist, who had absolutely no knowledge about national parks. One of the first questions he asked me on coming on duty was, "Tell me, what is a park superintendent?"

The Job

I entered my duty in the Washington Office on August 21, 1978. As chief of the Division of Natural Resources, my responsibilities, according to the approved department manual, included "all policy formulation and program standards, providing interpretation and advice about policy and guidelines, and preparing subject reports for all natural science research activities and for those resource management functions: (1) Resource Management Plans, (2) Aquatic Resources, including Fish, (3) Cave Systems, (4) Coastal Resources Management, (5) Climate, (6) Biocide Use, (7) Endangered Species, (8) Forest Insect and Disease, (9) Vegetation Management (Restoration/Rehabilitation),

spective, was that his agenda was incompatible with that of the National Park Service and Fish and Wildlife Service, agencies dedicated to resource protection that he oversaw. It was immediately clear that any progress I was to make in natural resource protection for the national parks would require diligence and persistence.

Although the position of associate director for science and technology had been approved, no one had yet been chosen for that position. I, and most everyone else, had assumed that Ted Sudia or another capable scientist would be chosen. But when I arrived in Washington, I found the situation almost unbearable. NPS

(10) Wildland Fire Management, (11) Wildlife and Surplus Animals, (12) Non-Native Species, and (13) Human Impact upon the Resources."

Because my position was a new one, based on a recent reorganization, it took me more than a year for my program to become fully staffed. By March 1980, I had divided my responsibilities into three subdivisions: (1) Science, with John Dennis as chief; (2) Resources Management, with George Gardner as chief; and (3) Fire Management, with Dave Butts as chief. Division employees at that time included twenty-six at the Washington Office and an additional five individuals at the Interagency Fire Center, located in Boise, Idaho.

My office was first located in the Interior Building, but as the division evolved, we moved to a separate building at the corner of 11th and L Streets, about ten blocks away from Department of the Interior. At first I was concerned about not being immediately available to the director's office, but I soon discovered that distance was often to my advantage. Betty also worked in the 11th Street building as a program analyst for the NPS Lands Division. Our commute was made easier by both being at the same location.

Prior to our move to Washington, I had been selected to participate in an international workshop in Egypt. From November 3 to 12, Betty and I were in Cairo, where I participated in the First International Workshop on the Management of Wildlife in Arid Ecosystems. The meeting was organized by the Egyptian Academy of Scientific Research and Technology. The purpose of the workshop was to introduce representatives of several countries to Egypt's arid land wildlife problems and to draw attention to the plight of threatened and endangered species in arid zones. As a secondary purpose, a smaller group from the NPS was asked to evaluate Egypt's natural resources for potential preservation as national parks.

Funds for the workshop, at least for US participation, came from an agreement between the two countries that allowed Egypt to reduce its debt to the United States by that amount. Betty was able to join me throughout our stay, and special collateral activities, such as a visit to the Egyptian Museum, were scheduled for the spouses not attending the workshops. Spouses were also invited to join us at restaurants and to attend field trips. On our arrival in Cairo, all the American citizens were invited to stay the first night at the American embassy. The next day and the remainder of our stay were at a good local hotel.

The first four days were principally spent in meetings, where various problems and solutions were discussed. Several of the participants presented preselected papers. I presented a paper titled "The Surveillance of Wildlife in Arid Ecosystem Monitoring Programs." The majority of presenters and participants came from the United States. Only a few Egyptians participated, although a number of important conservationists from other countries attended. The US contingency included Ariel Appleton, conservationist from Arizona; Arthur Singer, who painted the birds in the Bruun bird guide; Larry Mason and Richard Warner, US Fish and Wildlife Service; and Rick Cook, Roy Johnson, Larry May, and me of the National Park Service. Other participants represented the countries of Bahrain, France, Great Britain, Greece, Holland, India, Indonesia, Italy, Kuwait, Mali, Pakistan, Qatar, Saudi Arabia, Spain, Sudan, Thailand, United Arab Emirates, Uganda, Upper Volta, and Yemen.

Of all the people making presentations, I was most impressed by Dr. Bertrand des Clers, director of the International Foundation for the Conservation of Game (IGF), Paris; Antonio Machado, regional biologist of the Institute for the Conservation of Natural Areas (ICONA) in the Canary Islands; Dr. Bertel Bruun, author of *The Larousse Guide to Birds of Britain and Europe*, from the United Kingdom; and Dr. Jane Bock, University of Colorado.

I was unimpressed with the workshop itself, although I did meet some fine people, and some of the discussions were extremely interesting. But I generally felt we were talking to ourselves.

A lot of money was spent to let us preach to the saved. I am not sure if Egypt gained any significant benefit from the workshop.

On field trips we were treated to some exceptionally fine cultural sites and opportunities. Guided by Dr. Hassan Hafez, Egypt's undersecretary for agriculture, we were taken to numerous pyramids, mosques, monasteries, tombs, and statues, some of which were closed to the general public. I could not help being impressed with most of the cultural sites, most especially the Great Pyramid of Giza, the Sphinx, and the step pyramid at Saqqara. We also visited the Al-Muayyad Mosque in downtown Cairo. But none of the sites visited impressed me for their natural values. Vast stretches of Egypt's environment are desert with little or no life of any kind. The greenery of the Nile Valley is lush, but the majority of that vegetation is nonnative, and the greenery stops immediately beyond the influence of the Nile River. Except for one hunting preserve along the Suez road west of the valley, I saw no areas that would fulfill standards that the United States would use in recommending national park status. Once, near the Pyramid of Djoser, I walked away from the group and took a mile-loop walk. I found one single living thing, a moth that happened by. I did not find any other living plant or evidence of another living animal. All wildlife apparently is limited to the Nile Valley. Interestingly, in the

Author at Great Pyramid of Giza, Egypt, 1978

countryside were a number of castlelike structures of mud, often four stories tall, built for pigeons. Pigeon droppings provide farmers with important fertilizer.

The official field trips did provide an opportunity to see some of the country and record the birdlife encountered. A total of 127 species were recorded. On a trip to Wadi el Natrum, an isolated oasis deep in the desert northwest of Cairo, I saw my first hoopoe, a really strange bird with a long decurved bill, pinkish back, black-and-white banded wings, and a tall crest. Closely related to kingfishers, the hoopoe name comes from its characteristic call, a deep "hoo-poo-poo." Other birds of interest to me on this trip included hobby; little stint; pied flycatcher; rock and meadow pipits; crested lark; common bulbul; rock thrush; redstart; stonechat; wheatear; Isabelline; and ringed, Kentish, and spur-winged plovers.

On November 10, a day off for the participants, who mostly went sightseeing about the city, Roy Johnson, Lois Height, Betty, and I had a driver from the embassy take us on a birding trip to El Faiyum, a desert village along the Nile south of Cairo. It was my best birding day, as I recorded a number of lifers, including little egret; Egyptian goose; little ringed plover; lapwing; slender-billed and black-headed gulls; lesser sand-plover; Senegal coucal; little green bee-eater; brown-necked raven; tawny pipit;

lesser whitethroat; and willow, reed, sedge, and fan-tailed warblers.

The following day, on a field trip with the entire group east of Cairo to see the Suez Canal area, I added a few additional species: squacco heron, marsh harrier, marsh sandpiper, white-breasted kingfisher, Thekla lark, and bluethroat.

It was my opinion that the Egyptian public couldn't care less about a natural park. The scattered garbage and noncaring attitude evident around the pyramids and other similar nationally significant cultural sites proved that. The only site we saw that was seminatural was a hunting refuge that looked more like an enlarged goat corral, and it was closed to the public. I was shocked at the lack of attention given wildlife throughout Egypt's arid landscape.

Spain, 1978

Immediately after Egypt, Roy Johnson and I, along with our wives, traveled on to Spain for a five-day visit, from November 14 to 18. The Spain visit, arranged by the NPS Office of International Affairs and Spain's ICONA, was designed to provide us with an overview of Coto Doñana National Park and to help the ICONA personnel, administrators of the park, with whatever assistance we might be able to provide.

Our orientation began with a brief meeting

with Jose Luis Aboal, chief of ICONA's section on national parks, and Duncan Clement, American embassy science attaché, at the Madrid airport. We afterward flew on to Seville, where Juan Garay and Fernando Garcia met us at the airport and remained with us through the next five days. They, along with various other park personnel, gave us a thorough tour of the area and provided up-to-date information about their program and plans for the future of Coto Doñana.

During the final afternoon of our stay we met with Dr. Juan de Aizpuru, park superintendent, and additional staff members to discuss measures we thought could benefit the preservation of Doñana's natural resources, and we received informal requests for assistance from the National Park Service. The assistance they most wanted involved personnel training of a few of Doñana's staff in methods of management, interpretation, and resource management and also included visits to comparable US parks, such as Everglades and Padre Island. Eventually, two Doñana interpreters did attend an NPS interpretive training session at the Mather Training Center.

We thoroughly enjoyed our stay in Spain. It seemed to us that Coto Doñana National Park was well run with a professional staff of twenty full-time employees, eighteen of whom had responsibilities ranging from law enforcement

Author and Betty Wauer with rangers at Doñana National Park, Spain, 1978

to resource management. The ninety-seven thousand–acre park itself was considered one of Europe's richest and most important natural resources. It is located in southern Spain at the mouth of the Guadalquivir River, which flows into the Mediterranean Sea just north of the

Strait of Gibraltar. Because of its geographic location, millions of Europe's migratory birds pass through the park each spring and fall. The park also contains a huge diversity of additional wildlife, including such threatened species as the Mediterranean lynx, white-faced duck, and imperial and short-toed eagles.

On the downside, we learned that Doñana was experiencing major developments along its borders, a tremendous population of red deer that was causing severe impacts to the vegetation, and a significant impact from pesticides used by adjacent rice farmers. I later discovered that part of the problem was that ICONA's mission to protect all the park's natural resources was in direct conflict with that of the National Institute of Agriculture Reform and Development (IRYDA), whose mission was to reclaim arable land. Their method was to encourage the use of pesticides and herbicides on private lands alongside parklands. These problems are likely to be resolved only with the acquisition of the adjacent farmlands to provide adequate buffers to the park's natural ecosystem.

Of course, I recorded all of the birds seen during our excursions in the field and around Doñana Palace, the park's research center and our base of operations, as well as around the resort town of Matalascañas, where we stayed. Perhaps the most common and widespread of the larger birds were red kites, somewhat like a reddish Mississippi kite. Magpies, the same species as our black-billed magpie, were fairly common and widespread as well. Some of the other birds in these areas included griffon vultures; quail; blue rock thrush; robin (the Eurasian species); white wagtail; black redstart; and Bonelli's, Dartford, and Sardinian warblers.

On three of our days in the park area we were given official field trips to three different regions, thus allowing us to see more of the park and to record whatever bird species we encountered. On November 15, we recorded 58 bird species along the park's northern border, 62 species within the southern marshlands on November 16, and 24 species in the northwestern corner of the park on November 17. Highlights included more than five hundred flamingos, thousands of graylag geese, and fewer numbers of red-crested pochards, marsh harriers, pin-tailed sandgrouse, nightingales, carrion crows, blue and great tits, skylarks, blackbirds, wood larks, and spotless starlings, plus lone grasshopper and Orphean warblers on November 15.

The birds of the day on November 16 were three imperial eagles, seen extremely well but from some distance. They reminded me of golden eagles but with pale shoulder patches and a faintly banded tail. And we had super looks at azure-rumped magpies, thinner than the other magpie and one of Spain's endemic species. In addition, we saw more than a hundred red-legged partridges, large chukarlike birds with black streaks on the chest. Other highlight species this day included white storks, ruddy shelducks, oystercatchers, green woodpeckers, and goldcrests. November 17 was not as productive, although we added greater and lesser spotted woodpecker, crested tit, brambling, and yellowhammer.

Betty and I loved Spain. The people were extremely friendly, the steam-brewed coffee was superb, and especially after having just spent a few days in Egypt, which was one of the most crowded and filthy places we ever visited, we found Spain to be clean, neat, and beautiful.

Alaska, July 12–27, 1979

Because of the anticipated additions to National Park Service lands in Alaska, as part of the Alaska National Interest Lands Conservation Act, Director Russ Dickinson asked me to go to Alaska and visit the proposed additions so that he would have "someone in the Washington Office with basic knowledge of the new areas." The Alaska legislation, consisting of 186 pages, was an unparalleled conservation act. It eventually was passed in the Senate, and Public Law 96-487 was signed by President Jimmy Carter on December 2, 1980. It set aside 44 million acres in thirteen units of the National

Park Service, it added twenty-five free-flowing Alaska rivers to the National Wild and Scenic River System, and the nation's wilderness system increased by 56.4 million acres.

Glacier Bay's Humpback Whales

When Alaska Regional Director John Cook learned that I was coming to Alaska, he asked me also to visit Glacier Bay National Park to assess the alleged impact that increased numbers of cruise ships entering the bay were having on humpback whales.

My first stop in Alaska, in company of John Dennis from my staff, was at Juneau on July 13 and on to Glacier Bay National Park the following morning. There we met with Superintendent John Chapman and his staff and received a briefing on what was considered a serious decline in summering humpbacks in direct correlation with increased cruise ship activity. They told us that the decline was brought to the park's attention by Juneau schoolteacher Charles Jurasz, who had spent thirteen consecutive summers in Glacier Bay fishing and photographing humpbacks. It was Jurasz, through his photography, who first learned to identify individual whales by the animal's fluke shapes, white pigmentation, and scarring patterns. He had even accumulated life histories of some individual Glacier Bay whales.

Historically, ten to twenty-four humpbacks

fed in the waters of Glacier Bay and its inlets most of each summer. Female humpbacks calve in warmer Pacific waters off the California and Mexico coasts but bring their calves north to Glacier Bay for the summer months to feed on the abundant fisheries. In 1978, Jurasz discovered that seventeen of the twenty known humpbacks in Glacier Bay abruptly departed the bay soon after entry. Jurasz reasoned that their departure was due to vessel disturbance, and it was his concern that created a stir within the National Park Service and my subsequent visit. After all, the humpback whale is a listed endangered species, and Glacier Bay whales represent about one-third of the approximately sixty individuals believed to summer in southeastern Alaska; the world's population was estimated to be four to five thousand. The humpback is the second rarest of the world's great whales and was a highly visible species, both politically and environmentally.

My involvement was primarily to assess Jurasz's credibility. So we spent two days together, including an overnight on his fishing boat out on the bay. There was no question about Jurasz's knowledge and enthusiasm, and I was soon convinced that his concern was a real one. That conviction was fortified when a whale breached nearby the boat in the early morning. Chuck stated that the breaching was due to one of the cruise ships starting a motor sixty miles

up the bay. When I questioned such an assumption, he radioed the ship and they stated that they had just started up. In my mind, that provided a direct correlation between humpbacks and cruise ships.

I also recorded all the birds seen during my visit, 52 species, of which Kittlitz's murrelet, tufted puffin, and spruce grouse were lifers. The dozens of Kittlitz's murrelets we saw across the bay were the most exciting, as this little pelagic species is unique among the world's seabirds because it is primarily associated with the Pleistocene-remnant coastal glaciers of the North Pacific. Glacier Bay is home to over 50 percent of the world's remaining breeding population. And because of global warming and the receding glaciers, it may be one of our most endangered species.

John and I next flew to Anchorage, where we visited with John Cook in the regional office. My recommendations, based on my Glacier Bay visit and the Endangered Species Act of 1973, which required the Park Service to take steps to avoid any action that causes harassment to endangered species or threatens their survival, were in three parts. First, contact the cruise ship industry and ask for a voluntary drawback of vessels to the 1976 level, before the time when humpback declines were first detected. Maintain that 1976 level until the following research is completed and guidelines are completed.

Glacier Bay and cruise ship, Alaska, 1979

Second, publish temporary regulations restricting the number of vessels entering the bay and prohibiting close approach to the whales. Third, initiate a series of research studies to determine adequate food availability, whale behavior relative to vessel movement and noise, and the bay's acoustic environment. The latter two topics would require consultation with the National Marine Fisheries Service (NMFS). John Cook agreed with my recommendations.

Shortly after my Alaska visit, I received a telephone call from Cook, reporting what he believed to be a positive discussion with the president of the cruise ship company, who agreed with John's suggestions. But a few months later, a second call informed me that Cook had been told by Secretary of Interior Watt that the cruise ship president had complained to him that Cook was trying to destroy his business and that he (Cook) was being transferred out of Alaska to be superintendent of Great Smoky Mountains National Park; that Cook's deputy director, Doug Warnock, was being transferred to be superintendent of Redwoods National Park; and that Glacier Bay superintendent, John Chapman, was being transferred to be the chief ranger at the Rocky Mountain Regional Office. All because Cook and company had done what they thought best for the park resources.

However, in spite of the personnel changes, most of the suggested research was undertaken during the next few years. And in June 1983, NMFS issued a biological opinion that stated in part: "If the amount of vessel use were allowed to increase without limit in Glacier Bay . . . the associated disturbance would be likely to jeopardize the continued existence of the Southeast Alaska humpback whale stock."

The National Park Service then established permanent regulations for protection of the humpbacks that limited the number of vessels that can enter the bay during the summer months and also prohibited the harvest of certain species of fish and crustaceans that are prey species of the humpbacks. In addition, the park hired a biologist whose responsibilities included monitoring the number of humpbacks that enter the park's waters, determining how long individuals remain, and recording feeding and social behavior.

Onward to Alaska's North Slope

Next was our trip to see more of Alaska, including the proposed park areas on the North Slope. We first drove from Anchorage to Denali National Park, where we spent time with Superintendent Frank Betts, Chief Ranger Gary Brown, and Resource Manager John Dalle-Molle. My initial impression of this park was that it was a truly magnificent area with incomparable scenery. However, the park was experiencing considerable abuse from the abundance of visitors at a few locations. The ninety-mile road from park headquarters to Wonder Lake bisects

Aerial view of Alaska Range, Alaska

Kurupa Lake and distant campsite, Gates of the Arctic, Alaska

My Wild Life

the park, providing opportunities for backpackers to wander throughout that could not help leading to major impacts on the wilderness values and dangerous people-bear interactions. The scenes at the Eielson Visitor Center and at Wonder Lake are more similar to those at Yosemite Valley and Fishing Bridge than in an Alaskan wilderness. I realized that it is physically easier, due to airline transportation, for most Americans to visit this park than it is to visit Yellowstone.

After three days at Denali we continued on to Fairbanks, where we briefly visited with Fred Dean at the University of Alaska about his various research pursuits in Denali and elsewhere in Alaska. And the next morning we boarded a Grumman Goose 789 aircraft, piloted by John Warner, to continue northward. We flew over thousands of acres of tundra, mountains, rivers, and lakes first to Bettles, north of the Arctic Circle; and then on to the Noatak; Gates of the Arctic; Kobuk Valley's dunes and Salmon River drainage; again over Noatak's Grand Canyon; and eventually to Cape Krusenstern. We saw lots of country but got little more than a poor understanding of the area's true significance. I did get a magnificent perspective of its grandness, vastness, and remoteness, but I had only minimal time on the ground. We did stop to visit Embryo Lake in the upper Noatak, Kurupa Lake in the northern edge of the Gates, and Tulugak Lake in the lower-middle Noatak Valley.

At each of these three overnight stops we pitched tents, spent numerous hours wandering over the tundra and climbing onto the adjacent hilltops, and discussing various natural resource issues. The most pertinent topics included the Northwest caribou herd, Alaska's fire-management program, and the lack of research personnel and insufficient funds for Alaska, especially for the new park units. At each lake, Bill Palleck, from the Alaska Regional Office, spent the first hour or so fishing for our dinners. Bill's daily catch was one of the true highlights of the trip!

I of course recorded all of the birds found at each site; there was sufficient light at that time of year to bird from very early morning until almost midnight. Some of the most impressive birds, for me, included a couple of Pacific loons; harlequin ducks, including a female with thirteen young; and rock ptarmigans, hoary redpolls, tree sparrows, Lapland longspurs, wheatears, and snow buntings.

After a day in Kotsebue and a visit to Cape Krusenstern, we flew south to Deering and over Chimisso Wilderness, where I spotted a white morph gyrfalcon directly below us. Then the following morning (July 26) we headed back to Anchorage.

State of the Parks

On my return from Alaska, I was informed that the National Park Service had received a request from Congressmen Phillip Burton and Keith G. Sebelius for a State of the Parks report to be due September 15, 1979. Recognizing the potential of such a report, I immediately checked with the NPS Congressional Liaison Office to find out who was expected to coordinate the report. I was informed that no one had yet been given the responsibility, and the various divisions were reluctant. When I volunteered, they were happy to pass it on.

After considerable discussion with my staff, we packaged a seven-part questionnaire that was sent to every national park unit for a response. Although there was initial foot-dragging by some of the parks, most recognized the opportunity to give greater visibility to their natural and cultural resource problems. From January to April 1980, some 310 park units provided a response that was then computerized. Printouts of each park's threats were sent to the appropriate regional offices so that the parks could make appropriate changes and return them; the revisions would serve as the original threats database.

State of the Parks—1980: A Report to the Congress was submitted to Congressmen Burton and Sebelius in May. And an additional two thousand copies were printed and sent to every member of the House and Senate park subcommittees, to every NPS region and park, and to other congressmen, the press, special-interest groups, and other interested persons on request. Fewer than forty copies were left. The media immediately picked up on the sorry conditions of the parks, and several hundred articles appeared in newspapers and magazines; throughout much of 1981 the issue continued to receive attention from the press, special-interest groups, and the public.

The most significant findings in our report stated that (1) park units representing all size and use categories, and all types of ecosystems, reported a wide range of threats affecting their resources. These threats, which emanate from both external and internal sources, are causing severe degradation of park resources. (2) A surprising 75 percent of the 4,345 reported threats to park resources have been classified by on-site park observers as inadequately documented by either private or government research; and (3) the Park Service must significantly expand its research and resource management capabilities to deal with known and suspected threats to park resources.

Throughout this process, I had been working closely with Destry Jarvis, of the National Parks Conservation Association (NPCA), and Clay Peters and Cleve Pinnix, staffers for Congressman Burton and Sebelius, respectively. Those three individuals had written the initial request for the State of the Parks report. And the four of us then developed an additional request to the Park Service, signed by Burton and Sebelius, for a follow-up report that (1) would further analyze the findings, (2) describe short-term preservation/mitigation actions under way and anticipated, and (3) describe a long-term prevention/mitigation plan.

In July and August, after receiving the request for the follow-up report, I established a Threats to Parks Working Group to help guide this second effort. Members included George Gardner, Craig Shafer, and John Dennis from my office; Audrey Dixon, Science Projects; Al Vietl, Ranger Activities and Protection; Doug Scovill and Hugh Miller, Cultural Resources; Ed Drotos and Stan Lock, National Capital Region; Phil Metzger, Interior Department Office of Policy; Bill Shands, Conservation Foundation; and Destry Jarvis, NPCA. The group met four times and established generic prevention/mitigation activities for input into a response.

A second request for information to every national park was sent on August 26, and responses were incorporated into a revised Threats Information Management System in November. And on January 2, 1981, the "State of the Parks: A Report to the Congress on a Servicewide Strategy for Prevention and Mitigation on Natural and Cultural Resources Management Problems" was submitted to Congressmen Burton and Sebelius. This report provided a short- and midrange strategy for pre-

vention and mitigation of park threats, as well as a rather extensive listing of various activities under way and planned within the parks. The new chairman of the Subcommittee on Public Lands and National Parks, Representative John E. Seiberling, acknowledged the report on February 18. And on March 4, Senator Henry M. Jackson asked for additional details about mitigation activities by the NPS from Secretary Watt. Watt's response included a commitment for monthly progress reports, although I was told to stop these within a few months.

Perhaps the most significant program included in the second report was the establishment of natural resource management training, both for current employees such as superintendents and midlevel employees, and a new Natural Resource Management Trainee Program. This latter program was designed to increase the number of professional natural resource management specialists in the field. By October 1982, participating parks had selected thirty-seven trainees to go through an extensive two-year training program. This program continued for a number of years, and Resource Management Divisions have since become a reality in the majority of the national parks. I believe that this program was one of my more significant accomplishments during my career in the National Park Service.

Also in conjunction with the prevention/

First Natural Resource Management Program trainees
(author is seated in front center; Jon Jarvis is to his left), 1982

mitigation report preparation, my staff completed a system for ranking all of the identified resource problems (significant resource problems, or SRPs) to be used in a problem identification workshop scheduled for mid-February. That February 18–19 workshop, part of a regional directors' meeting in Washington, D.C., established a list of forty-three SRPs, categorized as "minimal essential." The result was a

$10 million add-on to the NPS fiscal year 1983 budget for SNR projects, and Congress appropriated an additional $750,000 for regional science programs.

The Threats to the Parks initiative provided significant gains in the Park Service's ability to identify and prescribe corrective actions for threatened resources; however, follow-up monitoring of the program declined precipitously

Barro Colorado
Island dock, Panama

once I and a few other key individuals moved on to other assignments.

Nevertheless, the George Wright Society, an organization established to encourage good natural and cultural resources management within the national parks, presented me with the Francis H. Jacot Memorial Award at its meeting on November 16, 1988. The award was "For Outstanding Contribution to and Enhancement of Natural Resources Management Programs within National Parks and Reserves." It was presented by the president of the society, Christine Schonewald-Cox, and the conference chairperson, R. Roy Johnson.

Panama, June 1979

The trip to a conference in Panama took place after the initial State of the Parks questionnaires were sent to the parks and before the responses arrived. The five-day conference, "Technical Meeting on Conservation of Migratory Animals of the Western Hemisphere and Their Ecosystems," was sponsored by the Organization of American States. I found it to be worthwhile regarding the contacts but of little value to me as a representative of the National Park Service.

I was able to spend two early mornings birding the immediate area of Panama City. And on day four we visited Barro Colorado Island, where we were able to spend a few hours bird-ing on the trails near the research station. A few of the birds encountered along the trails included double-toothed kite, crested guan, violaceous trogon, plain-brown woodcreeper, plain zenops, slaty antshrike, checkered-throated and white-flanked antwrens, spotted antbird, forest elaenia, lesser greenlet, red-throated anttanager, and white-shouldered and gray-headed tanagers.

Barro Colorado contains an impressive mature forest with minimum human impact. Operated by the Smithsonian Institution, the island serves as a control area for the surrounding area of Panama, which has some major developments. My birding companions, who seemed more interested in seeing birds than participating in the various sessions, included Earl Baysinger, Richard Fyfe, Eugene Morton, and Robert Pasquale.

Mountain Lions and New Mexico Ranchers

In September 1981, Under Secretary of Interior Arnett received a letter from William S. Huey, secretary of New Mexico Natural Resources Department, requesting permission for New Mexico employees to pursue and destroy mountain lions in Carlsbad Caverns National Park. According to Huey, local ranchers had complained that lions from Carlsbad Caverns were killing sheep outside the park and then returning to the park. Arnett told Director Dickinson to prepare a letter giving that permission; the responsibility for preparing a response landed on my desk.

I immediately visited with Associate Director Stan Albright about a modified approach to Arnett's order for full concurrence, although Dickinson had stated that there had been earlier examples of such cooperation between NPS and various states. But I was unsure how sincere Dickinson was about this. I thought it would be appropriate to postpone such clear-cut concurrence as long as possible. So, along with my assistant Bill Supernaugh, who coordinated wildlife issues, I responded with a draft letter to Huey from Arnett that expressed concern about livestock losses in New Mexico but included a statement about NPS policy regarding the killing of wildlife within the parks. Arnett was not happy about my initial draft, as well as a second-draft letter, and then stated that he wanted to give clear-cut permission. He finally signed a third letter that he dictated on January 26, 1982, which included the following steps:

1. A cooperative agreement between the National Park Service and the State of New Mexico will be prepared and executed.
2. The Service will undertake a research program to determine the population density, range, territory, and related information on lion ecology. The State will be a full cooperator in the design implementation and completion of this phase of the program.
3. A noted lion investigator will be contracted by the Park Service to initially collar lions for the research project. The research will be a joint effort between the State of New Mexico and National Park Service and will be closely coordinated with local ranchers.
4. At the end of a 2-year research effort, the Service will develop a lion management plan implementing the results and recommendations of the jointly developed program.

The Southwest Regional Office immediately prepared a Request for Proposals for an ecological study of mountain lions in the vicinity of Carlsbad Caverns and Guadalupe Mountains National Parks. Estimated price was not to exceed $30,000.

The Park Service also responded to a tort claim by Arthur Hughes of Carlsbad for "property damage in the amount of $26,000," alleging that "an undetermined number of mountain lions residing within the Park . . . left the Park, entering claimant's ranch in the State of New Mexico, and killed 400 lambs and 100 ewes belonging to the claimant."

As might be expected, the media picked up

on the controversy, and it wasn't long before several newspapers carried articles pro and con. For instance, the title of Byron Spice's *Albuquerque Journal* article of January 29, 1982, was "Mountain Lions Lose Hideaway at Carlsbad Park." Spice quoted rancher David Kincaid that he had lost 150 sheep to three mountain lions during three weeks in June, that "it was going on every night," with the mountain lions killing 10, 15, 20 sheep at a time.

Sometime in late February I visited with Laura Loomis (NPCA) about this issue. I expressed concern about what could possibly force the Park Service into making a change in policy regarding the full protection of wildlife within the parks. NPCA then submitted a Freedom of Information request for a full set of related documents between the secretary of the Interior and New Mexico Natural Resources Department. And on April 2, Brant Calkins, Southwest representative of the Sierra Club, representing his organization; NPCA; and the Defenders of Wildlife hand-carried a letter to NPS Southwest Regional Director Kerr that stated: "We are reviewing the steps necessary to file litigation if any hunting of mountain lions is contemplated by the National Park Service, any state agency, or any individual." The letter also stated: "Again, we remind you that the killing of any mountain lion would be illegal, and we ask you to deny or rescind any approval of such killing."

By late April two draft documents were circulated for review, a Memorandum of Understanding and an Environmental Assessment/ Finding of No Significant Impact. And on May 26, 1982, the Sierra Club and Defenders of Wildlife filed a suit in the US District Court for the District of New Mexico against James G. Watt and G. Ray Arnett, stating that the "Plaintiffs seek judgment declaring that defendants' actions in permitting mountain lions to be trapped, tracked and killed in, or removed from, Carlsbad Caverns and Guadalupe Mountains National Parks in New Mexico and Texas are unlawful." The purpose was to block the proposed Memorandum of Understanding, which would allow state trappers to enter the national parks to kill lions.

By fall 1982, letters from interested citizens and various congressmen begin to arrive, all in support of wildlife protection within the parks. And by October, Michael K. Deaver, deputy chief of staff and assistant to the president, asked the secretary of the Interior for details. The response to that request stated that the National Park Service had already initiated the first phase of the two-year research project and that no control action will take place until a public review of the environmental assessment and a Memorandum of Understanding are completed.

Because this issue became so controversial, a full Environmental Impact Statement was essential. Although the document was completed and received much public attention, it was never fully approved. The entire issue died during 1983.

Grizzly Bears

In early 1981, I was informed that I was to chair the Interagency Grizzly Bear Steering Committee, a group consisting of representatives from the National Park Service, US Forest Service, US Fish and Wildlife Service, and the states of Idaho, Montana, and Wyoming. Members included Superintendent John Townsley and Dick Knight, Interagency Grizzly Bear Study Team (IGBST), from Yellowstone, and Regional Chief Scientist Neil Reid, all from NPS; Regional Forester Craig Rupp and Roger Bay, Intermountain Forest and Range Experimental Station, from USFS; John Spinks, Office of Endangered Species, and Chris Servheen, Grizzly Bear Recovery Coordinator, from USFWS; Lloyd Oldenburg, Idaho Fish and Game Department; Eugene Allen, Montana Fish and Game Department; and Earl Thomas, Wyoming Game and Fish Department. I held my first meetings in Denver on March 12–13, 1981.

Ted Sudia had been the previous chairman, and on my appointment it was necessary to catch up with the purpose and background of this group in a hurry. I visited with Ted about his earlier activity and was impressed with his perspective. I already was aware, of course, that grizzly bear populations had severely declined in recent years, but I was not prepared for the politics involved. As background, I learned that grizzly bear numbers had declined in the past 280 years from 50,000 bears occupying the entire area west of the Mississippi River to fewer than 1,000 bears occurring in only six isolated localities. Of these six places, only two, the Yellowstone and the Northern Continental Divide ecosystems, contained populations that were still large enough to exist in a self-perpetuating condition. Because of this drastic decline in population, and because of serious ongoing and predictable threats to grizzly bear habitat caused by human needs for resource use and land development, the grizzly population in the lower forty-eight states had been listed as a Threatened Species under provisions of the Endangered Species Act.

Of the fewer than 1,000 grizzlies in the coterminous states, approximately 200 to 350 lived in the Yellowstone ecosystem. Management of these bears had evoked a great deal of controversy during recent years, spurring several actions: (1) the initiation in 1973 of a six-agency Interagency Grizzly Bear Study Team to study the bears and their habitats and to provide information that would support effective decision making; (2) the convening in 1974 of a National Academy of Sciences committee to review the status of the Yellowstone

Dick Knight collaring a grizzly at Yellowstone National Park

My Wild Life

grizzly bear population; (3) the inclusion of this population as a Threatened Species in 1975; (4) the cooperative preparation in 1979 of joint guidelines for managing grizzlies in the Yellowstone ecosystem; (5) the preparation in 1980 of a draft Grizzly Bear Recovery Plan, which stated that an all-out, concerted effort must be taken if the status of the grizzlies is to be improved and which also suggested specific steps to be taken, including an interagency enforcement capability and a monitoring system to address population trends; and (6) a December 1980 technical review of the results of, and a recommendation for, the future of the IGBST.

The March 1981 Steering Committee recommended the continuance of the current study through 1988, to place as many radio collars as possible on bears during 1983 and 1984, especially subadults and females, and to monitor the collared bears during the following three to four years. We also recommended a change in the composition of the Steering Committee by adding three federal land managers from NPS, USFWS, and USFS, and Recovery Plan Coordinator Chris Servheen. The regional offices of the NPS and USFWS had requested greater involvement in decision making, in spite of each already having representation on the committee.

And in August 1981, Representative Mike Williams and Senators Seiberling and Ryan held an Interior Subcommittee Hearing on grizzly bear management at Glacier National Park, which I attended. Joe Cutter, a resident of West Yellowstone, spoke at the hearing:

Right this minute, within two hundred miles of Yellowstone, there are at least five hundred illegal grizzly bear claws being offered for sale to those folks whose vogue is festooning their person with these gee-gaws. . . . They were obtained by poachers working around the park's borders, and in one case, actually heisting a live bear from inside the park. . . . In the past thirty days alone, I personally have reported to the US Fish and Wildlife Service Enforcement Division, either in face-to-face meetings, by telephone, or through contacts, twelve flagrant violations. . . . For example: three bear carcasses, one of which was a large grizzly, hanging in a frozen-meat locker at a restaurant less than twenty miles from Yellowstone's west gate. A trayful of approximately thirty grizzly claws on sale in the showcase of an Ennis, Montana, sporting goods store. An Indian jewelry dealer in Bozeman, Montana, who purchased two sets of grizzly claws from an Idaho/Targhee National Forest sheepman. A man in the vicinity of Quake Lake who is offering not only an impressive selection of grizzly claws but two dozen eagle talons and an assortment of eagle feathers. An individual in Cooke City, Montana, who was offering three grizzly hides and telling prospective customers that he could get anything they wanted in grizzly parts.

A follow-up investigation of these and other reports by "undercover" USFWS officers only caused the sales of grizzly parts and related activities to move underground.

On September 8, 1981, Secretary Arnett requested a briefing on the overall grizzly bear program. Arnett seemed pleased with my briefing, but there was no known follow-up. On August 17, 1982, in a memorandum to members of the Steering Committee, I wrote:

> Evidence persists that the population of grizzly bears within the greater Yellowstone ecosystem has seriously declined in recent years. Unless some change occurs to reduce the grizzly's mortality rate soon, the probability of retaining this wildland species in Yellowstone National Park is minimal. . . . The IGBST is reasonably certain that today's population is less than 200 individual grizzlies. . . . Solution: We no longer have the luxury of time to research the remaining parts of the puzzle. The Yellowstone grizzly bear picture is presently sufficiently clear enough! Any additional delays in mitigation, actions that the bear management community has known it must take for several years, will likely result in the loss of grizzly bears from the greater Yellowstone ecosystem. It is imperative that highest priority be given to eliminating grizzly bear mortality. Only immediate and broadscale protection can save the grizzly. Increased protection efforts must be united by all of the pertinent land managers. Without it we will only be documenting the demise of the grizzly bear within the Yellowstone ecosystem.

My memorandum to Steering Committee members was cleared by the NPS director. And I also provided copies to friends in NPCA who "leaked" it to the press, creating considerable public and Interior Department concern. I was fortunate to be on a trip to Mexico when Arnett called for me to report to his office. Within two weeks, the *New York Times* reported that the Yellowstone grizzly was "imperiled." On October 6, the National Park System Advisory Board Chairman Robin Winks sent a letter to Secretary Watt stating their "deep concern for a progressive decline of the grizzly bear in the Yellowstone ecosystem and other occupied habitats south of the Canadian border. . . . This Board regards it as imperative that the National Park Service intensify in every possible way its program of protective management of grizzly bear habitat in Yellowstone and Glacier National Parks."

By October 1982, when the Steering Committee met to review recent activities, committee responsibilities had been limited to deal only with research within the Yellowstone ecosystem. Chris Servheen chaired that meeting, and my role was limited. Although the Steering

Lüneburger Heide Nature Park, Germany, 1983

Committee met again in November to approve the proposed 1983 research program, in December when the three federal regional directors met with the three state governors, they agreed on restructuring the interagency committees "so that there would be fewer committees and one which will possess greater management authority to approve specific activities within the Yellowstone and Northern ecosystems," according to my memo of December 8 to the NPS director. My involvement with the Interagency Grizzly Bear Steering Committee came to an end.

Germany, 1983

From June 5 to 15, 1983, I participated, as the lone NPS representative, in the "International Working Conference—New Directions for Conservation of Parks" held in West Germany. The conference was co-sponsored by the National Parks Conservation Association, the Federation of Nature and National Parks of Europe, and the Northern Germany National Conservation Academy (NGNCA). Coordinators of the workshop were Paul Pritchard (NPCA), Henry Makoski (Lüneburger Heide Nature Park), and Hans Kopp (NGNCA). All participants were guests of Industrialist Alfred Toepfer, chairman of a private benefit organization dedicated to conserve Lüneburger Heide Nature Park.

All the working sessions were conducted at Lüneburger Heide Nature Park, and field trips were taken to Lauenberg Lakes Nature Park near Hamburg; Wassensea National Park near Bredstedt, at the northern tip of West Germany; and, during the final five days, Bayerischer Wald National Park, in the southeastern corner of West Germany.

The main purpose of the conference was to discuss methods of safeguarding and enhancing Europe's natural areas. Germany had sixty-four parks, but only two were national parks, while the remainder were nature parks with multiple uses and are considered to be "managed landscapes." No virgin forests exist in Germany, and all forests are managed for the production of timber. It was the first time that I understood my father's perception of beauty. He was born in Dresden and spent his first twelve years in an area where even the forests were arranged. That did not, however, limit his love of the outdoors, and my love of nature was undoubtedly a result of his influence.

One of the most interesting workshops, "Nature and National Parks and Equivalent Reserves," was led by Dr. Joe Sax, University of Michigan, who discussed differences and similarities between US and European systems. Differences include that (1) most European countries are small, the size of many US states; (2) most US protected areas are much larger than European areas; the average European preserve is less than one thousand hectares; (3)

one-third of all US parklands was first owned by federal or state governments, but almost all European lands are privately owned; (4) a good part of the United States (the West and Alaska) was relatively undisturbed, but European lands have all been previously used; and (5) the US park system is an old one (1872) with set standards and laws firmly established; this is not true for most European parks.

Similarities between US and European systems include that (1) both controlling "Departments" have conflicting missions; (2) both possess a wide range of area types from protected to full recreational uses; (3) both experience international conflicts; and (4) both are experiencing increasing recreational use demands.

I gave presentations during two of the eight workshops. In "Nature Conservation in Parks," I gave a talk on the evolution of resource management in the US national parks, and in "Interpretation in Parks," I presented a summary of interpretation that outlined five levels of interpretation/information. The workshops were, in my opinion, excellent, and I came away with a much better understanding of national park management as it applies outside the United States.

But I must admit that I most enjoyed what little outdoor time was available during the workshops and the considerable outdoor time during the field trips. My bird list at the end of the meeting included 128 species, many of

which were lifers. Some of my most memorable sightings were at Lüneburger Heide Nature Park. Those included a singing male cuckoo that repeated its "cuckoo" song over and over; tawny owls that I first heard (like a great horned owl) but then had a close-up view a few days later; a white-tailed eagle, closely related to our bald eagle but without the white head; a green woodpecker feeding on the ground like a flicker; meadow pipits singing in flight; a pair of crested tits feeding young in a cavity in a birch tree; a black redstart that was much more colorful than the illustrations in my field guide; and a bullfinch male in full breeding plumage.

On our trip to the North Sea, lapwings were numerous, and I had a number of close-up sightings. What a strange-looking shorebird! At Bredstedt, the birds of the day were a pair of ruffs, the male with a majestic white ruff, and several male tufted ducks with long tufts. And at Bayerischer Wald National Park, I had my only sightings of a kingfisher, a little blue and green bird, and a dipper, very different from our American dipper, a reddish bird with a snow-white throat.

The last evening we all were treated to an outdoor barbecue at Bayerischer, where we drank schnapps and beer and had good conversation. Several German women dressed in local costume were serving beer from coolers in colorful German mugs. But each refilling took several minutes to let the beer settle to eliminate the foam. But at one point I filled my own mug, simply tilting the mug to let the beer flow slowly with the minimum of foam. When one of the women observed this, she turned to another and remarked, "Look how he is doing that." Apparently, filling a mug in that manner had never been seen before.

England

En route home from Germany, I stopped for a few days in London; Betty flew in from Maryland to join me. From June 17 to 22, we played tourist in London and the adjacent countryside, visiting the Royal Botanic Gardens at Kew, Stonehenge, and Bath. Some of the most memorable sites visited in London included Buckingham Palace, where we saw the changing of the guard, the Houses of Parliament, Westminster Abbey and Cathedral, and the Tower of London. It was one of our most enjoyable vacations.

Although we spent very little time searching for birds, I did keep a list of all the birds seen while in Great Britain, a total of 43 species. Most were only duplicates of what I already had seen in Germany. The only lifer was a pied wagtail at the gardens at Kew. Very much like a white wagtail, it is mostly confined to the British Isles but does occur sporadically along the northern European coastlines.

Transition

During the first few months of 1983, I became painfully aware that I needed a change; an additional reorganization in which I was to be reassigned under Associate Director Richard Briceland was taking a toll. A Washington Office reorganization had occurred in 1982, placing my office under Associate Director Stan Albright, but Arnett was now intent on moving it back under Briceland. His way of dealing with Wauer! I visited with Director Russ Dickinson, longtime friend from the Zion days, who fully understood my concern. He postponed my reassignment and told me to hang tough, that he would arrange a comparable field assignment as soon as possible. I also contacted John Cook at Great Smoky Mountains about my situation, and very soon he offered me an assistant superintendent position at the Smokies. Betty and I decided that it would be wise to take that job, to get out of the puzzle palace as soon as possible.

Arrangements were soon in place for a transfer, and I moved to Tennessee in May. My official reassignment as assistant superintendent for resource management and science did not, however, take place until October 2, 1983. There were people and places in the D.C. area that we would miss, but we looked forward to being in a park environment again.

9
Great Smoky Mountains National Park, Tennessee and North Carolina

Great Smoky Mountains National Park is the most visited park in the entire National Park System. It is the premier national park in the eastern United States! It contains a highly diverse natural environment, including more than sixteen hundred kinds of flowering plants and one hundred tree species. Vegetation is divided into cove hardwood forests, hemlock forests, northern hardwood forests, spruce-fir forests, closed oak forests, and open oak and pine stands. In addition, the highland "balds" are unique and a significant environment in their own right.

The Smoky Mountains wildlife is equally diverse, including fifty kinds of mammals and two hundred kinds of birds. The two megafaunal species—black bear and white-tailed deer—get most of the attention, but the park also contains several endangered or threatened species.

There is little doubt about the biological sig-nificance of the Great Smoky Mountains, but the traffic can be horrendous during much of the year, especially when crossing the mountains between Tennessee and North Carolina. And the entrance highway on the Tennessee side, between Sevierville and park headquarters, can be jammed all summer. In spite of the crowds in and around the park, once a hiker is a mile or so away from the highways, the number of people encountered declines rapidly. My problem with hiking the park's superb trail system, including the Appalachian Trail, is that there are so many streams, so much running water, that hearing bird songs at any distance is nearly impossible.

We decided to buy a house in Sevierville rather than Pigeon Forge or Gatlinburg, so we had a fifteen-mile daily commute. But Sevierville was far less touristy than Pigeon Forge and Gatlinburg, and the house was just what we needed on the edge of town and with a great backyard. The Sevierville house was our favorite of all the houses we have lived in. And while living there, we developed good friends in the Pigeon Forge and Gatlinburg communities, especially Stu and Pat Coleman, John and Dani Cook, and Pat Miller. Sevierville also offered greater accessibility to Knoxville and other areas in Tennessee.

The Job

Park headquarters, where my office was located, was at Sugarlands, just inside the park in a gorgeous setting among a cove hardwood forest. My position, however, as one of two assistant superintendents, was my most boring assignment throughout my Park Service career. The two divisions within my responsibilities— science and resource management—had very capable chiefs, and I felt that I was little more than an interloper. John Piene was my chief scientist, head of the Uplands Lab, and Stu Coleman was my chief of resource management. I got along very well with both of them, as well as the various employees within each division, especially Bill Cook, wildlife biologist and fisherman, and Peter White, botanist.

My relationship with Jerry Eubanks, the other assistant superintendent, was not as comfortable, although Jerry was extremely kind and helpful. He had been the only assistant before I arrived, and because I had had a long relationship with Superintendent John Cook, who had gone out of his way to help me escape the Washington, D.C., scene, it was only natural to have created some animosity. Jerry had previously supervised both John Piene and Stu Coleman.

Because I believed that my two divisions were in good hands, I turned my principal attention to managing the Biosphere Reserve program. Great Smoky Mountains National Park was a principal component of that program, along with adjacent US Forest Service areas that were coordinated by John McCrone, professor at Western Carolina University. John and I agreed completely with the goal and steps necessary to strengthen this multiagency program.

In addition, because of my recent involvement with the State of the Parks program, in which all the parks had assessed their resource threats, I set up a workshop in which fifteen staff members participated. I asked Gary Machlis, University of Idaho, to coordinate the workshop. Utilizing the "Nominal Group Technique," we were able to examine each of the park's forty-three reported threats and rank them to help determine management priorities. The five highest rankings were given to (1) lack of exotic plant and animal management, (2) the need to

Visitor center and park headquarters, Great Smoky Mountains National Park

Black bear high in tree, Cades Cove, Great Smoky Mountains National Park

set and communicate priorities on workforce and funds, (3) air quality impacts, (4) lack of adequate commitment to resource management by management, and (5) inadequate database for resource management.

These combined data provided some important insights into both priority setting and staff concerns and attitudes. The data also revealed that some portion of the park's problems may have related to inadequate information transfer and understanding of the issues and actions under way and anticipated. Although many of the park's resource problems related to external politics or inadequate funding, many were internal and the result of either inappropriate priority setting or a lack of communication or training. The exercise provided me with greater insight into what I could do to give better guidance for resource protection. I, therefore, spent more efforts on the completion of the park's Resource Management Plan (RMP). It seemed strange to me that I was actually involved with writing (revising) a plan for which I had written the original guidelines years earlier. Prior to my guidelines, NPS had required Scientific Research Plans (SRPs) for some of the larger natural parks; a half dozen or so of those plans had been completed. But my RMP guidelines incorporated what I considered the best of the SRPs into a new, more management-oriented plan that could better benefit management and thus be better accepted. The revised RMP placed major emphasis on the park's black bears, wild hogs, and protection of the unique habitats.

Black Bears

Bears were a constant concern because of the potential interface with visitors. They are extremely smart and opportunistic and would readily take advantage of any food that a camper or hiker might not secure. Although all of the park's campsites and key visitor use sites contained "bear-proof" garbage cans, backcountry campsites were not always so well provisioned. The Park Service also had placed high-line cables between two trees at several of the sites so that campers could hoist their packs high overhead out of a bear's reach. However, some bears had learned to climb one of the trees and to reach a pack by going hand-over-hand on the cable; they would then search the pack for whatever goodies might be available.

Most of the park's adult bears weighed between 200 and 300 pounds, although there is a park record of one individual that weighed in at 550 pounds. And they could be found throughout the park and at all elevations, but they were most numerous around areas of human use, such as campsites. Long-term research by Mike Pelton, University of Tennessee, suggested that the park's bear population was around fifteen hundred individuals. Although bears generally sleep a good deal during the winter months, they are not true hibernators, so they occasionally were found wandering about in winter. They normally return to their den without feeding. Females, however, spent most of their wintertime in dens, where their cubs are born.

Because of our concern about a potential bear attack, most probably if they were fed or teased, Park Service employees in the backcountry usually carried Halt, a strong macelike spray that when sprayed into the face of a wild animal can strongly irritate its eyes, nose, and skin. We believed that it was best for animals to develop a fear of human beings so they were unlikely to become too friendly. My one incident of using Halt occurred when I was hiking the Appalachian Trail with Pat Miller. We had stopped for lunch, and I was leaning against a tree eating a sandwich when I suddenly realized, heard more than anything else, that a bear was just behind me less than five feet away. It undoubtedly had been attracted to my food and had approached with no warning. On seeing it so near out of the corner of my eye, I grabbed my Halt, swiveled around, and sprayed the bear directly in the eyes. It immediately backed off, grunted, rolled once or twice, and ran off into the woods. In about a half hour, however, we found it feeding alongside an old log, presumably not the worse for wear. But it immediately ran away when it saw us watching it.

Bears have always been an important part of the Smoky Mountains ecosystem. And we discovered that the local Native Americans used bear parts in many ways, from food to clothing and ceremonial activities. We experienced this firsthand when we were invited to the Cherokee Pow Wow in Cherokee, North Carolina, in June

1985. Several members of the Park Service staff were special guests of the Cherokee community. We enjoyed most of the activities, the storytelling and dances, but the exception was the evening dinner. The Cherokees utilized bear grease in the majority of their foods. Betty and I had a really difficult time swallowing anything with bear grease.

Wild Hogs

Introduced European wild boar for hunting in 1962 was one of the park's principal threats, affecting all its truly significant natural systems. Hog numbers, estimated at about five hundred animals within the park, were already great, and it was obvious that the hogs were there to stay. My feeling was that it was better to protect some of the park's most significant resources, by fencing, for instance, than to spend valuable funds and labor in a massive reduction effort that may produce some results but was hardly worth the effort in the long term. Current control efforts included both trapping and direct reduction (killing) by park personnel, and on the North Carolina portion of the park local hunters received permits to trap hogs and utilize the meat.

Once introduced into the park, these wild creatures began to interbreed with feral domestic pigs, producing an extremely wild and aggressive hybrid. They are also extremely prolif-ic, able to produce two broods of three to eight piglets annually. They reach sexual maturity in about eighteen months. And they are able to subsist on almost anything, from plant life, including roots that are dug up, to a wide diversity of animal life. They can feed on invertebrates as well as any vertebrate they can catch. And they have no natural enemies, although young occasionally fall prey to bears and bobcats. The only worthwhile control is direct shooting or trapping.

Mountain Lion Survey

Although mountain lions had once resided within the park, none had been recorded for many years. But rumors of lions persisted. Many of the locals swore that lions lived within the park, coming outside at night to kill livestock. After searching for telltale signs along the Appalachian Trail, without finding any lion tracks, kills, or other evidence, I decided to ask my old friend Roy McBride to visit the Smokies to find evidence that lions still existed in the park. I contacted Roy in West Texas and asked him if he would be willing to come to the Smokies to resolve this issue once and for all. Roy had studied mountain lion populations in the Big Bend Country, and I knew that if anyone could find lions, he could. The Park Service funded Roy's travel, accommodations, and expenses for a ten-day survey. He thoroughly covered the park, especially the Appalachian Trail, where lions would most likely be found, but he found no evidence of mountain lions. Other NPS employees and I were fully convinced that mountain lions no longer existed in the Great Smoky Mountains.

Avian Population Studies

Because of the impacts from wild hogs on the park's nature resources, I initiated breeding-bird studies at three key sites. All three possessed either (1) unique, rare, or endangered species and/or habitats; (2) significant undisturbed habitats; (3) large intact natural systems; or (4) especially fragile flora and/or fauna and required species attention if they were to be perpetuated. The park staff already had listed these as Special Protection Sites (SPSs).

Three of the SPSs—Abrams Creek Floodplain (ACF) in Cades Cove and two Beech Gap sites, West Beech Gap (WBG) and East Beech Gap (EBG) near Indian Gap along the Clingmans Dome Road—were considered "severely" threatened by wild hogs. All three sites were to be fenced in fall 1984, using thirty-eight-inch "hog fencing" that permitted small wildlife, such as birds, rabbits, foxes, and rodents, to pass through the mesh and larger wildlife, such as deer and bears, to go over the top. The sites, intended as demonstration areas, were accessible to the public, and interpretive signs were

Wild hog, Great Smoky Mountains National Park

Hog fencing along Appalachian Trail, Great Smoky Mountains National Park

installed at strategic places along the fence. The Beech Gap fence was installed so that it crossed the Appalachian Trail, forcing hikers to walk through one end of the exclosure itself.

My three study plots were laid out and marked with flagging prior to the 1984 breeding-bird season and installation of the fencing. Birds were censused on the 5-hectare ACF site for 2 hours nine times (total of 18 on-site hours) between April 10 and June 10. I censused each of the two 1.5-hectare WBG and EBG sites for 1.5 hours on eleven occasions (total of 16.5 on-site hours each) between June 2 and July 29. All censuses were undertaken between 6:00 and 9:30 a.m., by slowly walking the center lines and back and forth to the sides of the units with occasional stops for better bird identification as necessary. All avian species and their activities detected were recorded on field sampling forms and later transferred to permanent summary sheets to illustrate the number of individuals detected within the study sites.

Results of my surveys revealed that of the 41 bird species recorded within the ACF study site, only 12 were found to breed on-site: yellow-billed cuckoo, downy and pileated woodpeckers, Acadian and great crested flycatchers, blue jay, Carolina chickadee, tufted titmouse, white-breasted nuthatch, blue-gray gnatcatcher, red-eyed vireo, and brown-headed cowbird. The additional 23 species were considered to breed nearby, and 6 species were transients. The actual mean population of the 41 species recorded on nine censuses on ACF was 24.08, but the adjusted density (to 40 hectares) amounted to 191.5.

A total of 15 species were recorded within the WBG study site. Six of these were found to be breeding: hairy woodpecker, black-capped chickadee, red-breasted nuthatch, solitary vireo, black-throated green warbler, and dark-eyed junco. An additional 6 species were considered to breed nearby, and 3 species were transients. The actual mean population of the 15 species was 23.46, but the adjusted density was 610.2.

A total of 16 species were recorded within the EBG site. Seven of these were found breeding: hairy woodpecker, black-capped chickadee, red-breasted nuthatch, American robin, solitary vireo, black-throated green warbler, and dark-eyed junco. Six additional species were considered nearby breeders, and 3 species were transients. The actual mean population of the 16 species was 18.72, and adjusted density was 486.6.

Population totals suggested that, in spite of the greater number of birds recorded on the ACF, the Beech Gaps possessed a much higher avian density. These data provided valuable insight into the significance of Beech Gap communities within the Southern Appalachians. My study could easily be replicated for future comparisons. The differences between my 1984 baseline and future studies can contribute worthwhile information on the impact of wild hogs. That difference may help explain or justify continuance of hog control in the short- and long-term resource management programs at Great Smoky Mountains National Park.

In spite of being bored with the job, we enjoyed a number of activities available to us in the Smokies. We thoroughly enjoyed our visits to Silver Dollar City, later to be bought by Dolly Parton and renamed Dollywood, because of the music and crafts. We actually bought season tickets and took in the Silver Dollar City ambience as often as possible.

In addition, we traveled to a number of other places of interest during our three years in the Smokies: Nashville for music and a place to take visiting kids and parents; Asheville, North Carolina, for a couple of meetings and to enjoy the ambience; and nearby Knoxville and the University of Tennessee. At UT I worked with the local television crew in developing a program about the Biosphere Reserve program, which was utilized as an educational program for the various communities and the Park Service and Forest Service employees.

Finally, on one of Betty's trips back to visit kids in Texas, she brought along a tiny beagle puppy that she had purchased when we lived in the D.C. area. She said that if you ever want lots of attention, bringing a cute beagle puppy with you works very well. Because of the beagle's behavior of tugging on all sorts of things, including socks when your shoes were off, we named him Tug. He had a typical beagle personality, enthusiastic and rambunctious, but with his own set of ideas. Tug was also smart and could learn. After moving to Sevierville, I taught him to retrieve the newspaper on the walkway in front of the house. On one morning when I let him outside to fetch the paper, I told him to pee. Without any more encouragement he ran to the paper, lifted his leg, and peed on the paper. Then he wouldn't bring the paper in. I had to go fetch it myself.

Transition

One of my colleagues in the Southeast Regional Office, Jay Gogue, was fully aware that I was not satisfied with my situation at the Smokies; I remained bored and underutilized. Jay suggested a possible assignment in the Caribbean. The secretary of the Interior had recently informed the Park Service that it should be involved in the Caribbean Basin Initiative, and the Director's 12-Point Plan stated that "all levels of the NPS must have an integrated approach to the management of both natural and cultural resources. To that end the Park Service will identify natural and cultural resource needs through the Park System and will establish priorities for meeting and carrying out those needs." As far as I was concerned, that was one purpose of RMPs, but who was to argue with "new directions" from on high?

The Southeast Region, responsible for the Caribbean parks, had pretty much ignored some of their natural and cultural resource responsibilities at Virgin Islands National Park on St. John; Buck Island Reef National Monument and Christiansted National Historic Site on St. Croix; and San Juan National Historic Site in Puerto Rico. In addition, the National Park Service was expected to become involved with the Columbus five hundredth–anniversary celebrations in 1992.

After some discussion about the various resources and concerns, and learning that John Cook was willing to give up my salary and support costs for a reassignment, I worked out a deal that would first include an April visit to the islands. This would allow me to acquaint myself with the resources and the major issues and to decide whether or not Betty and I would enjoy such an assignment in the Caribbean. From April 7 through April 26, I visited various sites throughout the islands and talked with numerous individuals about such an assignment and possible office space.

On returning to the Smokies and after discussing such a move with Betty, we decided that a Caribbean assignment would be an exciting opportunity and a likely end to my Park Service career.

My Wild Life

10
Virgin Islands

My initial trip to the Virgin Islands (VI) was an exciting and fascinating experience. I had never before spent any time on tropical islands, so the entire scene was foreign to me. And the idea of working in such a remote, different environment was rather romantic and exotic. But it was first important to see the area to decide whether or not Betty and I could live in such a different place. On April 7, I left Knoxville at 8:05 a.m. and flew to Atlanta, then to San Juan, Puerto Rico, and on to the Virgin Islands, arriving at St. Croix at 5:00 p.m. A long day!

I planned to spend four days on St. Croix, the largest of the three Virgin Islands. Arriving late in the afternoon, I checked into the Holger Danski Motel in Christiansted and then walked around town, as there was still plenty of light to see the town and surroundings. And almost immediately I recorded 9 bird species, 4 of which were lifers: Zenaida dove, green-throated carib, Antillean crested hummingbird, and pearly-eyed thrasher. Most abundant, however, were the little bananaquits, buzzing about almost everywhere. Even at the restaurant where I ate, bananaquits were busy checking the sugar at each table for a handout. The local name of this little yellow and black, long-billed honeycreeper most appropriately is "sugarbird."

The next morning I met Christiansted's superintendent Tom Bradley and several members of his staff. Tom was most gracious and encouraging, and we had several very good discussions about his program at Christiansted and Buck Island and also his concern about the Salt River area and the upcoming Columbus quincentennial. Tom had arranged a boat trip that first morning to Buck Island, a short distance offshore. There I was told about the ongoing mongoose trapping program, an effort

Christiansted National Historic Site, St. Croix

My Wild Life

to rid Buck Island of these nonnative mammals that were feeding on ground lizards, an endangered species. Although I did not see a mongoose or a ground lizard, I did see lots of white-crowned pigeons, Caribbean elaenias, and black-whiskered vireos. And that afternoon I met with two regional office officials, Bob Deskins and Jack Ogle, along with the three Caribbean superintendents—Noel Pachta from Virgin Islands National Park, Ping Crawford from San Juan National Historic Site, and Tom Bradley—about my possible move to the Caribbean. The meeting went very well, and each of the superintendents was asked to send me a memorandum on his ideas about what I could do for him if I decided to make the move to the Caribbean.

The next morning I met with Fred Sladen, biologist for the Virgin Islands Fish and Wildlife Service, about his concerns about the Virgin Islands' natural resources. I discovered that Fred had an excellent understanding about the Virgin Islands' resource problems, and I also learned that Fred was an avid birder with a good perspective on the need for wildlife protection. We became close friends.

Salt River

The following morning Tom and I made a trip to see Salt River Bay, a beautiful area and one of the most significant historical and biological sites anywhere in the Caribbean. Here was the only place on US soil where Christopher Columbus landed in 1493 (second voyage) and where the first encounter between Europeans and native peoples occurred. That encounter, in which one sailor and one Carib Indian were killed, represents the cultural apex as well as the beginning of the long-term decline of the Carib civilization. The area also contained pre-Columbian burial grounds, the ruins of a ceremonial plaza and ballpark built in the 1200s or 1300s, and sites of French and British fortresses.

Biologically, Salt River contained a rare continuum of habitats. The fresh water that flows off the forested hillsides into the Salt River drainage forms a freshwater wetland before it passes through a mangrove forest and enters the Salt River Bay estuary. The Salt River mangroves, prior to Hurricane Hugo in 1989, were the largest intact mangrove forest in the Virgin Islands. Mangroves provide a filtering system to cleanse the water that flows seaward so that when the flow reaches the estuary, it carries important nutrients necessary to support the seagrass beds, coral gardens, and reef beyond. Each of these marine habitats provides important nurseries for the area's fisheries. The final stage of the Salt River continuum is a steep-sided submarine canyon that drops off dramatically to fifteen thousand feet.

The various habitats within the immediate

area of Salt River Bay, including a salt pond along the eastern shore, supported 27 territorial or federally threatened and endangered plants and animals. The 3 endangered plants were swamp fern, malpighia, and Vahl's boxwood. Three endangered sea turtles—green, hawksbill, and leatherback—had been found either on the beach or in the bay. And 21 of the area's threatened or endangered species were birds, 6 of which were endangered: brown pelican, peregrine falcon, snowy and piping plovers, and roseate and least terns. The remaining are threatened species: great blue and tricolored herons, great and snowy egrets, black-crowned night-heron, white-cheeked pintail, ruddy duck, West Indian whistling-duck, osprey, clapper rail, willet, royal and Sandwich terns, white-crowned pigeon, and bridled quail-dove.

Most of April 11 was spent with Fred, visiting numerous other localities within the western half of St. Croix, from Caledonia to Frederiksted. The highlights of the day were three bridled quail-doves and a mangrove cuckoo within the rain forest at Caledonia. The first of my three quail-doves was sitting on a low limb of a huge kapok tree, allowing me a marvelous view of this lifer; the other two were found walking on the ground, more typical for this pigeonlike dove. We could hear others within the forest; their calls were a deep, mournful "who-whooo" note, descending toward the end but slightly loudest in the middle. And I was surprised to find a mangrove cuckoo in the upland forest rather than in the lowland mangroves. But I was to learn that this long-tailed, buff-colored bird is more numerous in forested areas than in mangrove habitats.

St. John

Late that afternoon I flew to St. Thomas, where Noel and Sammy Pachta met me at the airport and then drove me around the island. We then took a boat across the channel to St. John, had dinner at Frank's (restaurant), and drove up to the superintendent's home atop a high hill. It had an incredible view of much of Virgin Islands National Park and several of the other islands, including some of the British Virgin Islands. I stayed with the Pachtas during my four days on St. John; we had become acquainted years earlier while working together at Big Bend. And each day we drove the island, visiting numerous localities of natural and cultural resource interest and also visiting with some of the park staff, as well as Rob Norton, biologist with the Virgin Islands Fish and Wildlife Service.

The best bird on St. John for me was the Lesser Antillean bullfinch; it was fairly common in the drier areas of St. John, but it is rarely found elsewhere in the Virgin Islands. And the day we hiked the Reef Bay Trail I had a good

El Yunque National Forest, Puerto Rico

look at a Puerto Rican flycatcher, and on April 17, on a boat ride around St. John with Noel and Rob, I had my first observation of red-billed tropicbirds. I also spent a partial day on St. Thomas, talking with folks at the Caribbean Conservation Association office about possible office space and sightseeing. I added two lifers that day: troupial, a large oriole, and a couple of brown-throated parakeets.

Puerto Rico

On April 19, I crossed back over to St. Thomas and flew to Puerto Rico, where I stayed at El Convento, a marvelous hotel in old-town San Juan. That afternoon I walked around El Morro, part of San Juan National Historic Site. Once again, a number of lifers were available with little difficulty on my part: blue-throated and monk parakeets, red-legged thrush, Greater Antillean grackle, bronze mannikin, and saffron and Java finches. I was surprised to find the two monk parakeets feeding on the ground with the grackles. But the red-legged thrush impressed me the most! This large, red-legged bird, with a black-streaked white throat, also has a large, bright red bill and red eye rings. Truly a remarkable creature!

I spent the next two days seeing the historic site and talking with Ping and his staff about ways I possibly could help them in Puerto Rico as well as about office space that could be made available. I was not overly impressed with what I could possibly do in Puerto Rico, although during the next two days on annual leave, when I rented a vehicle and drove around the island, I was extremely impressed with Puerto Rico's scenery and birdlife. At El Yunque National Forest I found several target species: Puerto Rican screech-owl, Puerto Rican woodpecker, Puerto Rican tody, Puerto Rican parrot, Puerto Rican emerald, Puerto Rican tanager, Puerto Rican bullfinch, and, the most elusive of all, an elfin woods warbler.

I stayed overnight at Loquillo, a guest house high in the mountains, and afterward drove on to Guanica, located at the southwestern corner of the island, where I stayed at the Copamarina Hotel. In the Guánica Forest Reserve I found several additional lifers: West Indian nighthawk, Puerto Rican nightjar, Puerto Rican flycatcher, Adelaide's warbler, and shiny blackbird. Adelaide's warblers were numerous among the coastal scrub, feeding on low shrubs and on the ground. Every now and then one would put its head back and sing a song that, to me, was very similar to that of a Colima warbler of Big Bend National Park. Adelaide's were very perky warblers with yellow underparts that reminded me of Grace's warblers.

During the remainder of my stay in Puerto Rico, I added three more lifers along the Fish

Hatchery Road near Maricao: a green mango and a Puerto Rican cuckoo and a loggerhead kingbird that I watched catch and eat three lizards. The evening of April 26 found me at a hotel near the San Juan airport. I left for home the next morning.

Back at home in Sevierville, and after discussing this rather radical change in scenery with Betty, we agreed to the move. We also decided to live on St. Croix so I could use the administration at Christiansted National Historic Site for paperwork, as suggested by Tom Bradley; to use office space at the Caribbean Research Institute, located at the University of the Virgin Islands on St. Croix; and to rent a condo along Christiansted Harbor. After a few months in the condo, however, we purchased a mobile home and located it along the edge of campus, where I could walk to my office. That allowed Betty the use of our vehicle. She worked as personal secretary for Mrs. Henry J. Kaiser for two and a half years.

Thus, after rather lengthy correspondence with the Southeast Regional Office, where I was to report to Associate Director Bob Deskins, and with various others in the Islands, my new assignment officially took place on August 5, 1986.

The Job

My next step was to prepare a description for my new position. The principal point of that document was to develop a "Caribbean-wide strategy plan for the long-term perpetuation of the abundant cultural and natural resources which exist on National Park Service administered lands within the Caribbean Basin. These internationally recognized resources include fortifications and other historic structures, historic scenes, unique marine and terrestrial ecosystems, and cultural and natural resource collections."

By January 1987, after visiting several pertinent sites and talking with dozens of knowledgeable people, I had packaged a document titled "A Systematic Approach to Comprehensive Resource Management for the Caribbean National Parks," which listed seven generic concerns: (1) decline of the coral reefs and seagrass beds, (2) decline of the native terrestrial plant and animal communities, (3) decline of the threatened/endangered species populations, (4) decline of the fisheries (fish, conch, and lobster), (5) degradation of the historic structures and sites, (6) degradation of the archeological values (marine and terrestrial), and (7) loss of archival materials. Each element included pertinent prevention and mitigation activities.

I then established a coordinating committee to provide guidance for a prevention/mitigation

University of the Virgin Islands, St. Croix

program. That committee consisted of me as chairman; Pachta, Bradley, Crawford, and Fred Sladen; Ed Towle, Island Resource Foundation (IRF); George Tyson, IRF historian; Jessie Thomson, Columbus Jubilee Committee; and a representative of the National Parks Conservation Association. We met, along with several additional invited individuals, several times over the next few months, eventually developing two documents: "The Historic Resources of the U.S. Virgin Islands" and "Virgin Islands Wildlife Resources," written by the Cultural Resource Group and the Wildlife Committee, respectively. Each, containing forms for public comments, was sent out to a wide assortment of people throughout the Virgin Islands' historical, conservation, and political communities.

The Wildlife Resource document consisted of fourteen elements:

1. Threatened/Endangered Species Conservation and Monitoring
2. Sea Turtle Monitoring
3. Seabird Protection and Monitoring
4. St. Croix Ground-Lizard Monitoring
5. Bat Ecology
6. Status of Amphibians and Reptiles
7. Management of Mongoose Populations
8. Deer Management
9. Free-Ranging Animal Control
10. Wetland Inventory, Assessment, and Management

11. Shoreline Erosion and Sediment Control
12. Environmental Assessment/Long-Term Ecosystem Monitoring
13. Information Management
14. Museum Collections Management in the Virgin Islands.

Each element included a description of the issue, pertinent management objectives, and corrective actions necessary.

Soon after the completion of these documents, my tenure in the Islands ended with my retirement. The implementation of the various projects was left to those individuals who had helped prepare the documents. However, it had been our intention early on that many of the identified natural and cultural resource sites could fit very well into a Territorial Park System. Governor Farrelly expressed his interest but did not take any additional steps to establish a Territorial Park.

Life in the Virgin Islands

Our move to the Virgin Islands resulted in a significant change in scenery and responsibilities, and new personal interests began almost immediately; Betty and I began snorkeling and seashell collecting. During that first winter we swam throughout the winter months, although the water was too cool for most of the local people. But by our second winter we had acclimatized sufficiently that the winter water was too cool even for us. We did continue to spend considerable time shelling, however, searching the beaches and surf line for seashells. We had discovered a new passion that we thoroughly enjoyed together. And over the three years in the Caribbean, shelling on St. Croix as well as on several of the other islands of the West Indies, we accumulated thousands of seashells that totaled 581 species. After retirement I sent the entire collection to Dr. Walter Sage at the American Museum of Natural History for his assessment. Of the 581 species, he corrected my identification of only 6. And a year later I donated the entire collection to the Corpus Christi Museum of Science and History.

Bird Study

During 1987, I established four driving transects on St. Croix to document avian populations throughout a full twelve-month period. The principal objective of this study was to establish a baseline that could be compared with data gathered in exactly the same manner at some future date, perhaps after a hurricane. Although my study included a full year of data, any two- or three-week series of data gathered at another time could be utilized for comparisons. The most useful period of time to replicate the transect data was during the spring months, March through June, when the largest number of native species are breeding and when the birds are most influenced by their environment.

Each of my 1987 transects was started about fifteen minutes before sunup, approximately every two weeks. Count techniques were similar to those established by the US Fish and Wildlife Service for the Breeding Bird Survey, with three exceptions: (1) all stops were preselected to allow for duplication, (2) fewer than 50 stops were involved per transect, and (3) instead of a single count, 20 or 21 censuses were undertaken on each transect. The four transect routes included (A) the South Shore Route that followed St. Croix's south-central shoreline (Highway 60) for 10 miles; (B) the North Shore Route that followed the north-central shoreline (Highway 80) for 7 miles; (C) the Castle Burke Route that crosses St. Croix south to north at midisland for 5 miles; and (D) the Rain Forest Route that runs 6 miles into the northwestern mountains and includes the Creque Dam Scenic Road and Northside Drive (Highway 63). The four routes included 85 stops that were dominated by pasture/field habitat (37%) and followed by thorn woodland (20%), deciduous forest (12%), semi-evergreen forest (10%), coastal hedge/grassland (6%), and mangrove woodland (1%).

A total of 80 bird species were recorded on the four transects during the twelve-month study. These included 62 species on the South Shore, 51 on the Rain Forest, 44 on the Castle Burke, and 39 on the North Shore transects. Total individuals recorded were greatest on the South Shore transect (8,734), followed by Castle Burke (7,803), Rain Forest (6,704), and the North Shore routes (4,883). Total numbers of individuals recorded per stop, a better measure of habitat preference, revealed that the Castle Burke route provided the highest population, followed by the South Shore, Rain Forest, and the North Shore transects.

Further assessment of the avifauna included the percentage of stops on which a species was recorded. On the South Shore transect, only 1 of the 62 species recorded—bananaquit—was found on more than half of the total 650 stops (number of censuses taken times the number of stops). Seven additional species were recorded on at least one-third (217) of the 650 stops: Zenaida dove, common ground-dove, smooth-billed ani, Caribbean elaenia, northern mockingbird, yellow warbler, and black-faced grassquit.

On the North Shore transect, only the pearly-eyed thrasher was recorded on more than half of the 546 stops. An additional 3 species were recorded on two-thirds (182) or more of the stops: gray kingbird, yellow warbler, and bananaquit.

On the Castle Burke transect, 4 of the 44 species were recorded on more than half of the 304 stops: scaly-naped pigeon, gray kingbird, pearly-eyed thrasher, and bananaquit. Six additional species—cattle egret, Zenaida dove, northern mockingbird, black-whiskered vireo, yellow warbler, and black-faced grassquit—were recorded on at least one-third (101) of the stops.

On the Rain Forest transect, 5 of the 51 species were recorded on at least half of the 483 stops: scaly-naped pigeon, Zenaida dove, gray kingbird, pearly-eyed thrasher, and bananaquit. No additional species were found on one-third of the 161 stops.

The highest numbers of birds were recorded during fall migration, which generally runs from August to early November. This was most obvious for the Rain Forest route, where species recorded increased more than 50 percent above norm from mid-September through October. Fall migration extends over a longer period at wetland habitats at lower elevations, beginning by late July and lasting to at least late October.

I also identified 16 species that could be used as indicator species for each transect and that could be monitored for long-term changes in the environment. For instance, brown pelican,

Mangrove forest in Salt River, St. Croix, 1988

My Wild Life

white-cheeked pintail, white-crowned pigeon, and bridled quail-dove are considered threatened or endangered or unique and of special importance. Other selected species, such as scaly-naped pigeon, Zenaida dove, Caribbean elaenia, and yellow warbler, are especially common in occurrence, and any change in status should be easily detected and could be directly related to impacts upon their environment.

Mangroves

Maybe because I had never before spent any time in mangroves, this habitat piqued my curiosity, so I spent considerable time during my residency birding the Sugar Bay mangroves, a fifteen-acre western backwater of Salt River. This same area was already listed in the *Directory of Neotropical Wetlands* (1986) as "threatened by the development of two marinas, the construction of private dwellings, and hotel development." To make my counts more legitimate, I used a point-count method of documenting the birdlife between October 1, 1986, and March 31, 1987. On 12 counts I recorded a total of 20 species (all passerines) and individual numbers that ranged from a low of 31 on October 1 to a high of 128 individuals on October 26.

Of the 20 species recorded within the Sugar Bay mangroves, 15 (75%) occur in the West Indies only as a migrant/transient and/or winter resident. Species considered as migrants only included yellow-throated vireo; blue-winged, magnolia, Cape May, yellow-rumped, prairie, blackpoll, black-and-white, worm-eating, and hooded warblers; northern parula; American redstart; ovenbird; and common yellowthroat. Five species—Caribbean elaenia, pearly-eyed thrasher, black-whiskered vireo, yellow warbler, and bananaquit—are permanent residents. Black-whiskered vireo numbers fluctuate during the year, and there is a sharp increase during the spring and summer months. And there may be an increase of yellow warblers during the fall months as migrants pass through the area.

More than one-half of the total number of recorded passerines had traveled southward from their breeding grounds for several thousand miles to secure winter habitat in the Sugar Bay mangroves. They remain there for fully one-half of the year, from October through March, during which time they are dependent upon the stability of the Sugar Bay mangrove habitat.

The population high on October 26 is a fair representation of the peak of Caribbean migration. Totals remained fairly constant through mid-December, dropped off somewhat during January and February, and increased again by late March. The higher total in late March probably represents an increased activity level that would occur prior to departure for their breeding grounds in North America.

British Virgin Islands, 1987

Betty and I flew to Tortola to attend a meeting of the Caribbean Conservation Association from September 9 to 13. Our accommodations and the meeting were at the Prospect Reef Hotel in Tortola. The British Virgin Islands is a British crown colony of more than fifty islands and cays within an area of fifty-nine square miles. The principal island of Tortola is twenty-five square miles, followed by Anegada at thirteen, Virgin Gorda at eight, and Jost Van Dyke at three; the remainder are much smaller. But it is on the smaller islands and cays where at least thirteen species of seabirds are known to nest.

Our field trip during the meeting visited Gorda Peak National Park, where we walked to an observation station near the 1,370-foot summit. The principal area of interest in this park is the jumble of huge granite boulders at the shore that offers unique snorkeling opportunities, including underwater passageways and grottos of the Baths. The adjacent designated marine preserve includes the sunken *Rhone*, a 310-foot royal mail ship that was wrecked off the coast of Salt Island during the hurricane of 1867. Today, it provides one of the very best diving sites in the Caribbean.

I managed to record 9 species of birds during our Virgin Gorda visit, 2 waterbirds—least and Sandwich terns—and 7 terrestrial species: American kestrel, scaly-naped pigeon, mangrove cuckoo, smooth-billed ani, Caribbean elaenia, northern mockingbird, and black-faced grassquit.

Following the meeting, Betty and I drove to Sage Mountain National Park, a ninety-two-acre area that contained the last remnant of a cloud forest community that once covered most of the central highlands of Tortola. A pair of Caribbean martins were playing overhead while we were investigating the forest. And two raptors—red-tailed hawk and American kestrel—were taking advantage of the thermals rising from the warmer lowlands. Forest birds found that morning included scaly-naped pigeons, Zenaida doves, pearly-eyed thrashers, bananaquits, and black-whiskered vireos.

We walked the Sage Mountain Trail to the seventeen hundred–foot summit, where the view was spectacular. We had a grand, sweeping panorama of dozens of bright green islands, each surrounded by varying shades of blue. The island of St. John, US Virgin Islands, dominated the scene to the southwest. The British island of Jost Van Dyke lay below us to the west. The smaller British islands of Norman, Peter, Salt, Cooper, and Ginger rose out of the sea like stepping-stones between St. John and Virgin Gorda, the long gray-green island that lay almost directly to the east.

Also along the trail were two hummingbirds: the tiny Antillean crested hummingbird and

The Baths on Cerro Gorda, British Virgin Islands

larger green-throated carib. These were bright green jewels among the vast array of multicolored flowers of bottle brush, ixora, giant fire dart, and coral plant.

Later in the day, we found the same hummingbird species at the Botanical Gardens in Road Town, Tortola's largest town and capital of the British Virgin Islands. Established in 1979, the 2.8-acre gardens are managed by the National Parks Trust as a recreational and educational facility. Different sections of the gardens are dedicated to various groups of plants: rain forest, bamboo and other grasses, bromeliads, heliconias and philodendrons, and orchids.

We left for St. Croix and home the following day, but our visit provided us with a better understanding of our nearest foreign islands. And although I recorded only 31 bird species during our visit, seeing the various species in the Sage Mountain forest was most memorable.

Martinique, 1988

From August 30 to September 3, I visited the French West Indies island of Martinique to attend the annual meeting of the Caribbean Conservation Association (CCA). The meeting was held at the Meridian Hotel in Trois-Îlets, a tourist area across the bay from the capital city of Fort-de-France. We stayed at the Hôtel La Pagerie, a less expensive but comfortable and convenient hotel nearby.

Robert Norton (fellow birder from Tortola) and I met at Antigua and flew on together to Martinique, arriving early on the evening of August 28. We had purposely arrived a day early to spend some extra field time. But we mistakenly decided to rent a car at Trois-Îlets, rather than at the airport, and discovered that the rental offices had closed by the time we checked into our hotel. We were unable to obtain a vehicle before 7:00 a.m. the following morning.

By 7:30, however, we were on the road to the Caravelle Peninsula. Alden and Gooders (1981) reported that the white-breasted thrasher, a species endemic to Martinique and nearby St. Lucia, "may still be seen around Ferret Point" on the Caravelle Peninsula. It was one of our most wanted but difficult-to-find species.

The drive from Trois-Îlets to the town of La Trinité, near the entrance to the Caravelle Peninsula, took less than an hour. And after a breakfast of greasy eggs and bread, we drove east toward the "nature park" situated on the outer half of the peninsula. It took us a short time to find the signed Ferret Trail parking area, where we left the car and bushwhacked our way downhill through rather thick brush, occasionally finding portions of the trail. Later on, when we were returning to the car, we found a partially paved route nearby that would have made our downhill travels much easier.

The habitat that we were seeking was located along the lower slopes between the fringe mangroves and brushy hillsides. It was there that we found our bird. In fact, we found three individuals, all in the mid- to upper foliage of the vegetation. The birds were attracted to our squeaking and spishing noises, and their approach was quiet but not overly cautious.

We also observed several Lesser Antillean saltators and heard calls or songs of two other bird species of interest to us. Two Lesser Antillean flycatchers and two bare-eyed robins were calling nearby, but we saw neither of these birds. In fact, I mistakenly identified the robin songs as those of Martinique orioles. It wasn't until we later observed bare-eyed robins at another location that we discovered the error.

We left the Caravelle Peninsula at about noon, stopped for a fast lunch on the La Trinité Bay beach, and then drove back to the airport area. The remainder of the afternoon was spent in the area of Le Lamentin, driving various roads around Fort-de-France Bay, where we found a few ponded areas while trying to locate a ringed kingfisher, but without success. In the early evening I returned to the airport to meet Betty, and then we returned to the hotel and joined Rob for dinner.

The meeting of the CCA began the next morning, and that afternoon the entire contingency traveled to the Macabou Coastal Forest Preserve on the southeastern coast. We spent a couple of hours there, which contained a littoral woodland similar to that which Rob and I had visited on the Caravelle Peninsula. We did not see a white-breasted thrasher, although I again heard songs of bare-eyed robins.

Our next field time was during the early morning of September 2, when Rob, Betty, and I returned to an area near Le Diamant that we had passed on our afternoon field trips two days before. We returned to the CCA meeting by midmorning, but Rob and I went back to the Diamant site that evening. It was there at dusk, after chasing several supposed oriole songs back and forth across a little valley, that we finally observed three bare-eyed robins well enough to realize that our oriole songs were indeed robin songs. Afterward, before returning to our hotel, we spent a couple of hours driving the roadways within the area looking for a white-tailed nightjar, but to no avail.

On the morning of September 3, Rob, Betty, and I left the hotel early in the morning and drove into the north-central mountains. Although the weather was rather cloudy and damp, the beginning of what later turned into Hurricane Gilbert, we succeeded in finding all of the highland birds we searched for in the area of Pitons du Carbet.

Several rufous-throated solitaires were recorded from the roadway. We had a long, excellent look at one subadult perched in an open tree very close to the road. Another was seen flycatching over the roadway. And their melodic songs were fairly common everywhere in the highlands.

Our most productive site was just south of the junction of roads D1 and N3, within a small eastern drainage that contained a small stream flowing through cloud forest vegetation; tree ferns were abundant. It was there that we found Lesser Antillean swifts, purple-throated caribs, a pair of blue-headed hummingbirds, and, finally, a Martinique oriole. We had excellent looks at this endemic species, which at first looked very much like a black-cowled oriole. But it seemed to possess a deeper-colored chestnut head, neck, and upper breast. And from a sample of one, it seemed more arboreal than its black-cowled cousin, creeping or foraging among the vegetation, wrenlike.

Also in the Pitons du Carbet area, we were surprised to find several human hunters, shotguns in hand, lining the roadway. This situation probably explains why we found no pigeons or doves there, species that would normally be a prominent part of the upland forest community.

That afternoon was spent driving the coastlines from St. Pierre on the northwestern coast and Basse-Pointe to St. Marie on the northeastern coast. Two village weaver colonies were found along the northeastern coast; one tree held eight nests, which apparently were in use by the birds that were perched nearby and feeding in the adjacent vegetation. At Le Prêcheur, we observed at least 75 brown noddies flying approximately one-quarter mile offshore, all flying low over the water heading north. And later near St. Marie we recorded more than 60 Sandwich terns feeding offshore.

Late afternoon found us in the vicinity of Le Lamentin, where we birded the racetrack area and the marina. This marina site had been suggested by a local birder as a good place to find the white-tailed nightjar, Martinique oriole, and grassland yellow-finch. We found only the yellow-finch, as well as more than 50 red bishops, many of which were in bright breeding plumage.

We again tried to find a ringed kingfisher in the marina area, without success. We did record a few shorebirds at the adjacent salt flats. However, several hunters were posted in blinds along constructed dikes that crossed the flats, and they were shooting any and all shorebirds that ventured close enough. Shotgun firing was heard all the while we were in the vicinity, and this activity undoubtedly limited bird use of the area.

The following morning, Betty and I drove Rob to the airport to catch his flight home, and we continued northwest. We turned south at Le Robert and followed the coastline all the way to the end of the southwestern peninsula to Savane de Pétrification, an area of open water and salt flats. But once again the area was busy with hunters. I added only a lone injured whimbrel and a pair of semipalmated sandpipers to our trip list.

On September 5, when it rained almost the entire day, we visited a reservoir in the vicinity of Ducos early in the morning and returned to the marina by 9:30 a.m. Although the reservoir was reasonably large and seemed to contain adequate vegetation along the shoreline to support birds, I did not find a single waterbird. We then drove back to the marina and spent a couple of hours walking into the mangroves, through the very soggy mud and wet grasses, in search of seashells. Three days earlier we had discovered several fringed murexes and crown conchs among the piles of dredged materials. We collected several reasonably clean specimens of these beautiful shells.

Later in the afternoon we rode the ferry to and from Fort-de-France and Trois-Îlets. I recorded a couple of magnificent frigatebirds flying overhead and approximately 40 brown noddies feeding on the Trois-Îlets side of the bay. The following morning we took a flight back through Antigua and on to St. Croix. I had recorded 55 bird species. Three of those—bare-eyed robin, white-breasted thrasher, and Martinique oriole—were lifers.

Saving Salt River Bay

While living on St. Croix, especially during the latter half of my residency, I probably spent more of my time on this issue than any other. Although my initial work plan called for involvement only with the Columbus Jubilee Celebration, and I already had visited with a number of key Jubilee Committee members, my involvement increased substantially in August 1986. Fred Sladen asked me to help prepare a response to the NPS Natural Landmark Office regarding the extent of impacts on the Salt River Natural Landmark. Park Ranger Felix Revello had submitted a report to the Southeast Regional Office in March, stating that the Salt River site was threatened by a number of proposed developments. Realizing the significance of these threats, I sent copies of our response to all the local conservation organizations and numerous pertinent national conservation organizations, including several NPS offices and individuals.

My concern for the area increased in September and October when the Virgin Islands Department of Conservation and Cultural

Triton and Salt River Bays, St. Croix, 1988

My Wild Life

Affairs (DCCA) asked for public review of a Coastal Zone Permit Application by Sugar Bay Land Development, Ltd., to construct a major complex of a 288-unit hotel, 300 condo units, a 157-slip marina, and support facilities for Salt River, as well as to dredge a channel fifty feet wide to a depth of eight feet on Cape of the Arrows, within the Salt River Natural Landmark site. And in spite of the permit reviews being overwhelmingly against development, on December 4, the St. Croix Coastal Zone Management Committee (CZM) voted to approve the application, but with the inclusion of twenty-one conditions. The conditions were the result of a mid-November meeting with VI Senator Virden Brown, Tom Bradley, and me, a number of local citizens' groups (Jubilee Committee, Landmark Society, Virgin Islands Environmental Association [VICS]), two CZM Committee members, and Laura Loomis of NPCA.

Upon approval of the application, the issue became even more contentious and was given greater visibility. For instance, a *New York Times* article appeared on December 7 that described the "fight" to save the Salt River site. And the Jacksonville Corps of Engineers and Environmental Protection Agency visited the site on December 11 and 12 regarding the pending permits. I participated in that site visit, making a presentation about its significance.

On January 26, VICS attorney Nancy Young submitted an appeal of the CZM permit to the Board of Land Use Appeals. On February 2, the VI *Daily News* carried a front-page article stating that the EPA had asked the Corps to deny the marina/dredging permit. Yet, on April 6, the permits were completed and sent to Sugar Bay Land Development, with permission to begin development.

On July 22, the Board of Land Use Appeals finally heard testimony regarding the VICS appeal. NPS stated its objection to development within the National Natural Landmark site. But on August 7, the board denied the appeal. And on August 21, Attorney Young filed a petition for a rehearing. That appeal was also denied on December 22. The following day, Attorney Young filed a petition to the US District Court, asking the court to reverse the decision; that petition was joined by the Landmark Society, Jubilee Committee, VI League of Women Voters, NPCA, and National Wildlife Federation. The District Court issued a stay on September 15. And on December 2, the Corps of Engineers denied the permit to dredge and construct a marina.

In the meantime, on August 3–6, I traveled to Washington, D.C., to visit with several conservation organizations about the NPS Caribbean strategy, although Salt River issues took the greatest amount of time. I had brought along a fifteen-minute slide talk that was pre-

Salt River Exhibit, St. Croix

sented on several occasions. It was then that Congressman Morrison of Connecticut stated that he was considering the introduction of a bill for a Salt River National Park. I made sure that he was fully aware that NPS could become involved only if asked to do so by Congress.

On November 20, the Jubilee Committee and AT&T of the Virgin Islands sponsored a reception to commemorate the 494th anniversary of Columbus's landing at Salt River. That event was utilized as a fund-raiser for the quincentennial celebrations but also to give greater visibility to the site itself; more than five hundred people attended.

This issue began to take a more positive turn in February 1988, when VI Delegate to Con-

gress Ron de Lugo stated that the Christopher Columbus landing site in Salt River was in jeopardy and told the NPS it should move quickly to do a comprehensive study of the area for possible national park designation. In April I unveiled the Salt River Exhibit that I had designed, a traveling exhibit that first was placed on view at the Christiansted Public Library, then at the Whim Plantation, where more than three hundred people attended the opening, and was later moved into a Christiansted bank.

On July 12, VI Governor Farrelly and NPS Regional Director Robert Baker signed a cooperative agreement for planning, management, training, and advisory on a Columbus Landing State Park. NPS immediately initiated planning. And by mid-July, CZM planners called for a building moratorium "to allow the VI Government time to correct failings of its Coastal Zone Management program."

By the beginning of 1989, park site planning was moving ahead, and any additional developments were being stalled at every turn. On January 10, I briefed Congressman Bruce Vento (chairman of Interior Subcommittee for National Parks and Public Lands), Delegate de Lugo, and Governor Farrelly on the alternatives in the draft planning document. And on January 19, I also briefed Sierra Club defense attorney Bob Dreher and Wilderness Society Assistant Director Brien Culhane on the alternatives.

Dreher issued a statement to the *Daily News* stating: "The conservationists' fight against Virgin Grand resort planning at St. Croix's Salt River could be a precedent-setting case likely to draw national attention."

Considerable time and energy went into the numerous briefings, meetings, and other public relations activities during the remainder of the spring months. At one point, Brad Northrup, vice president of The Nature Conservancy, visited the site and offered to purchase the Salt River lands for a park. At a March 15 presentation to sixty-five members of the St. Croix Chamber of Commerce, they expressed support for the park project. On March 18, the *Daily News* reported that "developer offers to sell Salt River land." And on March 27, VI Senator Holland Redfield stated that "Interior is 100 percent in favor of efforts to acquire the property to preserve it from private commercial development."

On the evening of May 10, a Salt River Park public meeting, sponsored by the VI League of Women Voters, attracted three hundred people. Testimony strongly favored the comprehensive park alternative. The *Daily News* headline the following day read: "People, Officials to Farrelly: Take Stand, Save Salt River."

It still was more than two years before Congress took a stand to save Salt River. On November 5, 1991, H.R. 2927, "to provide for the

Briefing Governor Farrelly, Congressman Bruce Vento, Delegate to Congress Ron de Lugo, and NPS Regional Director Robert Baker at Salt River, St. Croix

establishment of the St. Croix, VI, Historical Park and Ecological Preserve," was introduced by Congressman Bruce Vento; three dozen other congressmen co-sponsored the bill. In April 1992, a 912-acre national park became a reality, with a dedication ceremony on November 14, 1993, held in conjunction with the five hundredth anniversary of Columbus's landing at Salt River in 1493.

• • • • •

Additional West Indies Visits

All during our stay in the Virgin Islands Betty and I took every opportunity possible to visit other Caribbean Islands. We spent time on Puerto Rico, the British Virgin Islands, and Dominican Republic in the Greater Antilles, and Saba, Anguilla, St. Martin, Antigua, Montserrat, Guadeloupe, Dominica, and Martinique in the Lesser Antilles. And after retiring, before moving back to Texas, Fred Sladen and I visited the few additional islands that Betty and I had not been able to visit: St. Lucia, St. Vincent, Barbados, Grenada, and Jamaica. And a year later I also traveled to Cuba with Canada's Long Point Bird Observatory tour to see the birdlife of that island. I eventually accumulated all of my notes on my West Indies birding trips into a book in 1996, *A Birder's West Indies: An Island-by-Island Tour*.

Post-Hurricane Bird Survey

I had sent a copy of my original report (1988) on my 1987 bird surveys to the US Fish and Wildlife Service offices in Washington, D.C., and Puerto Rico. On September 18, 1989, St. Croix suffered a direct hit from Hurricane Hugo, which remained over the island for an extended period of twelve hours. All of the island's vegetation was subjected to severe damage, most especially areas with tall, mature vegetation.

Within a few weeks after the storm, Hilda Diaz-Soltero, USFWS official in Puerto Rico, contacted me to see if I would be willing to return to the island in the spring to redo my St. Croix transects to document changes in the avifauna. I readily agreed, especially since USFWS would fund my return.

Eight months after Hurricane Hugo, from May 6 to 18, 1990, I replicated my 1987 transects. And Joe Wonderle, Institute of Tropical Forestry in Puerto Rico, also conducted vegetation surveys. We jointly prepared a report of our findings that was later published in the *Wilson Bulletin*. Our abstract stated:

Surveys revealed 33 species both before and after the hurricane, of which 30 species were detected during both samples. However, the average number of birds per stop was significantly lower after the storm's passage than before. No pattern was evident in the changes of aquatic species, but this may reflect limited sample sizes. Among terrestrial species, higher proportions of nectarivores and fruit/seed-eaters declined than insectivores or raptors, suggesting that the storm's greatest stress occurred after its passage rather than during its impact. Populations of the Pearly-eyed Thrasher declined on one transect and increased on another, a pattern consistent with inner-habitat migration. The fruit/seed diet, low population size, and restriction to remnant forest fragments of the Bridled Quail-Dove may explain the significant population decline of this species and its disappearance from traditional sites.

Species that increased in numbers were not surprising, as they included predators and other species that might take advantage of prey, less competition, or more open terrain. Cattle egrets, red-tailed hawks, American kestrels, Caribbean elaenias, and northern mockingbirds increased in numbers. Declines were found in species whose diets consisted primarily of nectar, fruit and seeds, and insects. These included the three nectar feeders: green-throated carib, Antillean crested hummingbird, and bananaquit; five insect eaters: mangrove cuckoo, smooth-billed ani, gray kingbird, black-whiskered vireo, and yellow warbler; and eight fruit/seed eaters: helmeted guineafowl (non-native), rock dove, scaly-naped and white-crowned pigeons, Zenaida dove, common ground-dove, bridled quail-dove, and black-faced grassquit.

I had recorded only one lone hummingbird on my transects, and I was told by some of the locals who fed hummers that they believed that by placing sugar water out immediately after the storm, they had been instrumental in saving the hummers. Because the storm stalled over the island for so long, no nectaring plants remained.

Hurricane Hugo

Following my return from St. Croix, I wrote up a few paragraphs about my trip that included the following information: Hurricane Hugo struck the tiny Caribbean Island of St. Croix, US Virgin Islands, on September 17, 1989. The storm's 200+ mph winds (local estimate) mutilated every part of the island throughout the night, actually stalling there for several hours with the eye centered over the western half. The National Hurricane Center reported that "the eye moved over St. Croix at 0600 UTC on the 18th with a forward speed of eight knots" with surface winds "estimated at 120 knots" (138 mph).

When people finally emerged from their places of safety later that morning, they found complete havoc. Overnight, 90 percent of the island homes had been severely damaged or destroyed, all of the trees and shrubs had been broken and defoliated, and the remaining vegetation had been turned brown by the excessive salt water and abrasion.

It was reported time and again that the scene was "like the aftermath of a nuclear explosion." Galvanized roofing dotted the landscape. Skeletons of old structures and deserted vehicles, which previously had been well hidden by vegetation, were evident everywhere. Walls and ceilings from one house became obstructive eyesores in neighbors' yards. The abundant, nightmarish happenings during Hugo could fill numerous books, and many of the Hugo stories were indeed "stranger than fiction."

Understandably, after such a major catastrophe, there was little immediate concern about the condition of native vegetation and wildlife. Island residents were first attentive to their personal needs. Most experienced a tremendous burst of energy to restore their lives and those of their loved ones. That energy often turned to depression when they discovered how impossible it was to rebuild their lives to pre-Hugo conditions. Most of their physical necessities were either destroyed or in short supply. And the local administration's lack of organizational skills necessary to address those shortcomings was obvious to most residents. Eight months later many people were still waiting for shipments of necessary supplies to rebuild their homes. In the meantime, many survived in one or two makeshift rooms or with complete dependency on others. Except for two insurance companies that declared bankruptcy because of the storm, most insurance claims paid adequately and within a reasonable time frame.

As for St. Croix's wildlife, a few people found dead and dying birds right after the storm, mostly doves and pigeons, and there was one report of a dead hummingbird. Scaly-naped pigeons and Zenaida doves became yard birds wherever seed was provided. And almost everyone I talked with mentioned the complete absence of hummingbirds. Although a few hummers were seen immediately after the storm, they disappeared within a few days. The loss of flowering plants was undoubtedly to blame.

Fred Sladen was one of the few island residents to check on certain bird habitats soon after Hugo. He found little blue and green herons and cattle egrets nesting within the mangroves on the Buccaneer Hotel grounds in October. By early February 1990, he found Zenaida doves, gray kingbirds, pearly-eyed thrashers, and American kestrels nesting "in good numbers."

It was evident that most of the resident bird species had made it through the storm, and their populations will probably recover in time. However, the real concern is for the species that might be missing or so badly impacted that they might never recover. And to what extent were the species affected and what community changes resulted from Hugo?

Overview

Our general stay in the Virgin Islands was fantastic from my point of view, but Betty had numerous concerns. She missed her family and flew back to Texas twice each year to see her kids, parents, and siblings. And the lack of security on St. Croix was troublesome. She never felt safe; robbery and rapes occurred on a reg-

Salt River Bay National Historical Park and Ecological Preserve, St. Croix

ular basis. Our vehicle was broken into on nine occasions. Once, while snorkeling along the East End, we returned to find both back wheels gone. Later I was able to find my same wheels at a local tire shop and buy them back.

Most visitors to the Virgin Islands experience only the magnificent scenery, the Caribbean culture, some very good restaurants, and the ambience at shopping centers, but nonnatives who live there day in and day out are subject to minority status. And the effects of some of that can be difficult to endure. We learned early on to carry reading material with us wherever we went; everything that required dealing with the local bureaucracy took many times longer than it did in the States. But given the same opportunity again, we probably would take it.

Transition

I had originally agreed to stay in the Caribbean for three years. And as the end of that assignment became a reality, we had to decide to either remain in the Park Service or retire. Although most of my thirty-two-year career had been unbelievably satisfying, the more we thought about our options, the more we decided it was time to try something different. I had always wanted to write full-time, and I had lots of ideas. So with exciting thoughts for the future, we decided it was time to move on. My retirement became effective in May 1989. We left St. Croix and returned to the mainland and our new home in Victoria, Texas.

Afterword

When the life you have chosen (or has it chosen you?) allows you to spend your entire career working in, writing about, and having an impact on the most beautiful parts of the United States—the national parks—how can life get any better?

So after retirement you sit back and do nothing and wish you were back in the good old days. Right? No! For Ro life just kept getting busier and better with each year. Before the ink was dry on his retirement papers (May 1989), he was traveling all through the "other" islands in the Caribbean. He couldn't leave there without seeing them all. And of course he eventually wrote a book about his experiences in the area, *A Birder's West Indies: An Island-by-Island Tour* (1996).

Early in the three-year assignment to the Virgin Islands, a decision was made to settle eventually in Texas. So in 1987 on a trip to visit my family, I selected and we purchased a house (with a yard to Ro's specifications) fifteen miles northwest of Victoria, Texas.

Ro didn't decide to retire solely to write full-time, but that was the motivating factor. During the time he worked for the NPS, he spent most of his weekends and vacation time traveling to look at birds. He always kept journals documenting the trips and birds recorded, a great resource for his writing.

After his retirement and the last travels in the Islands, Ro arrived in Texas in June 1989 and was soon out looking at birds in South Texas. Our house, with some remodeling, was—from 1989 to December 2009—a very comfortable home; it was the longest time either of us had lived in one house.

Once the house was in good shape with pictures on the wall, books on the shelves, and the kitchen in cooking order, Ro decided it was time for a trip to visit families we hadn't seen in recent years. So he and I went on an extended

Betty and Ro Wauer in
the Maderas del Carmen.
Photograph by Sally
Finkelstein.

trip through West Texas to New Mexico, then Utah and Wyoming, and on to California, Oregon, and Washington, then back through Arizona and home. Our families do live in nice places to visit, and checking out the birds along the way only made good sense.

This trip also sparked a long-held desire in Ro—a book(s) about birds in the national parks. After some time with talks, proposals, and so on, the desire turned into reality, and the years of 1991–95 saw the two of us in a fifth-wheel, traveling to every national park in the United States and Canada. These trips were absolutely wonderful and were brought to a close by four outstanding weeks in Alaska and a flight to Hawaii for a two-week visit. The resultant books included the *Visitor's Guide to the Eastern National Parks* (1992), *Rocky Mountain Parks* (1993), *Central National Parks* (1994), *Northwestern National Parks* (2000), and *Southwestern National Parks* (2004).

Between the long national park trips, Ro made numerous trips to Big Bend National Park to conduct bird and cacti seminars and bird population studies. Birding trips included the Lower Rio Grande Valley, the Texas Gulf Coast, the Pineywoods, and many other places. He also traveled to Belize, Guatemala, and the US Virgin Islands in 1990; Cuba in 1991; Trinidad in 1992; and made trips to Mexico in 1989, 1990, 1994, and 1995. Books that came about from this period and a bit beyond were *A Naturalist's Mexico* (1992), *A Field Guide to Birds of the Big Bend* (1996), *A Birder's West Indies* (1996), *Birds of Zion National Park and Vicinity* (1997), *For All Seasons: A Big Bend Journal* (1997), *Birding Texas* (1998), *The American Robin* (1999), *Heralds of Spring in Texas* (1999), *Naturally South Texas* (2001), and *The American Kestrel* (2005).

The constant urge to travel, be outdoors, and write about it took a dramatically different course in late 1996. Ro had turned our one-and-a-half-acre yard into a great area to attract birds. The yard backed up to an extensive tree-covered pasture, so that and some strategic bird feeders meant he always had birds around. But he was always trying to attract more, so he planted some additional bushes that hummingbirds like. Well, not only did hummingbirds like them but so did butterflies!

It wasn't long until Ro was totally hooked on butterflies. Each year our yard sported another area of flower beds full of butterfly plants; and each year we attracted new species. When we moved from the Victoria area in 2009, we had by far the best butterfly garden in Victoria County. Our yard list included 133 butterfly species and 182 species of birds.

By springtime of 1997 it seemed to me that things became kind of frenetic, as if Ro's major thought was, "Think of all the areas I've been while birding and then think of all the butterflies that I paid no attention to. I have to hurry." At this same time, all the scheduled talks, walks, tours and seminars, and the book and magazine writing commitments were still going on. So even though I thought Ro traveled more than anyone but a traveling salesman, I began to see it could be adjusted to a higher level.

The years 1997 through 2005 saw Ro traveling more than he ever had; he traveled back and forth over each section of Texas. He made twenty-four trips to Big Bend, thirty-three trips to the Valley, and spent many days in the Hill Country. He went on fifteen trips to Mexico. In those same years the two of us usually made a trip out west to see family, and the routes were drawn to include the most butterflies possible. Three more books came about because of these travels: *Butterflies of West Texas Parks and Preserves* (2002), *Butterflies of the Lower Rio Grande Valley* (2004), and *Finding Butterflies in Texas* (2006). Four Quick Reference guides were also published: *Butterflies of South Texas including the Lower Rio Grande Valley* (2009), *Butterflies of Texas Big Bend Country* (2010), *Butterflies of North Texas* (2010), and *Butterflies of the Rocky Mountains* (2012).

During 1997 through 2004, while Ro was mostly on the road, I was busy with a business venture and also very involved in family genealogy and research. We went on some trips together but mostly crossed paths when Ro was at home between trips.

Then sometime in the spring of 2005, another dramatically different course of events happened. Ro's backyard was absolutely beautiful by then with all kinds of butterflies, and I started noticing them enough to start asking what they were. And Ro started asking me to come out and see one or the other until finally, I went back in the house, got paper and pen, and wrote down "White-striped Longtail, 05-05-2005, TX (yard)."

Ro seemed only too happy to show me all the nice places to go see butterflies all around our local area. Then a trip to Colorado in July was awesome—both the scenery and the butterflies—a Big Bend/Davis Mountain trip in August, the Gulf Coast, Hill Country, and Panhandle area in September, and a trip to the Lower Rio Grande Valley in October. In November Ro was a leader on a trip to Mexico, and I went along. We saw 270 butterflies! It was a fantastic trip, but I went home wondering how a person was supposed to remember all those butterflies.

Then in early December Ro gave me a birthday treat—a butterfly trip to the Valley. What? You thought Ro bought diamonds? The trip turned out to be so much fun with new butterflies and lots of people running around trying to see them all and take pictures, and I was totally hooked, too. I finally went over to the dark side and knew that I would probably never spend more than a week or maybe two weeks at any one time at home again. Ro just seemed pleased to have a full-time travel buddy again.

The years 2006 through 2009 went much the

same way as 2005; six trips to Big Bend, two to the Davis Mountains, six trips to the Valley, a number of trips to the Pineywoods, Gulf Coast, the Panhandle, and other spots in Texas. There were two trips to California and Oregon, one to Arizona, and six trips to Mexico. Sadly, Mexico is no longer in our travel plans.

Ro wrote weekly nature articles for the *Victoria Advocate* for twenty-one years, led and/or participated in numerous butterfly counts, still participated in some of the local bird counts, and gave talks to many of the local clubs. Victoria County was a great place to live.

But I thought it was time to think of downsizing and moving closer to some of the kids. Ro reluctantly agreed that it was a wise choice. For a while he insisted on taking his yard with him, and it took hours of persuasion to talk him out of that. After a few exploratory trips, the decision was made to buy a home in Bryan, Texas.

We moved in December 2009 into a small but nice house in a fifty-five-and-above only neighborhood. The very small, totally inadequate yard, according to Ro, was reason enough for him to adopt a local place to go weekly. Lick Creek Park, a 515-acre area in College Station, is just a twenty-minute drive from the house.

After twenty-plus years in the country, the move to Bryan/College Station was a bit of a shock to both of us. The cars and activity level when the fifty thousand–plus college students are in the area are amazing. But there are pluses, too. There are many conveniences not available when living in the country, the people are nice, and it is a beautiful part of Texas.

We haven't traveled as much since moving to Bryan, but that has more to do with the drought than anything else. We have gone on a few trips, the favorite being a three-week trip in 2010 to Idaho, Wyoming, and Montana. Ro was born in Idaho Falls and spent a number of summers in the Jackson Hole area. We joined a group of friends in Jackson for a week of butterflies in the Rocky Mountains. We saw many beautiful butterflies, enjoyed the friendship, and the scenery was spectacular. It just doesn't get much better.

Ro still keeps records of the butterflies he sees, gives lots of talks, and leads some walks. He has finished his autobiography about his years in the National Park Service, important to both of us. Our very small yard is looking better all the time. It has about as many flower beds as it will hold, and it is really pretty. Now all we need are some rains to bring on the butterflies. Then the two of us, but especially Ro, will be content.

Betty Newman Wauer, July 2013

Appendix: Scientific Names

Mammals

Badger (*Taxidea taxus*)

Bear, black (*Ursus americanus*)

Bear, grizzly (*Ursus arctus*)

Beaver (*Castor canadensis*)

Beaver, mountain (*Aplodontia rufa*)

Bighorn (*Ovis canadensis*)

Bobcat (*Lynx rufus*)

Burro (*Equus asinus*)

Caribou (*Rangifer tarandus*)

Chipmunk (*Tamias* sp.)

Coyote (*Canis latrans*)

Deer, mule (*Odocoileus hemionus*)

Deer, red (*Cervus elaphus*)

Deer, white-tailed (*Odocoileus virginianus*)

Elk (*Cervus elaphus*)

Flying squirrel (*Glaucomys sabrinus*)

Fox, gray (*Urocyon cinereoargenteus*)

Ground-squirrel, golden-mantled (*Spermophilus lateralis*)

Hog, wild (*Sus scrofa*)

Jackrabbit, black-tailed (*Lepus californicus*)

Javelina (*Pecari tajacu*)

Kangaroo rat (*Dipodomys* sp.)

Lion, mountain (*Puma concolor*)

Lynx (*Lynx canadensis*)

Lynx, Mediterranean (*Lynx lynx*)

Marten, pine (*Martes americana*)

Mongoose (*Herpestes* spp.)

Moose (*Alces alces*)

Mouse, deer (*Peromyscus* sp.)

Mouse, harvest (*Reithrodontomys* sp.)

Mouse, house (*Mus musculus*)

Mouse, white-footed (*Peromyscus leucopus*)

Opossum (*Didelphis virginiana*)

Raccoon (*Procyon lotor*)

Sea lion (*Zalophus californianus*)

Shrew, desert (*Notiosorex crawfordi*)

Whale, gray (*Eschrichtius robustus*)

Whale, humpback (*Magaptiera novacangliae*)

Wood rat (*Neotoma* sp.)

Birds

Anhinga (*Anhinga anhinga*)
Ani, groove-billed (*Crotophaga sulcirostris*)
Ani, smooth-billed (*Crotophaga ani*)
Antshrike, slaty (*Thamnophilus atrinucha*)
Ant-tanager, red-throated (*Habia fuscicauda*)
Antwren, checkered-throated (*Myrmotherula fulviventris*)
Antwren, spotted (*Hylophlax naevioides*)
Antwren, white-flanked (*Myrmotherula axillaries*)
Auklet, Cassin's (*Phychoramphus aleuticus*)
Bananaquit (*Coereba flaveola*)
Bee-eater, green (*Merops orientalis*)
Bishop, red (*Euplectes franciscanus*)
Blackbird (*Turdus merula*)
Blackbird, melodious (*Dives dives*)
Blackbird, red-winged (*Agelaius phoeniceus*)
Black-hawk, common (*Buteogallus anthracinus*)
Blackpoll (*Dendroica striata*)
Bluethroat (*Kuscinia svecica*)
Brambling (*Fringilla montifringilla*)
Bulbul, common (*Pynonotus barbatus*)
Bullfinch (*Pyrrhula pyrrhula*)
Bullfinch, lesser Antillean (*Loxigilla noctis*)
Bullfinch, Puerto Rican (*Loxigilla portoricensis*)
Bunting, snow (*Plectrophenax nivalis*)
Caracara, crested (*Caracara plancus*)
Cardinal, northern (*Cardinalis cardinalis*)
Carib, green-throated (*Eulampis holosericeus*)
Chat, yellow-breasted (*Icteria virens*)
Chickadee, black-capped (*Poecile atricapillus*)
Chickadee, Carolina (*Poecile carolinensis*)
Chukar (*Alectoris chukar*)
Chuck-will's-widow (*Caprimulgus carolinensis*)
Condor, California (*Gymnogyps californianus*)
Cormorant, Brandt's (*Phalacrocorax penicillatus*)
Cormorant, neotropical (*Phalacrocorax brasilianus*)
Cormorant, pelagic (*Phalacrocorax pelagicus*)
Coucal, Senegal (*Centropus senegalensis*)
Cowbird, brown-headed (*Molothrus ater*)
Cowbird, shiny (*Molothrus bonariensis*)
Crossbill, white-winged (*Loxia leucoptera*)
Crow, carrion (*Corvus corone*)
Crow, fish (*Corvus ossifragus*)
Cuckoo (*Cuculus canotus*)
Cuckoo, mangrove (*Coccyzus minor*)
Cuckoo, Puerto Rican (*Saurothera vieilloti*)
Cuckoo, squirrel (*Piaya cayana*)
Dipper (*Cinclus cinclus*)
Dipper, American (*Cinclus mexicanus*)
Dove, mourning (*Zenaida macroura*)
Dove, rock (*Columba livia*)
Dove, white-winged (*Zenaida asiatica*)
Dove, Zenaida (*Zenaida aurita*)
Duck, harlequin (*Histrionicus histrionicus*)
Duck, ruddy (*Oxyura jamaicensis*)
Duck, tufted (*Atthya fuligula*)
Duck, white-faced (*Dendrocygna fuligula*)
Eagle, bald (*Haliaeetus leucocephalus*)
Eagle, golden (*Aquila chrysaetos*)
Eagle, imperial (*Aquila heliaca*)

Eagle, short-toed (*Circaetus gallicus*)

Eagle, white-tailed (*Haliaeetus albicilla*)

Egret, cattle (*Bubulcus ibis*)

Egret, great (*Archea alba*)

Egret, little (*Egretta garzetta*)

Egret, snowy (*Egretta thula*)

Elaenia, Caribbean (*Elaenia martinica*)

Elaenia, forest (*Myiopagis gaimardii*)

Emerald, Puerto Rican (*Chlorostilbon maugaeus*)

Euphonia, yellow-throated (*Euphonia hirundinacea*)

Falcon, peregrine (*Falco peregrinus*)

Falcon, prairie (*Falco mexicanus*)

Finch, house (*Carpodacus mexicanus*)

Flamingo (*Phoenicopterus* sp.)

Flicker, red-shafted (*Colaptes cafer*)

Flycatcher, Acadian (*Empidonax virescens*)

Flycatcher, ash-throated (*Myiarchus cinerascens*)

Flycatcher, brown-crested (*Myiarchus tyrannulus*)

Flycatcher, great crested (*Myiarchus crinitus*)

Flycatcher, lesser Antillean (*Myiarchus oberi*)

Flycatcher, Pacific-slope (*Empidonax difficilis*)

Flycatcher, pied (*Ficedula hypoleuca*)

Flycatcher, Puerto Rican (*Myiarchus antillarum*)

Flycatcher, vermilion (*Pyrocephalus rubinus*)

Frigatebird, magnificent (*Fregata magnificens*)

Gallinule, common (*Gallinule chloropus*)

Gallinule, purple (*Porphyrula martinica*)

Gnatcatcher, black-tailed (*Polioptila melanura*)

Gnatcatcher, blue-gray (*Polioptila caerulea*)

Godwit, marbled (*Limosa fedoa*)

Goldcrest (*Regulus regulus*)

Goldfinch, Lawrence's (*Carduelis lawrencei*)

Goose, Egyptian (*Alopochen aegyptiacus*)

Goose, graylag (*Anser anser*)

Goshawk, northern (*Accipiter gentiles*)

Grackle, greater Antillean (*Quiscalus niger*)

Grassquit, black-faced (*Tiaris bicolor*)

Grassquit, yellow-faced (*Tiaris olivacea*)

Grebe, least (*Tachybaptus dominicus*)

Greenlet, lesser (*Hylophilus decurtatus*)

Grosbeak, crimson-collared (*Rhodothraupis celaeno*)

Grosbeak, rose-breasted (*Pheucticus ludovicianus*)

Ground-dove, common (*Columbina passerine*)

Grouse, spruce (*Falcipennis canadensis*)

Guan, crested (*Penelope purpurascens*)

Guineafowl, helmeted (*Numida meleagris*)

Gull, black-headed (*Larus ridibundus*)

Gull, Heermann's (*Larus heermanni*)

Gull, slender-billed (*Chroicocephalus genei*)

Gull, western (*Larus occidentalis*)

Gyrfalcon (*Falco rusticolus*)

Harrier, marsh (*Circus spilonotus*)

Hawk, Cooper's (*Accipiter cooperii*)

Hawk, crane (*Geranospiza caerulescens*)

Hawk, Harris's (*Parabuteo unicinctus*)

Hawk, red-shouldered (*Buteo lineatus*)

Hawk, red-tailed (*Buteo jamaicensis*)

Hawk, rough-legged (*Buteo lagopus*)

Hawk, sharp-shinned (*Accipiter striatus*)

Hawk, zone-tailed (*Buteo albonotatus*)

Heron, boat-billed (*Cochlearius cochlearius*)
Heron, great blue (*Ardea herodias*)
Heron, green (*Butorides virescens*)
Heron, little blue (*Egretta caerulea*)
Heron, squacco (*Ardeola ralloides*)
Heron, tricolored (*Egretta tricolor*)
Hobby (*Falco subbuteo*)
Hoopoe (*Upupa epops*)
Hummingbird, Anna's (*Calypte anna*)
Hummingbird, Antillean crested (*Orthorhynchus cristatus*)
Hummingbird, blue-headed (*Cyanophaia bicolor*)
Hummingbird, blue-throated (*Lampornis clemenciae*)
Hummingbird, Costa's (*Calypte costae*)
Hummingbird, Lucifer (*Calothorax lucifer*)
Jay, blue (*Cyanocitta cristata*)
Jay, Mexican (*Aphelocoma ultramarina*)
Junco, dark-eyed (*Junco hyemalis*)
Junco, gray-headed (*Junco hyemalis*)
Junco, Oregon (*Junco hyemalis*)
Kestrel, American (*Falco sparverius*)
Kingbird, Couch's (*Tyrannus couchii*)
Kingbird, gray (*Tyrannus dominicensis*)
Kingbird, loggerhead (*Tyrannus caudifasciatus*)
Kingbird, thick-billed (*Tyrannus crassirostris*)
Kingfisher (*Alcedo atthis*)
Kingfisher, green (*Chloroceryle americana*)
Kingfisher, ringed (*Ceryle torquata*)
Kingfisher, white-breasted (*Halcyon smyrnensis*)
Kite, double-toothed (*Harpagus bidentatus*)
Kite, hook-billed (*Chonodrohierax uncinatus*)

Kite, Mississippi (*Intinia mississippiensis*)
Kite, red (*Milvus milvus*)
Kite, swallow-tailed (*Elanoides forticatus*)
Kite, white-tailed (*Elanus leucurus*)
Lapwing (*Vanellus vanellus*)
Lark, crested (*Galerida cristata*)
Lark, Thekla (*Galerida theklae*)
Lark, wood (*Lullula arborea*)
Longspur, Lapland (*Calcarius lapponicus*)
Loon, Pacific (*Gavia pacifica*)
Magpie, azure-rumped (*Cyanopica cyanus*)
Magpie, black-billed (*Pica pica*)
Magpie, yellow-billed (*Pica nuttalli*)
Mango, green (*Anthracothorax dominicus*)
Mannikin, bronze (*Lonchura malacca*)
Martin, Caribbean (*Progne dominicensis*)
Merganser, red-breasted (*Mergus serrator*)
Mockingbird, northern (*Mimus polyglottos*)
Motmot, blue-crowned (*Momotus momota*)
Murrelet, Kittlitz's (*Brachyramphus brevirostris*)
Nighthawk, lesser (*Chordeiles acutipennis*)
Nighthawk, West Indian (*Chordeiles gundlachii*)
Night-heron, black-crowned (*Nycticorax nycticorax*)
Nightingale (*Luscinia magarhynchos*)
Nightjar, Puerto Rican (*Caprimulgus noctitherus*)
Nightjar, white-tailed (*Caprimulgus cayennensis*)
Noddy, brown (*Anous stolidus*)
Nutcracker, Clark's (*Nucifraga columbiana*)
Nuthatch, brown-headed (*Sitta pusilla*)
Nuthatch, red-breasted (*Sitta canadensis*)
Nuthatch, white-breasted (*Sitta carolinensis*)

Oriole, Altamira (*Icterus gularis*)

Oriole, black-cowled (*Icterus dominicensis*)

Oriole, black-vented (*Icterus wagleri*)

Oriole, Martinique (*Icterus bonana*)

Oriole, Montserrat (*Icterus oberi*)

Oriole, orchard (*Icterus spurious*)

Oriole, Scott's (*Icterus parisorum*)

Osprey (*Pandion haliaetus*)

Ovenbird (*Seiurus aurocapillus*)

Owl, barn (*Tyto alba*)

Owl, barred (*Strix varia*)

Owl, elf (*Micrathene whitneyi*)

Owl, flammulated (*Otus flammeolus*)

Owl, great gray (*Strix nebulosa*)

Owl, great horned (*Bubo virginianus*)

Owl, long-eared (*Asio otus*)

Owl, mottled (*Strix virgata*)

Owl, saw-whet (*Aegolius acadicus*)

Owl, spotted (*Strix occidentalis*)

Owl, tawny (*Strix aluco*)

Oystercatcher (*Haematopus ostralegus*)

Oystercatcher, black (*Haematopus bachmani*)

Parakeet, brown-throated (*Aratinga pertinax*)

Parakeet, monk (*Myiopsitta monachus*)

Parakeet, olive-throated (Aztec) (*Aratinga astec*)

Parrot, Puerto Rican (*Amazonia vittata*)

Partridge, red-legged (*Alectoris rufa*)

Parula, northern (*Parula americana*)

Parula, tropical (*Parula pitiayumi*)

Pelican, brown (*Pelecanus occidentalis*)

Phainopepla (*Phainopepla nitens*)

Phoebe, eastern (*Sayornis phoebe*)

Phoebe, Say's (*Sayornis saya*)

Pigeon, red-billed (*Columba flavirostris*)

Pigeon, white-crowned (*Columba leucocephala*)

Pintail, white-cheeked (*Anas bahamensis*)

Pipit, meadow (*Anthus pratensis*)

Pipit, rock (*Anthus petrosus*)

Pipit, tawny (*Anthus campestris*)

Plover, Kentish (*Charadrius alexandrinus*)

Plover, mountain (*Charadrius montanus*)

Plover, piping (*Charadrius melodus*)

Plover, ringed (*Charadrius dubius*)

Plover, snowy (*Charadrius alexandrinus*)

Plover, spur-winged (*Vanellus spinosus*)

Pochard, red-crested (*Netto rufina*)

Ptarmigan, rock (*Lagopus mutus*)

Puffin, tufted (*Fratercula cirrhata*)

Pygmy-owl, northern (*Glaucidium gnoma*)

Pyrrhuloxia (*Cardinalis sinuatus*)

Quail (*Coturnix coturnix*)

Quail, California (*Callipepla californica*)

Quail, Montezuma (*Cyrtonyx montezumae*)

Quail, mountain (*Oreortyx pictus*)

Quail-dove, bridled (*Geotrygon mystacea*)

Rail, clapper (*Rallus longirostris*)

Raven, brown-necked (*Corvus ruficollis*)

Raven, common (*Corvus corax*)

Redpoll, hoary (*Carduelis hornemanni*)

Redstart (*Phoenicurus phoenicurus*)

Redstart, American (*Setophaga ruticilla*)

Redstart, black (*Phoenicurus ochrures*)

Redstart, painted (*Myioborus pictus*)

Roadrunner, greater (*Geococcyx californianus*)

Robin (*Erithacus rubecula*)

Robin, American (*Turdus migratorius*)

Robin, bare-eyed (*Turdus nudigenis*)

Robin, rufous-backed (*Turdus rufopalliatus*)

Rock-thrush, blue (*Monticolia solitarius*)

Ruff (*Philomachus pugnax*)

Saltator, lesser Antillean (*Saltator albicollis*)

Sandgrouse, pin-tailed (*Pteracies alchata*)

Sandpiper, marsh (*Tringa stagnatilis*)

Sandpiper, semipalmated (*Calidris pusilla*)

Sand-plover, lesser (*Charadrius mongolus*)

Screech-owl, Puerto Rican (*Otus nudipes*)

Screech-owl, western (*Otus kennicottii*)

Shelduck, ruddy (*Tadarna ferruginea*)

Shrike, loggerhead (*Lanius ludovicianus*)

Skylark (*Alauda arvensis*)

Solitaire, rufous-throated (*Myadestes genibarbis*)

Sparrow, Bachman's (*Aimophila aestivalis*)

Sparrow, black-chinned (*Spizella atrogularis*)

Sparrow, golden-crowned (*Zonotrichia atricapilla*)

Sparrow, house (*Passer domesticus*)

Sparrow, olive (*Arremonops rufivigatus*)

Sparrow, rufous-crowned (*Aimophila ruficeps*)

Sparrow, swamp (*Melospiza georgiana*)

Sparrow, tree (*Spizella arborea*)

Sparrow, vesper (*Pooecetes gramineus*)

Sparrow, white-throated (*Zonotrichia albicollis*)

Starling, spotless (*Sturnus unicolor*)

Stint, little (*Calidris minuta*)

Stonechat (*Saxicolis rubicola*)

Stork, white (*Ciconia ciconia*)

Storm-petrel, black (*Oceanodroma melania*)

Swallow, cave (*Petrochelidon fulva*)

Swallow, cliff (*Petrochelidon pyrrhonota*)

Swan, trumpeter (*Cygnus buccinator*)

Swift, lesser Antillean (*Chaetura martinica*)

Swift, Vaux's (*Chaetura vauxi*)

Swift, white-throated (*Aeronautus saxatalis*)

Tanager, gray-headed (*Eucometis penicillata*)

Tanager, hepatic (*Piranga flava*)

Tanager, Puerto Rican (*Nesospingus speculiferus*)

Tanager, summer (*Piranga rubra*)

Tanager, western (*Piranga ludoviciana*)

Tanager, white-shouldered (*Tachyphonus luctuosus*)

Tern, least (*Sterna antillarum*)

Tern, roseate (*Sterna dougallii*)

Tern, royal (*Sterna maxima*)

Tern, Sandwich (*Sterna sandivicensis*)

Thrasher, California (*Toxostoma redivivum*)

Thrasher, Crissal (*Toxostoma crissale*)

Thrasher, Le Conte's (*Toxostoma lecontei*)

Thrasher, long-billed (*Toxostoma longirostre*)

Thrasher, pearly-eyed (*Margarops fuscatus*)

Thrasher, white-breasted (*Ramphocinclus brachyurus*)

Thrush, red-legged (*Turdus plumbeus*)

Thrush, rock (*Monticola saxatillis*)

Tiger-heron, bare-throated (*Tigrisoma mexicanum*)

Tinamou, thicket (*Crypturellus cinnamomeus*)

Tit, blue (*Cyanistes caeruleus*)

Tit, crested (*Lophophanes cristatus*)

Tit, great (*Parus major*)

Titmouse, black-crested (*Baeolophus atricristatus*)

Titmouse, tufted (*Baeolophus bicolor*)

Tody, Puerto Rican (*Todus mexicanus*)

Towhee, California (*Pipilo crissalis*)

Towhee, canyon (*Melozone fuscus*)

Towhee, spotted (*Pipilo maculatus*)

Trogon, violaceous (*Trogon violaceus*)

Tropicbird, red-billed (*Phaethon aethereus*)

Troupial (*Icterus icterus*)

Turkey, wild (*Meleagris gallopavo*)

Verdin (*Auriparus flaviceps*)

Vireo, Bell's (*Vireo bellii*)

Vireo, black-capped (*Vireo atricapillus*)

Vireo, gray (*Vireo vicinior*)

Vireo, red-eyed (*Vireo olivaceus*)

Vireo, solitary (*Vireo solitarius*)

Vireo, yellow-green (*Vireo flavoviridis*)

Vireo, yellow-throated (*Vireo flavifrons*)

Vulture, black (*Coragyps atratus*)

Vulture, griffon (*Gyps rueppellii*)

Wagtail, pied (*Motacilla aguimp*)

Wagtail, white (*Motacilla alba*)

Warbler, Adelaide's (*Dendroica adelaidae*)

Warbler, black-and-white (*Mniotilta varia*)

Warbler, black-throated green (*Dendroica nigrescens*)

Warbler, blue-winged (*Vermivora pinus*)

Warbler, Bonelli's (*Phylloscopus bonellii*)

Warbler, Cape May (*Dendroica tigrina*)

Warbler, Colima (*Vermivora crissalis*)

Warbler, Dartford (*Sylvia undata*)

Warbler, elfin woods (*Dendroica angelae*)

Warbler, fan-tailed (*Bassileuterus lachrymosa*)

Warbler, Grace's (*Dendroica graciae*)

Warbler, grasshopper (*Locustella naevie*)

Warbler, hooded (*Wilsonia citrine*)

Warbler, Lucy's (*Vermivora luciae*)

Warbler, magnolia (*Dendroica magnolia*)

Warbler, mourning (*Oporornis philadelphia*)

Warbler, Orphean (*Sylvia hortensis*)

Warbler, prothonotary (*Protonotaria citrea*)

Warbler, Sardinian (*Sylvia melanocephala*)

Warbler, sedge (*Acrocephalus schoenobaenus*)

Warbler, willow (*Phylloscopus trochilus*)

Warbler, worm-eating (*Helmitheros vermivorus*)

Warbler, yellow (*Dendroica petechia*)

Warbler, yellow-rumped (*Dendroica coronata*)

Waterthrush, northern (*Seiurus noveboracensis*)

Weaver, village (*Ploceus cucullatus*)

Wheatear (*Oenanthe oenanthe*)

Wheatear, Isabelline (*Iduna opaca*)

Whimbrel (*Numenius phaeopus*)

Whistling-duck, West Indian (*Dendrocygna arborea*)

Whitethroat, lesser (*Sylvia curruca*)

Willet (*Catoptrophorus semipalmatus*)

Woodcreeper, ivory-billed (*Xiphorhynchus flavigaster*)

Woodcreeper, plain-brown (*Dendrocincla fuliginosa*)

Woodpecker, downy (*Picoides pubescens*)

Woodpecker, greater (*Dendrocopos major*)

Woodpecker, green (*Picus viridis*)

Woodpecker, ivory-billed (*Campephilus principalis*)

Woodpecker, ladder-backed (*Picoides scalaris*)

Woodpecker, lesser spotted (*Dendrocopos minor*)

Woodpecker, Nuttall's (*Picoides nuttallii*)

Woodpecker, pileated (*Dryocopus pileatus*)

Woodpecker, Puerto Rican (*Melanerpes portoricensis*)

Woodpecker, red-headed (*Melanerpes erythrocephalus*)

Woodpecker, smoky-brown (*Veriliornis fumigatus*)

Wren, Bewick's (*Thryomanes bewickii*)

Wren, brown-throated (*Troglodytes brunneicollis*)

Wren, cactus (*Campylorhynchus brunneicapillus*)

Wren, canyon (*Catherpes mexicana*)

Wren, rock (*Salpinctes obsoletus*)

Wrentit (*Chamaea fasciata*)

Yellow-finch, grassland (*Sicalis luteola*)

Yellowhammer (*Emberiza citrinella*)

Yellowthroat, common (*Geothlypis trichas*)

Yellowthroat, gray-crowned (*Chamaethlypis poliocephala*)

Zenops, plain (*Xenops minutus*)

Reptiles

Chuckwalla (*Sauromalus sauros*)

Coachwhip (*Masticophis flagellum*)

Coachwhip, western (*Masticophis flagellum testaceus*)

Gecko, Mediterranean (*Hemidactylus turcicus*)

Gila monster (*Heloderma suspectum*)

Horned-lizard, Cedros Island (*Phrynosoma cerroense*)

Horned-lizard, coastal (*Phrynosoma coronatum*)

Kingsnake, common (*Lampropelis getula*)

Lizard, desert night (*Xantusia vigilis*)

Lizard, ground (*Ameiva polops*)

Lizard, side-blotched (*Uta stansburiana*)

Lizard, spiny (*Sceloporus olivaceus*)

Lizard, Texas alligator (*Gerrhonotus liocephalus*)

Lizard, western fence (*Scelophorus undulates*)

Racer, western yellow-bellied (*Coluber constrictor*)

Rattlesnake, Mohave (*Crotalus scutulatus*)

Rattlesnake, Panamint (*Crotalus mitchellii stephensi*)

Rattlesnake, speckled (*Crotalus mitchellii*)

Rattlesnake, western (*Crotalus atrox*)

Rattlesnake, western diamondback (*Crotalus atrox*)

Sea turtle, green (*Chelonia mydas*)

Sea turtle, hawksbill (*Eretimochelys imbricata*)

Sea turtle, Kemp's ridley (*Lepidochelys kempii*)

Sea turtle, leatherback (*Dermochelys coreacea*)

Sea turtle, Pacific ridley (*Lepidochelys olivacea*)

Sidewinder (*Crotalus cerastes*)

Snake, California lyre (*Trimorphodon bisculatus*)

Snake, common garter (*Thomnophis siratis*)

Snake, gopher (*Pituophis melanoleucus*)

Snake, long-nosed (*Rhinochelius lecontei*)

Snake, spotted night (*Hypsiglena torquata*)

Tortoise, desert (*Gopherus agassizii*)

Tortoise, Texas (*Gopherus berlandieri*)
Turtle, western pond (*Actinemys marmorata*)
Whiptail, California (*Masticophis lateralis*)

Amphibians

Salamander, tiger (*Ambystoma tigrinum*)

Fish

Bluegill (*Lepomis macrochirius*)
Fish, mosquito (*Gambusia affinis*)
Gambusia, Big Bend (*Gambusia gaigei*)
Goldfish (*Carassius auratus*)
Mackerel (*Scomber scombrus*)
Pupfish, Rio Grande (*Cyprinodon* sp.)
Shiner, Chihuahuan (*Notropis jemenzanus*)
Stoneroller, Mexican (*Campostoma ornatus*)
Sunfish, green (*Chaenobryttus cyanellus*)

Insects

Blue, square-spotted (*Euphilotes battoides*)
Checkerspot, Edith's (*Euphydryas editha*)
Hairstreak, bramble green (*Callophrys perplexa*)
Hairstreak, Sheridan's (*Callophrys sheridanii*)
Metatmark, Zela (*Emesis Zela*)
Satyr, Georgia (*Neonympha ateolata*)
Swallowtail, black (*Papilio polyxenes*)
Swallowtail, eastern tiger (*Papilio glaucus*)
Swallowtail, Palamedes (*Papilio palamedes*)
Swallowtail, spicebush (*Papilio troilus*)

Swallowtail, zebra (*Eurytids marcellus*)
Tortoiseshell, California (*Nymphalis californica*)
Viceroy (*Limenitis archippus*)
White, spring (*Pontia sisymbrii*)

Other Invertebrates

Abalone (*Haliotus* spp.)
Conch, crown (*Melongena melongena*)
Metastome, distorted (*Metastome* sp.)
Murex, fringed (*Murex* sp.)
Shrimp, fairy (*Branchinecta* spp.)
Shrimp, fairy (*Eulimnadia texana*)
Snail, agave (*Humboldtiana agavophile*)
Snail, distorted metastome (*Metastoma roemeri*)
Snail, Stockton Plateau three-band (*Humboldtiana texana*)

Plants

Agave (*Agave* spp.)
Bottle brush (*Callistemon cirrinus*)
Boxwood, Vahl's (*Buxus vahlii*)
Cactus, barrel (*Echinocactus wislizeni*)
Cactus, cotton-top (*Echinocactus polycephalus*)
Cardon (*Cereus pringlei*)
Coral plant (*Berberidopsis corallina*)
Creosotebush (*Larrea tridentata*)
Cypress, Arizona (*Cupressus arizonica*)
Fern, swamp (*Acrostichum danaeifolium*)
Fire dart, giant (*Malvaviscus arboreus*)
Hemlock, mountain (*Tsuga mertensiana*)

Ixora (*Ixora* spp.)
Joshua tree (*Yucca breviflora*)
Kapok (*Ceiba pentandra*)
Lechuguilla (*Euphorbia antisyphilitica*)
Mesquite (*Prosopis glandulosa*)
Ocotillo (*Fouquieria splendens*)
Pine, digger (*Pinus sabineana*)
Pine, ponderosa (*Pinus ponderosa*)
Pinyon, Mexican (*Pinus cembroides*)

Sources Consulted

Alden, Peter, and John Gooders. 1981. *Finding Birds around the World*. Boston: Houghton Mifflin.

Bailey, Vernon. 1905. *Biological Survey of Texas*. North American Fauna 25. Washington, DC: Government Printing Office.

Benson, Lyman. 1982. *The Cacti of the United States and Canada*. Stanford, CA: Stanford University Press.

Bissonette, John A. 1982. *Ecological Behavior of the Collared Peccary in Big Bend National Park*. Scientific Monograph Series No. 16. Washington, DC: US Department of the Interior, National Park Service.

Blake, Emmet Reid. 1953. *Birds of Mexico*. Chicago: University of Chicago Press.

Bond, James. 1985. *Birds of the West Indies*. Boston: Houghton Mifflin.

Conant, Roger. 1975. *A Field Guide to the Reptiles and Amphibians of Eastern North America*. Boston: Houghton Mifflin.

Gertsch, Willis J., and M. Soleglad. 1972. "Studies of North American Scorpions of the Genera *Uroctonus* and *Vejovis* (Scorpionida, Vejovidae)." *Bulletin of the American Museum of Natural History* 148:549–608.

Johnston, Richard F., and Robert K. Selander. 1964. "House Sparrows: Rapid Evolution of Races in North America." *Science* 144:548–50.

Oberholser, Harry C., and Edgar B. Kincaid, Jr. 1974. *The Birdlife of Texas*. Austin: University of Texas Press.

Peterson, Roger Tory, and Edward L. Chalif. 1973. *A Field Guide to Mexican Birds*. Boston: Houghton Mifflin.

Raffaele, Herbert A. 1983. *A Guide to the Birds of Puerto Rico and the Virgin Islands*. San Juan, Puerto Rico: Fondo Educativo Interamericano.

Scott, D. A., and M. Carbonell. 1986. *Directory of Neotropical Wetlands*. Richmond, UK: IUCN Conservation Monitoring Centre.

Selander, R. K., M. H. Smith, S. Y. Yang, W. E. Johnson, and J. B. Gentry. 1964. "Seasonal Variation in Gene Frequencies in the House Sparrow." *Science* 149:548–55.

Stebbins, Robert C. 1966. *A Field Guide to Western Reptiles and Amphibians*. Boston: Houghton Mifflin.

Viola, Herman J. 1993. *An American Warrior: Ben Nighthorse Campbell*. New York: Orion Books.

Welles, Ralph E., and Florence Welles. 1961. *The Bighorn of Death Valley*. Fauna of the National Parks Series No. 6. Washington, DC: US Department of the Interior.

Publications Authored and Coauthored by Ro Wauer

Beason, Robert C., and Roland H. Wauer. 1999. "Colima Warbler (*Vermivora crissalis*)." In *The Birds of North America*, no. 383, 1–12. Philadelphia: Birds of North America.

Hubbs, Clark, J. Johns, and Roland H. Wauer. 1977. *Habitat Management Plan for Big Bend Gambusia, Big Bend National Park, Texas*. Washington, DC: US Department of the Interior, National Park Service.

Hubbs, Clark, and Roland Wauer. 1973. "Seasonal Changes in the Fish Fauna of Tornillo Creek, Brewster County, Texas." *Southwestern Naturalist* 17 (4): 375–79.

Knudson, Ed, Charles Bordelon, and Roland H. Wauer. 2001. "Zela Metalmark (*Emesis zela* Butler): A New Record for Texas." *News of the Lepidopterists' Society* 43 (1): 199.

Turner, Frederick B., and Roland H. Wauer. 1963. "A Survey of the Herpetofauna of the Death Valley Area." *Great Basin Naturalist* 3–4:119–28.

Wauer, Roland H. 1957a. "Bird Notes from the Crater Lake Area." *Audubon Society of Portland Warbler*, November, 1–3.

———. 1957b. *Checklist of the Birds of Crater Lake National Park*. White City, OR: Crater Lake Natural History Association.

———. 1958a. "Checklist of the Birds of Pinnacles National Monument, California." National Park Service. Mimeograph.

———. 1958b. "General Report on the Vertebrates of Pinnacles National Monument." Typed report to National Park Service.

———. 1959. "The Ecological Distribution of the Birds of Pinnacles." Typed report to National Park Service.

———. 1960. "Rare Migrants to Death Valley National Monument." *Condor* 62:139.

———. 1962. "A Survey of the Birds of Death Valley." *Condor* 62:220–33.

———. 1964a. "The Ecological Distribution of the Birds of the Panamint Mountains, California." *Condor* 66:287–301.

———. 1964b. *A Guide to the Trails of Zion National Park*. Springdale, UT: Zion Natural History Association.

———. 1964c. "Hiking in Zion National Park." *National Parks Magazine*, December, 10–11.

———. 1964d. *Reptiles and Amphibians of Zion National Park*. Springdale, UT: Zion Natural History Association.

———. 1964e. "The Unpredictable Nelson Bighorn." *National Parks Magazine*, August, 10–11.

———. 1965a. "Genus and Species of Shrew New for Utah." *Journal of Mammalogy* 46:496.

———. 1965b. "Intraspecific Relationship in Red-shafted Flickers." *Wilson Bulletin* 77 (4): 404.

———. 1965c. "The Narrows of Zion—a Passageway of Time." *Summit Magazine*, March, 4–12.

———. 1965d. *The Narrows Trail*. Springdale, UT: Zion Natural History Association.

———. 1965e. *Pictograph Site in Cave Valley, Zion National Park, Utah*. Anthropological Papers No. 75. University of Utah Miscellaneous Papers No. 9. Salt Lake City: University of Utah Press.

———. 1965f. "Wintering Rufous-crowned Sparrows Found in Utah." *Condor* 67 (5): 447.

———. 1966a. "Eastern Phoebe in Utah." *Condor* 68 (5): 519.

———. 1966b. "Flammulated Owl Records Following May Storms in Zion Canyon, Utah." *Condor* 68 (2): 211.

———. 1967a. *Chisos Mountain Trails*. Big Bend National Park, TX: Big Bend Natural History Association.

———. 1967b. "Colima Warbler Census in Big Bend's Chisos Mountains." *National Parks Magazine*, November, 8–10.

———. 1967c. "First Thick-billed Kingbird Record for Texas." *Southwestern Naturalist* 12 (4): 485–86.

———. 1967d. "New Status for the Rufous-crowned Sparrow in Utah." *Wilson Bulletin* 79 (3): 348–49.

———. 1968a. *Check-list of the Birds of Big Bend National Park*. Big Bend National Park, TX: Big Bend Natural History Association.

———. 1968b. "The Groove-billed Ani in Texas." *Southwestern Naturalist* 13 (4): 452.

———. 1968c. "Hiking the Day before Yesterday." *Summit Magazine*, November, 6–13.

———. 1968d. "Northern Range Extension of Wied's Crested Flycatcher." *Condor* 70 (1): 88.

———. 1969. "Recent Bird Records from the Virgin River Valley of Utah, Arizona, and Nevada." *Condor* 72 (3): 331–35.

———. 1970a. *Guide to the Backcountry Roads and the River*. Big Bend National Park, TX: Big Bend Natural History Association.

———. 1970b. "The Occurrence of the

Black-vented Oriole, *Icterus wagleri*, in the United States." *Auk* 87 (4): 361–62.

———. 1970c. *Road Guide*. Big Bend National Park, TX: Big Bend Natural History Association.

———. 1971a. "Ecological Distribution of Birds of the Chisos Mountains, Texas." *Southwestern Naturalist* 16 (1): 1–129.

———. 1971b. *Hiker's Guide—Big Bend National Park*. Big Bend National Park, TX: Big Bend Natural History Association.

———. 1971c. "The Texas Big Bend Country." *Cactus and Succulent Journal* 38:51–54.

———. 1972. "Birds, Bird Study, and Conservation of Birds in Texas: A Panel Discussion." *Texas Ornithological Society* 5:14–22.

———. 1973a. *Birds of Big Bend National Park and Vicinity*. Austin: University of Texas Press.

———. 1973b. *Naturalist's Big Bend*. Santa Fe, NM: Peregrine Productions.

———. 1973c. "Report on Harlequin Quail Release, Big Bend National Park." Typed report to National Park Service.

———. 1973d. "Seasonal Changes in the Fish Fauna of Tornillo Creek, Brewster County, Texas." *Southwestern Naturalist* 18:105–10.

———. 1975. "A Case History of Land Use and Some Ecological Implications, the Chisos Mountains, Big Bend National Park, Texas." *Proceedings of the Second Resource Manage-*

ment Conference, SW Region, National Park Service: 70–82.

———. 1977a. "Changes in the Breeding Avifauna within the Chisos Mountains System." In *Transactions of the Symposium on Biological Resources of the Chihuahuan Desert Region, U.S. & Mexico*, Transactions of Proceedings Series No. 3, 597–608. Washington, DC: US Department of the Interior, National Park Service.

———. 1977b. "Distributional Relations of Breeding Avifauna of Four Southwestern Mountain Ranges." In *Transactions of the Symposium on Biological Resources of the Chihuahuan Desert Region, U.S. & Mexico*, Transactions of Proceedings Series No. 3, 567–78. Washington, DC: US Department of the Interior, National Park Service.

———. 1977c. "Interrelations between a Harris's Hawk and a Badger." *Western Birds* 8:155.

———. 1977d. "A Program of Research at Bandelier National Monument: A Postscript to the La Mesa Fire." Typed report to National Park Service.

———. 1977e. "Significance of Rio Grande Riparian Systems upon the Avifauna." In *Symposium on Importance, Preservation and Management of Riparian Habitats*, 165–74. Washington, DC: US Forest Service.

———. 1978a. *Action Plan for Restoration*

and Enhancement of Atlantic Ridley Turtle Populations, Playa de Rancho Nuevo, Mexico, and Padre Island National Seashore, Texas, 1978–1988.* Washington, DC: US Department of the Interior, National Park Service.

———. 1978b. "Head Start for an Endangered Turtle." *National Parks and Conservation Magazine* 52: 16–29.

———. 1978c. "Impacts of Feral Burros upon the Breeding Avifauna—Bandelier National Monument." Typed report to National Park Service.

———. 1978d. "The Surveillance of Wildlife in Arid Ecosystem Monitoring Programs." In *The First International Workshop on the Management of Wildlife in Arid Ecosystems*, held in Cairo, Egypt, November 4–8.

———. 1979. "Colima Warbler Status at Big Bend National Park, Texas." In *Proceedings of the First Conference on Scientific Research in the National Parks*, 469–72. Washington, DC: US Department of the Interior, National Park Service.

———. 1980a. "Great Blue Heron and Osprey Nest on Cardon Cactus on Tiburon Island, Sonora, Mexico." *Southwestern Naturalist* 24:184–85.

———. 1980b. "Parks in Peril." *Outdoor America* 45 (6): 6–9.

———. 1980c. *Role of the National Park Service Natural Resource Manager.* Cooperative Park Study Unit, University of Washington, UW-80-2.

———. 1980d. *State of the Parks—1980: A Report to the Congress.* Washington, DC: US Department of the Interior, National Park Service.

———. 1981. "State of the Parks: A Report to the Congress on a Servicewide Strategy for Prevention and Mitigation of Natural and Cultural Resources Management Problems." Typed report to Congress.

———. 1982. "The Greening of Natural Resource Management." *Trends* 19 (1): 2–6.

———. 1986a. "Baseline Studies on Avifauna Populations: Abrams Creek Floodplain and Beech Gap Special Protection Sites, Great Smoky Mountain National Park." Typed report to National Park Service.

———. 1986b. "Parks and Other Reserves as Island of Protection with Special Reference to the Chihuahuan Desert." *Chihuahuan Desert—U.S. and Mexico* 2:150–58.

———. 1987. "Caribbean Landing Point." *National Parks*, January/February, 20–21.

———. 1988a. "Avian Population Baseline for St. Croix, U.S. Virgin Islands." Typed report to US Fish and Wildlife Service.

———. 1988b. *The Historic Resources of the U.S. Virgin Islands.* Christiansted, VI: Antilles Graphic Arts.

———. 1988c. "New Hope for Salt River." *Sea Magazine,* August/September, 5–7.

———. 1988d. "Salt River's Terrestrial Fauna of Special Concern." Typed report to National Park Service.

———. 1989a. "Salt River Park Alternatives of Environmental Assessment." Typed report to National Park Service.

———. 1989b. "A Salt River Park—Last Chance for St. Croix!" Typed report to US Congress.

———. 1989c. "Virgin Islands Wildlife Resources." Typed report to National Park Service.

———. 1990. "Assessment of Changes in St. Croix Avifauna after Hurricane Hugo." Typed report to US Fish and Wildlife Service.

———. 1992. "Treasure Island." *National Parks*, September/October, 31–35.

———. 1996a. "Avian Ambassadors." *Birder's World*, October, 40–44.

———. 1996b. *A Birder's West Indies: An Island-by-Island Tour.* Austin: University of Texas Press.

———. 1997. *Birds of Zion National Park and Vicinity.* Logan: Utah State University Press.

———. 1999. "Avian Population Survey of a Tamaulipan Scrub Habitat, Tamaulipas, Mex." *Cotinga* 10:13–19.

———. 2000. *Butterfly Checklist: Big Bend National Park, Texas.* Big Bend National Park, TX: Big Bend Natural History Association.

———. 2001. *Breeding Avifaunal Baseline for Big Bend National Park, Texas.* TOS Occasional Publication No. 3. Texas Ornithological Society.

———. 2006. "Three New Butterflies Found at Big Bend National Park." *Southern Lepidopterists' News* 29 (2): 10–11.

———. 2010a. *Butterflies of Big Bend National Park and the Davis Mountains.* Austin, TX: Quick Reference Publishing.

———. 2010b. "Butterfly Richness and Abundance on the Rio Grande Floodplain." Written report to the National Park Service.

Wauer, Roland H., and George Burdick. 1975. "Range Extension of Mediterranean Gecko in Coahuila, Mexico." *Southwestern Naturalist* 19:446.

Wauer, Roland H., and Dennis Carter. 1965. *Birds of Zion National Park and Vicinity.* Springdale, UT: Zion Natural History Association.

Wauer, Roland H., and Don Davis. 1973. "Cave Swallows in Big Bend National Park, Texas." *Condor* 74 (4): 482.

Wauer, Roland H., and John Dennis. 1981. "Burro Impacts upon Avifauna." Typed report to National Park Service.

Wauer, Roland H., and Mark Flippo. 2008. "Avifaunal Changes in Big Bend National Park, Texas." In *Birds of the US-Mexico Borderlands: Distribution, Ecology, and Conservation,* 20–27. Studies in Avian Biology No. 37. Cooper Ornithological Society.

Wauer, Roland H., and Terry Johnson. 1984. "La
   Mesa Fire Effects upon Avifauna." In *La
   Mesa Fire Symposium,* Los Alamos National
   Laboratory, October 6–7, Los Alamos, NM.
Wauer, Roland H., and Ed Knudson. 2001. "De-
   finitive Destination: Big Bend National Park,
   Texas." *American Butterflies* (Spring): 4–17.
Wauer, Roland H., and Richard C. Russell. 1967.
   "New and Additional Records of Birds in
   the Virgin River Valley." *Condor* 69 (4):
   420–23.
Wauer, Roland H., and Kent Rylander. 1968.
   "Anna's Hummingbird in West Texas." *Auk*
   85 (3): 501.
Wauer, Roland H., and James Tucker. 1971.
   *Traveler's List and Checklist for Birds of North
   America.* Colorado Springs, CO: American
   Birding Association.
———. 1973. *Traveler's List and Checklist for
   Birds of Mexico.* Santa Fe, NM: Peregrine
   Productions.
Wauer, Roland H., John Vukonich, and Steve
   Cinnamon. 1981. "The Breeding Avifauna
   of Capulin Mountain National Monument,
   New Mexico." Typed report to National
   Park Service.
Wauer, Roland H., and Joe Wunderle. 1993.
   "The Effects of Hurricane Hugo on Bird
   Populations on St. Croix, U.S. Virgin Is-
   lands." *Wilson Bulletin* 104 (4): 656–73.

Index

murex, fringed, 203
Murrelet, Kittlitz's, 154

Narrows, Zion, The, 68, 69
National Academy of Sciences, 167
National Hurricane Center, 209
National Judo Bulletin, 3
National Marine Fisheries Service, 126, 129, 156
National Parks Conservation Association, 160, 166, 170, 172
National Parks & Conservation Magazine, 127
National Parks Magazine, 27, 87
National Park Service, 7, 17, 19, 50, 144, 156, 217
National Science Foundation, 63
Natural Landmark Program, 63
Natural Resources Management Plans, 118
Natural Resource Management Trainee Program, 161–62
Naturalist's Big Bend, 91
Naturalist's Mexico, 215
Naturally South Texas, 215
Nelson, Dick, 87
Newman, George, 110
News of the Lepidopterist' Society, 107
Newsone, "Buck," 79
New York Times, 170
Nichols: Betty, 80
nighthawk: lesser, 64; West Indian, 190
night-heron, black-crowned, 90, 188
nightingale, 150
nightjar: Puerto Rican, 190; white-tailed, 201, 202
Nile River, Egypt, 148
noddy: black, 202; brown, 203
Northington, David, 115
Northrop, Brad, 207
Norton, Rob, 188, 200, 201, 203

nuthatch: brown-headed, 124; red-breasted, 182; white-breasted, 182

Oberhansley, Frank, 58, 74
Oberholser, Harry C., 81, 104
Ogle, Jack, 187
Oldenburg, Lloyd, 167
opossum, 101
Oregon Caves National Monument, *16*
Organization of American States, 164
oriole: Altamira, 129–30; black-vented, 83; hooded, 90; Martininque, 292; orchard, 84; Scott's, 83; Wagler's, 83
osprey, *134*, 139, 188
ovenbird, 197
owl: barn, 41; barred, 124; elf, 81; flammulated, 61, *62*, 81; great gray, 13, 52; great horned, 30, 41, 60, 83; long-eared, 41; mottled, 131; saw-whet, 84; spotted, 59; tawny, 173
oystercatcher, 153; black, 139

Pachta: Noel, 187, 188; Sammy, 188
Packard, Robert, 115
Padre Island National Seashore, 112–13, *113*, 124, 126, 128–29
Palleck, Bill, 159
Panama, *163*, 163–64
panther (see mountain lion), 91
Panther Junction, Big Bend, 46, 79
parakeet: blue-throated, 190; monk, 190; olive-throated, 131
Parmeter, Mike, 75
Parque Natural de la Ballena Gris, Mexico, 138
Parr, Howard, 25, 28
parrot, Puerto Rican, 190
Parsons, Noel, 108